A WORLD ATLAS OF MILITARY HISTORY 1861-1945

A WORLD ATLA

by ARTHUR BANKS

OF MILITARY HISTORY

MODERN WARFARE

HIPPOCRENE
BOOKS, INC.
New York City

First Hippocrene edition, 1983
HIPPOCRENE BOOKS, INC.
171 Madison Avenue
New York, N. Y. 10016
Library of Congress Catalog Card Number 73-90857

ISBN 0 88254 454 3

CONTENTS

I Physical Features

1	Europe	2
2	Asia	3
3	North America	4
4	South America	5
5	Africa	6
6	Australasia	7

II The American Civil War

7	Eve of the American Civil War	10
8	The Opposing Forces in the American Civil War, 1861-1865	11
9	Eastern Theatre of War—Terrain and Communications	12
10	Western Theatre of War—Terrain and Communications	13
11	Military Organization	14
12	The American Civil War, 1861-1862	15
13	The American Civil War, 1863	16
14	The American Civil War, 1864-1865	17
15	The Battles of Ulysses S. Grant	18
16	The Battles of William T. Sherman	19
17	The Battles of Robert E. Lee	20
18	The Battles of "Stonewall" Jackson	21
19	The Battle of First Bull Run (Manassas), 21 July, 1861	22
20	The Battle of Second Bull Run (Manassas), 30 August, 1862	23
21	The Battle of Antietam, 17 September, 1862	24
22	The Battle of Fredericksburg, 13 December, 1862	25
23	The Vicksburg Campaign, November, 1862-July, 1863	26
24	The Battle of Chancellorsville, 1-6 May, 1863	27
25	The Battle of Gettysburg, 1-3 July, 1864	28
26	The Atlanta Campaign, May-September, 1864	29

| 27 | Lee's Retreat from Richmond-Petersburg to Appomattox, 31 March-9 April, 1865 | 30 |
| 28 | White Man Versus Red Man, 1865-1898 | 31 |

III Strife and Alignments

29	Strife in Africa, 1860-1899	34
30	Strife in Africa, 1899-1914	35
31	Strife in South America, 1864-1895	36
32	Strife in Central America, 1861-1900	37
33	The Unification of Italy	38
34	The Unification of Germany	39
35	The Franco-Prussian War, 1870-1871	40
36	The Russo-Turkish War, 1877-1878	41
37	Austria-Hungary, 1867-1918	42
38	The World following the Congress of Berlin, 1878	43
39	The Zulu War, 1879	44
40	'Scramble for Africa', pre-1914	45
41	The Battle of Tel-el-Kebir, 12-13 September, 1882	46
42	The Battle of Omdurman, 2 September, 1898	47
43	The Sino-Japanese War, 1894-1895	48
44	The Boer (or South African) War, 1899-1902	49
45	The "Boxer" Rebellion, 1900	50
46	The Russo-Japanese War, 1904-1905	51
47	Chief Armies of the World, 1906	52
48	Chief Navies of the World, 1906	52
49	The Italo-Turkish War, 1911-1912	53
50	Crises in North Africa and the Balkans, 1905-1912	54
51	World Empires of Britain, France and Germany, 1914	55
52	The First Balkan War, 1912-1913	56
53	The Second Balkan War, 1913	57
54	The Growth of the Russian Empire, pre-1914	58
55	The Growth of British and Russian Influence in Asia, pre-1914	59
56	The Middle East, pre-1914	60
57	Possessions of the United States, pre-1914	61

IV The First World War

58	Europe in 1914	64
59	War Plans and Concentrations	65
60	The Western Front in Outline, 1914-1918	66
61	The Eastern Front in Outline, 1914-1918	67
62	Opening Moves Involving Germany	68
63	Opening Moves Involving Other Powers	69
64	The German Drive to The Marne	70
65	The First Battle of The Marne	71
66	Prelude to Trench Warfare, Autumn, 1914	72
67	Battle of the Yser, 18-31 October, 1914	73
68	The Tannenberg Campaign, 20-31 August, 1914	74
69	The Ypres Salient, 1914-1915	75

70	The Static Western Front, 1915	76
71	The Mobile Eastern Front, 1915	77
72	Oceanic Warfare: The World Scene, 1914	78
73	The First Battle of the Atlantic, 1915-1918	79
	Europe: The Middle Years, 1915-1917;	
74	1. Land Events 1915	80
75	2. Land Events 1916	81
76	3. Land Events 1917	82
77	4. Naval Events, 1915-1917	83
78	The Dardanelles Fiasco in 1915	84
79	The Minesweeping Problem at the Dardanelles	85
80	The Gallipoli Fiasco in 1915	86
81	The Austro-German-Bulgarian Combined Assault upon	
	Serbia, October 1915	87
82	The Confrontation of the British and German Battle Fleets	
	at Jutland Bank on 31 May, 1916	88/9
83	The Verdun Battle, 1916	90
84	The Somme Battle, 1916	91
85	The Brusilov Offensive, June-October, 1916	92
86	The Rumanian Campaign, 1916	93
87	'Third Ypres' (Passchendaele), July-November, 1917	94
88	The British Tank-Spearhead Offensive at Cambrai, 1917	95
89	The German Somme and Lys Offensives, 1918	96
90	The German Aisne and Metz Offensives, 1918	97
91	The Allied Offensives, 18 July-11 November, 1918	98
92	The Allied Advance into Germany 1918	99
93	Military Casualties of the 1914-1918 War	100
94	Civilian Casualties and Expenditure, 1914-1918	101

V The Inter-War Years

95	The Russian Civil War, 1917-1922	104
96	The Graeco-Turkish War, 1919-1922	105
97	The Russo-Polish War, 1920	106
98	The Weimar Republic	107
99	Ireland	108
100	Italian Expansion, 1899-1939	109
101	Europe in 1925	110
102	Europe Between the World Wars	111
103	China, 1926-1933	112
104	China, 1933-1939	113
105	Strife in India, pre-1939	114
106	Spain: The Axis 'Training Ground', 1936-1939	115

VI The Second World War

107	Hitler's Road to War, 1936-1939	118
108	The Invasion of Poland by Germany (1 September) and	
	U.S.S.R. (17 September)1939	119
109	The Cruise of *Admiral Graf Spee*, 21 August-13 December,	

	1939	120/1
110	The Soviet-Finnish War, 30 November, 1939-12 March, 1940	122
111	*Weserubung Nord* and *Weserubung Sud*, 9 April-10 June, 1940	123
112	*Sichelschnitt* (Cut of the Sickle), 1940	124
113	Operations in the Vicinity of Dunkirk, 1940	125
114	Battle of Britain, 1940	126/7
115	German Plans for Invading Britain, 1940	128
116	The German Night 'Blitz' on Britain, September, 1940-May, 1941	129
117	Second Battle of the Atlantic	
	1. Phase One: July, 1940-April, 1941	130
	2. Phase Two: January-May, 1942	
	3. Phase Three: August, 1942-May, 1943	131
	4. Allied Convoy Routes and Bases	
118	The Mediterranean and North Africa, 1940-1941	132
119	British Naval Losses off Greece and Crete, 1941	133
	Rommel in North Africa	
120	Securing the Balkan Flank, Spring 1941	134
121	Operation 'Barbarossa'	135
122	The Japanese Assault on Pearl Harbor, 1941	136
123	Japanese Conquests, 1941-1942	137
124	The Japanese Assault on Burma, 1942	138
125	Defiant Malta	139
126	Allied Aid to the U.S.S.R.	140
127	Europe under the Axis, 1942	141
128	Strategy: Viewpoints and Intentions, Autumn, 1942	142
129	The German Rebuff at Alam Halfa, 31 August-2 September, 1942	143
130	Operation 'Torch', November, 1942	144
131	Allied Advances in the Mediterranean and Balkans, 1942-1945	145
132	The Conquest of Sicily, 10 July-17 August, 1943	146
133	The Campaign in Italy, 1943-1945	147
134	The Carrier Clash in Mid-Pacific in June, 1943	148
135	Allied Advances in Burma, 1944-1945	149
136	The Liberation of Western Europe, 1944	150/1
137	The Battle of the Bulge, 16 December, 1944-16 January, 1945	152
138	The Advancing Soviet Tidal Wave, 1944	153
139	Germany at Bay, January-May, 1945	154
140	Allied Advances in the Pacific, 1943-1945	155
141	The Reconquest of the Philippines, 1944-1945	156
142	1. The Iwojima Campaign, 19 February-16 March, 1945	157
	2. The Okinawa Campaign, 1 April-22 June, 1945	
143	Military Casualties of the 1939-1945 War	158
144	Civilian Casualties and Expenditure, 1939-1945	159
145	The World's Superpowers, 1945	160

ACKNOWLEDGEMENTS

During the preparation of this atlas, I was aided by a number of friends
and military organizations. I wish to express my gratitude and thanks to
Mrs J Campbell, Mr R Holmes, Mr E Jennings, Mr A Palmer and
Mr M Willis. In particular, the Imperial War Museum and the Royal
United Services Institute for Defence Studies were generous in the
facilities they placed at my disposal. I am also indebted to Messrs
Heinemann Educational Ltd for allowing me to reproduce twelve maps
which I originally drew for my *Military Atlas of the First World War.*

Arthur Banks

I
PHYSICAL FEATURES

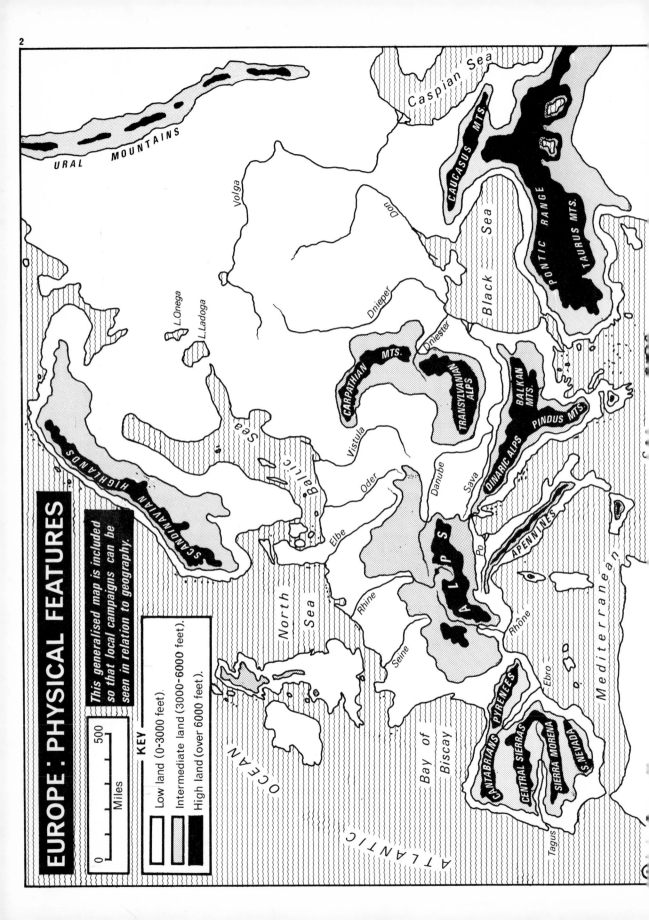

EUROPE: PHYSICAL FEATURES

This generalised map is included so that local campaigns can be seen in relation to geography.

KEY

☐ Low land (0-3000 feet).

▨ Intermediate land (3000-6000 feet).

■ High land (over 6000 feet).

Miles

0   500

URAL MOUNTAINS

Caspian Sea

Volga

Don

Dnieper

CAUCASUS MTS.

PONTIC RANGE

TAURUS MTS.

Black Sea

Dniester

L.Onega

L.Ladoga

CARPATHIAN MTS.

TRANSYLVANIAN ALPS

BALKAN MTS.

PINDUS MTS.

Vistula

Oder

Danube

Sava

DINARIC ALPS

SCANDINAVIAN HIGHLANDS

Baltic Sea

Elbe

A L P S

Po

APENNINES

North Sea

Rhine

Seine

Rhône

Mediterranean

Bay of Biscay

ATLANTIC OCEAN

CANTABRIANS

PYRENEES

CENTRAL SIERRAS

SIERRA MORENA

S. NEVADA

Ebro

Tagus

ASIA : PHYSICAL FEATURES

1000

Miles

0

PACIFIC

OCEAN

ARCTIC   OCEAN

EUROPE

AFRICA

Indigirka

Lena

Yenisei

Ob

Irtysh

Tobol

URAL MTS.

Ural

Volga

Don

Dnieper

Dniester

BLACK SEA

MEDITERRANEAN SEA

RED SEA

Tigris

Euphrates

CASPIAN SEA

ARAL SEA

L. Balkash

L. Baikal

Amur

Liao Ho

Hwang Ho

Wei

Yangtze

Sikiang

Red

SOUTH CHINA SEA

Mekong

Salween

Irrawaddy

KUNLUN MTS.

HIMALAYAS

MT. EVEREST

Hindu Kush

Indus

Ganges

Narbada

Godavari

Krishna

BAY OF BENGAL

ARABIAN SEA

INDIAN   OCEAN

KEY

☐ Low land (0-3000 feet).

▨ Intermediate land (3000-6000 feet).

■ High land (over 6000 feet).

This generalised map is included in order that local campaigns can be seen in relation to geography.

© Arthur Banks 1975

SOUTH AMERICA : PHYSICAL FEATURES

Caribbean Sea

ATLANTIC OCEAN

LLANOS

Orinoco

GUIANA HIGHLANDS

Branco

Negro

Japura

Putumayo

CHIMBORAZO

S E L V A

Jurva

Purus

Madeira

Tapajoz

Amazon

Tocantins

C. Araguaia

CAATINGAS

Sao Francisco

A N D E S

PACIFIC OCEAN

SAJAMA

OJOS DEL SALADO

ACONCAGUA

Pilcomayo

CHACO

GRAN

Paraguay

Parana

Parana

Uruguay

Parana

PAMPAS

ATLANTIC OCEAN

This generalised map is included so that individual campaigns can be seen in broad relation to local geography.

0   500
Miles

© Arthur Banks 1975

KEY

☐	Low land (0-3000 feet).
▦	Intermediate land (3000-6000 feet).
■	High land (over 6000 feet).
▲	Important heights.

AFRICA: PHYSICAL FEATURES

BLACK SEA

ATLANTIC OCEAN

CASPIAN SEA

MEDITERRANEAN SEA

SUEZ CANAL

Atlas Mts.

AHAGGAR

SAHARA DESERT

Libyan Desert

TIBESTI

Nile

RED SEA

Senegal

Gambia

Niger

L.Chad

MARRA

MT.DENDI

W.Shebeli

Juba

Ubangi

Congo

MT.KENYA

L.VICTORIA

ATLANTIC

Congo

Kasai

Kwango

MT. KILIMANJARO

L.TANGANYIKA

INDIAN OCEAN

OCEAN

L.NYASA

Cubango

Zambezi

This generalised map is included so that individual campaigns can be seen in broad relation to their geographical locations.

Kalahari Desert

Limpopo

Madagascar

Orange

Vaal

DRAKENSBERG

KEY

Low land (0-3000 feet).

Intermediate land (3000-6000 feet).

High land (over 6000 feet).

▲ Important heights.

© Arthur Banks 1975

0   500
Miles

AUSTRALASIA: PHYSICAL FEATURES

This generalised map is included so that individual campaigns can be seen in broad relation to their geographical locations.

KEY TO BOTH MAPS

▢ Low land (0-3000 feet).

▨ Intermediate land (3000-6000 feet).

▮ High land (over 6000 feet).

▲ Important heights.

NEW ZEALAND

L. TAUPO

Waikato

MT. EGMONT

TAPOAEAUKU

TASMAN SEA

Rakaia

Rangitata

Waitiki

PACIFIC OCEAN

MT. COOK

Clutha

Stewart I.

0   200

Miles

AUSTRALIA

CORAL SEA

Flinders

Georgina

Diamantina

Finke

L. Eyre

Alberga

Great Victoria Desert

Fortescue

Ashburton

Gascoyne

Murchison

Cuago

Darling

Macquarie

Lachlan

Murray

Great Dividing Range

MT. KOSKIUSKO

INDIAN OCEAN

TASMANIA

0   500

Miles

© Arthur Banks 1975

II

THE AMERICAN CIVIL WAR

EVE OF THE AMERICAN CIVIL WAR 1861

The political issues concerned not merely slavery, but also the doctrine of States' rights. The Northern States were mainly manufacturing and mining, whereas the Southern States were almost wholly agricultural (especially in the growth of cotton).

Mason & Dixon Line

12 April 1861, bombardment of fort marks opening of Civil War

THE TWO PRESIDENTS

1 *JEFFERSON DAVIS elected President of the Confederate States on 18 February 1861.*

2 *ABRAHAM LINCOLN inaugurated as President of the United States on 4 March 1861.*

CANADA

PACIFIC OCEAN

ATLANTIC OCEAN

Gulf of Mexico

MEXICO

MAINE
N.H.
VT.
MASS.
R.I.
CONN.
NEW YORK
PENNSYL-VANIA
NEW JERSEY
DELAWARE
MARYLAND
Washington D.C.
Richmond
VIRGINIA
N.CAROLINA
S. CAROLINA
Ft. Sumter
GEORGIA
FLORIDA
ALABAMA
MISSISSIPPI
LOUISIANA
TENNESSEE
KENTUCKY
OHIO
INDIANA
ILLINOIS
MICHIGAN
WISCONSIN
MINNESOTA
IOWA
MISSOURI
ARKANSAS
KANSAS
Unorganised Territory
TEXAS
DAKOTA TERRITORY
NEBRASKA TERRITORY
COLORADO TERRITORY
UTAH TERRITORY
NEW MEXICO TERRITORY
NEVADA TERRITORY
WASHINGTON TERRITORY
OREGON
CALIFORNIA

KEY

- Free States.
- Free Territories.
- Slave States.
- Slave Territories.
- Boundary between the United and Confederate States.

300
0
Miles

© Arthur Banks 1975

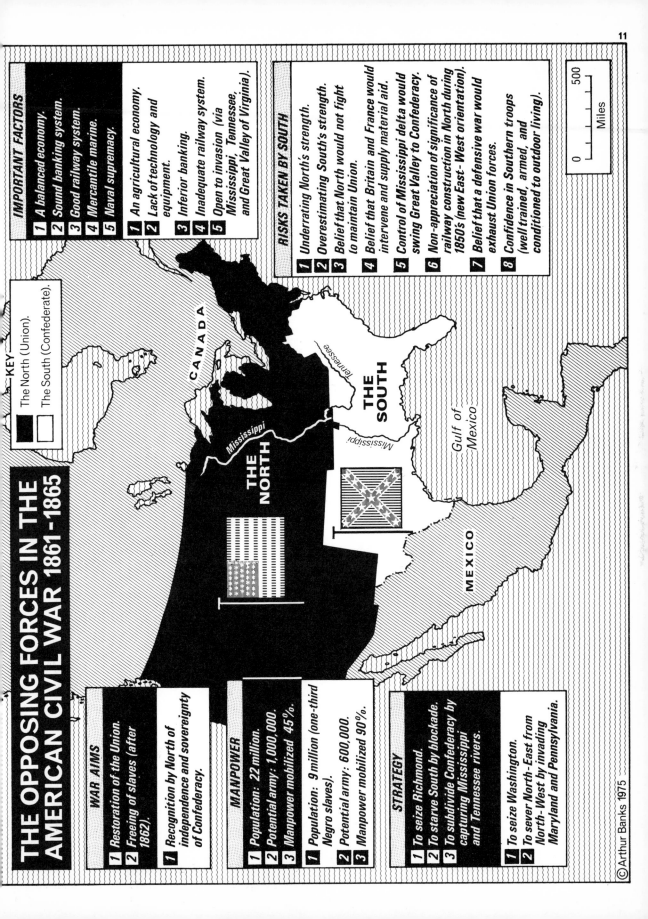

THE OPPOSING FORCES IN THE AMERICAN CIVIL WAR 1861-1865

KEY
- ◼ The North (Union).
- ◻ The South (Confederate).

IMPORTANT FACTORS

[North]
1. A balanced economy.
2. Sound banking system.
3. Good railway system.
4. Mercantile marine.
5. Naval supremacy.

[South]
1. An agricultural economy.
2. Lack of technology and equipment.
3. Inferior banking.
4. Inadequate railway system.
5. Open to invasion (via Mississippi, Tennessee, and Great Valley of Virginia).

RISKS TAKEN BY SOUTH
1. Underrating North's strength.
2. Overestimating South's strength.
3. Belief that North would not fight to maintain Union.
4. Belief that Britain and France would intervene and supply material aid.
5. Control of Mississippi delta would swing Great Valley to Confederacy.
6. Non-appreciation of significance of railway construction in North during 1850's (new East-West orientation).
7. Belief that a defensive war would exhaust Union forces.
8. Confidence in Southern troops (well trained, armed, and conditioned to outdoor living).

WAR AIMS

[North]
1. Restoration of the Union.
2. Freeing of slaves (after 1862).

[South]
1. Recognition by North of independence and sovereignty of Confederacy.

MANPOWER

[North]
1. Population: 22 million.
2. Potential army: 1,000,000.
3. Manpower mobilized 45%.

[South]
1. Population: 9 million (one-third Negro slaves).
2. Potential army: 600,000.
3. Manpower mobilized 90%.

STRATEGY

[North]
1. To seize Richmond.
2. To starve South by blockade.
3. To subdivide Confederacy by capturing Mississippi and Tennessee rivers.

[South]
1. To seize Washington.
2. To sever North-East from North-West by invading Maryland and Pennsylvania.

CANADA

THE NORTH

THE SOUTH

Mississippi

Tennessee

Mississippi

Gulf of Mexico

MEXICO

0 — 500
Miles

© Arthur Banks 1975

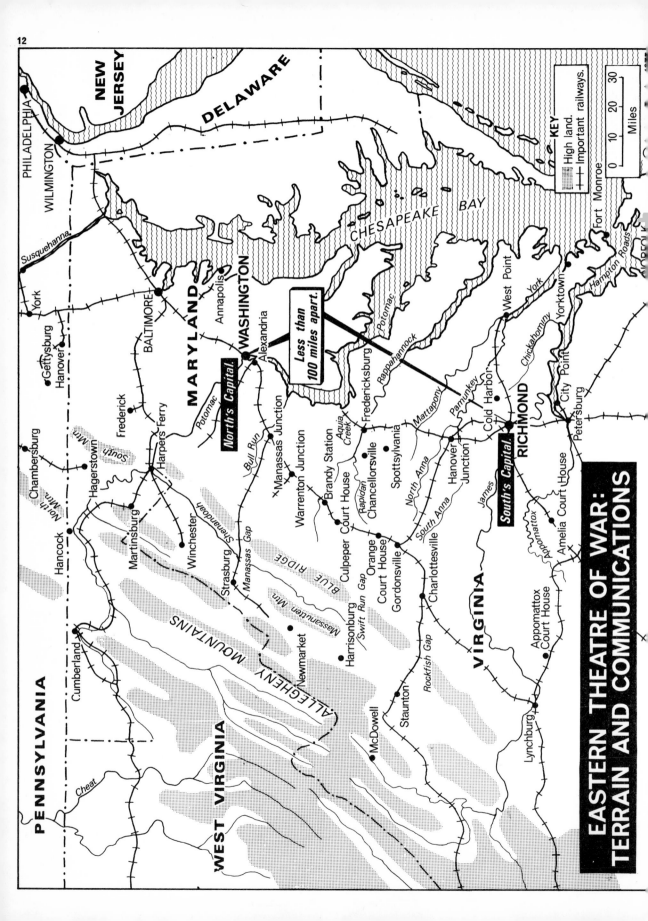

EASTERN THEATRE OF WAR:
TERRAIN AND COMMUNICATIONS

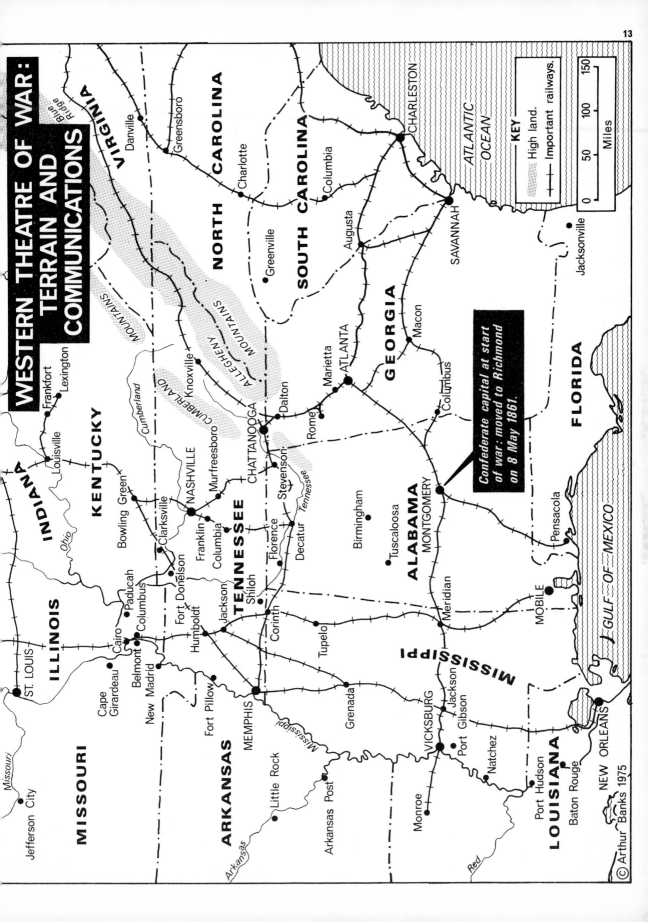

WESTERN THEATRE OF WAR: TERRAIN AND COMMUNICATIONS

KEY

High land.

Important railways.

0   50   100   150

Miles

VIRGINIA

Blue Ridge

Danville

Frankfort

Lexington

Louisville

KENTUCKY

Bowling Green

Clarksville

Greensboro

NORTH CAROLINA

Charlotte

Knoxville

CUMBERLAND MOUNTAINS

Cumberland

ALLEGHENY MOUNTAINS

Greenville

SOUTH CAROLINA

Columbia

CHARLESTON

ATLANTIC OCEAN

Augusta

SAVANNAH

INDIANA

Ohio

NASHVILLE

Murfreesboro

Franklin

Columbia

TENNESSEE

CHATTANOOGA

Dalton

Rome

Marietta

ATLANTA

GEORGIA

Macon

Columbus

Jacksonville

FLORIDA

ILLINOIS

ST. LOUIS

Cairo

Paducah

Columbus

Fort Donelson

Jackson

Humboldt

Florence

Stevenson

Tennessee

Decatur

Birmingham

Tuscaloosa

ALABAMA

MONTGOMERY

Pensacola

Confederate capital at start of war: moved to Richmond on 8 May 1861.

MISSOURI

Jefferson City

Cape Girardeau

Belmont

New Madrid

Fort Pillow

MEMPHIS

ARKANSAS

Little Rock

Arkansas Post

Arkansas

Mississippi

Humboldt

Shiloh

Corinth

Tupelo

Grenada

MISSISSIPPI

Jackson

VICKSBURG

Port Gibson

Natchez

Meridian

MOBILE

GULF OF MEXICO

Monroe

Port Hudson

Baton Rouge

NEW ORLEANS

LOUISIANA

Red

Missouri

© Arthur Banks 1975

MILITARY ORGANIZATION

Both sides commenced with similar organizations but changes occurred as the war progressed. Neither side started with army corps, but, in March 1862, the Union (on Lincoln's initiative) formed several of these. Strength of units varied considerably: commanders were given maximum and minimum figures to work to most of the tim

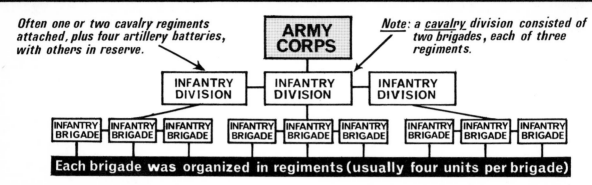

Often one or two cavalry regiments attached, plus four artillery batteries, with others in reserve.

Note: a cavalry division consisted of two brigades, each of three regiments.

ARMY CORPS

INFANTRY DIVISION — **INFANTRY DIVISION** — **INFANTRY DIVISION**

INFANTRY BRIGADE (×9)

Each brigade was organized in regiments (usually four units per brigade)

UNION INFANTRY REGIMENT

REGIMENTAL HEADQUARTERS

OFFICERS:
- COLONEL
- LIEUTENANT-COLONEL
- MAJOR
- ADJUTANT
- QUARTERMASTER
- SURGEON-MAJOR
- ASSISTANT SURGEONS (2)
- CHAPLAIN

ENLISTED PERSONNEL:
- SERGEANT-MAJOR
- QUARTERMASTER-SERGEANT
- COMMISSARY-SERGEANT
- PRINCIPAL MUSICIANS (2)
- HOSPITAL STEWARD

The regiment was the basic tactical unit of the United States army both in peace and war, and was similar to the British battalion. Its field strength averaged about 900 officers and men. In theory, Union and Confederate regiments were organized on similar lines but, in practice, there were many variations on the Conferate side: for example, the 55th. Alabama had battalions.

AVERAGE REGIMENTAL STRENGTHS AT BATTLE OF CHANCELLORSVILLE WERE:
UNION _____ 433 } Officers & men per regt.
CONFEDERATE __ 409 }

AVERAGE COMPANY STRENGTH AT BATTLE OF GETTYSBURG WAS 32 OFFICERS AND MEN.

COMPANIES (10) — *Note*: except heavy artillery regiments retained as infantry which had 12.

A B C D E F G H I K

Note: 'J' omitted

Maximum strength: 101 **COMPANY** Minimum strength: 83

CAPTAIN	SERGEANTS (4)	PRIVATES (64-82)
FIRST LIEUTENANT	CORPORALS (8)	
SECOND LIEUTENANT	MUSICIANS (2)	
FIRST SERGEANT	WAGGONER	

Usually six squadrons, each of two companies.

CAVALRY REGIMENT
THIS HAD **12** COMPANIES AND THESE WENT FROM 'A' TO 'M' (WITH 'J' OMITTED). 725 all ranks.

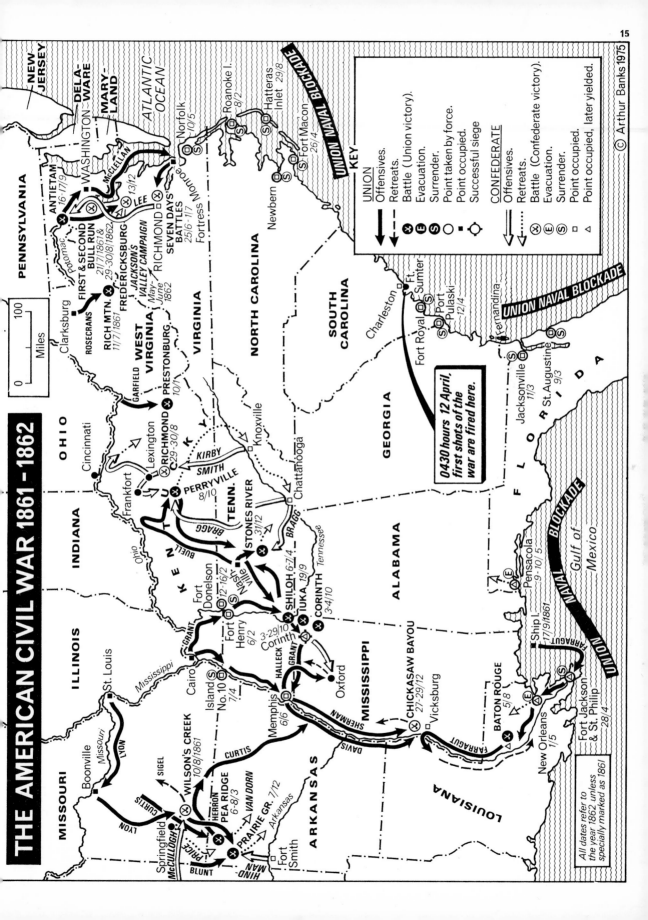

THE AMERICAN CIVIL WAR 1861–1862

© Arthur Banks 1975

KEY

UNION
Offensives.
Retreats.
Battle (Union victory).
Evacuation.
Surrender.
Point taken by force.
Point occupied.
Successful siege

CONFEDERATE
Offensives.
Retreats.
Battle (Confederate victory).
Evacuation.
Surrender.
Point occupied.
Point occupied, later yielded.

0430 hours 12 April, first shots of the war are fired here.

All dates refer to the year 1862 unless specially marked as 1861.

UNION NAVAL BLOCKADE

Gulf of Mexico

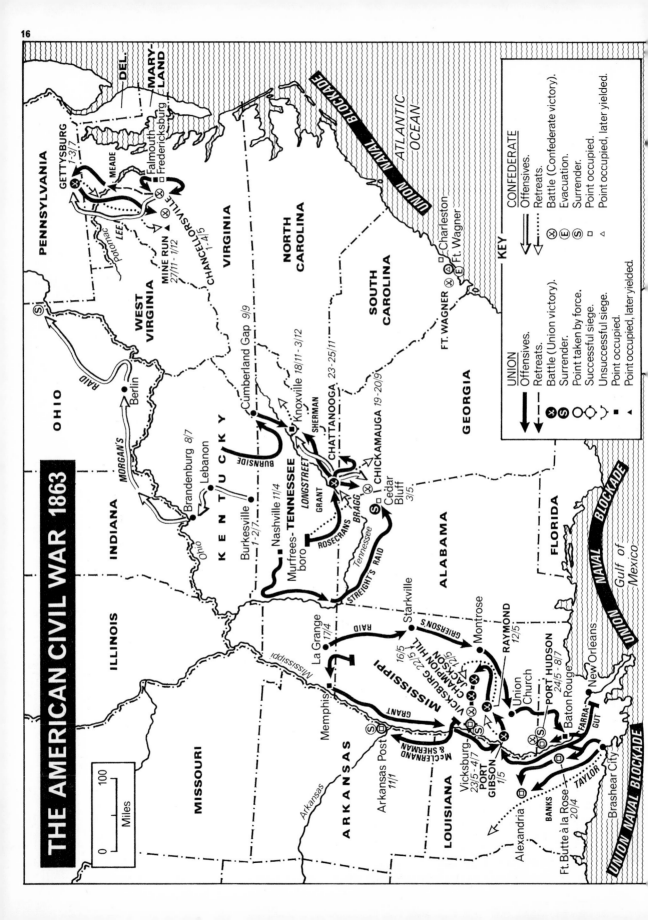

THE AMERICAN CIVIL WAR 1863

16

Miles
0   100

KEY

UNION
Offensives.
Retreats.
Battle (Union victory).
Surrender.
Point taken by force.
Successful siege.
Unsuccessful siege.
Point occupied.
Point occupied, later yielded.

CONFEDERATE
Offensives.
Retreats.
Battle (Confederate victory).
Evacuation.
Surrender.
Point occupied.
Point occupied, later yielded.

⊗ Ⓢ ○ ⌣ ■ ▲
⊗ Ⓔ Ⓢ □ △

OHIO
INDIANA
ILLINOIS
MISSOURI
ARKANSAS
KENTUCKY
TENNESSEE
MISSISSIPPI
ALABAMA
GEORGIA
LOUISIANA
FLORIDA
WEST VIRGINIA
VIRGINIA
PENNSYLVANIA
MARYLAND
DEL.
NORTH CAROLINA
SOUTH CAROLINA

ATLANTIC OCEAN
Gulf of Mexico

UNION NAVAL BLOCKADE
UNION NAVAL BLOCKADE

MORGAN'S RAID
Berlin
Brandenburg 8/7
Lebanon
Burkesville
Nashville 11/4
Murfreesboro
ROSECRANS
BURNSIDE
Cumberland Gap 9/9
Knoxville 18/11 - 3/12
SHERMAN
CHATTANOOGA 23 - 25/11
LONGSTREET
GRANT
BRAGG
CHICKAMAUGA 19 - 20/9
Cedar Bluff 3/5
STREIGHT'S RAID
Starkville
Montrose
RAYMOND 12/5
GRIERSON'S RAID
La Grange 17/4
GRANT
Memphis
Arkansas Post 11/1
Vicksburg 23/5 - 4/7
McCLERNAND & SHERMAN
PORT GIBSON 1/5
CHAMPION HILL 16/5
JACKSON 14/5
VICKSBURG 22/5 - 4/7
Union Church
PORT HUDSON 24/5 - 8/7
Baton Rouge
New Orleans
FARRAGUT
BANKS
Ft. Butte à la Rose 20/4
Brashear City
TAYLOR
Alexandria

Ohio
Mississippi
Arkansas
Tennessee

GETTYSBURG 1-3/7
MEADE
Falmouth
Fredericksburg
LEE
MINE RUN 27/11 - 1/12
CHANCELLORSVILLE 1-4/5
Potomac

FT. WAGNER
Charleston
Ft. Wagner

NAVAL BLOCKADE

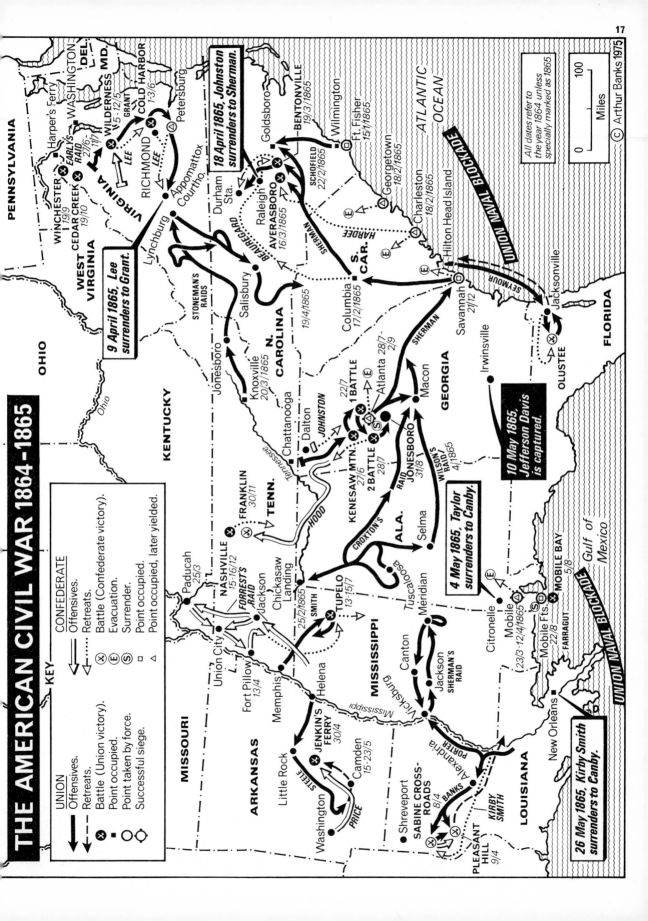

THE AMERICAN CIVIL WAR 1864-1865

© Arthur Banks 1975

All dates refer to the year 1864 unless specially marked as 1865.

0   100
Miles

KEY

UNION
— Offensives.
⟶ Retreats.
Ⓧ Battle (Union victory).
■ Point occupied.
○ Point taken by force.
◇ Successful siege.

CONFEDERATE
— Offensives.
⟶ Retreats.
Ⓧ Battle (Confederate victory).
Ⓔ Evacuation.
Ⓢ Surrender.
□ Point occupied.
△ Point occupied, later yielded.

9 April 1865, Lee surrenders to Grant.

18 April 1865, Johnston surrenders to Sherman.

10 May 1865, Jefferson Davis is captured.

4 May 1865, Taylor surrenders to Canby.

26 May 1865, Kirby Smith surrenders to Canby.

PENNSYLVANIA

OHIO

WEST VIRGINIA

VIRGINIA

Harper's Ferry
WASHINGTON
MD.
DEL.
WINCHESTER 19/9
CEDAR CREEK 19/10
EARLY'S RAID 27/6-11/7
WILDERNESS 5-12/5
COLD HARBOR 1-3/6
GRANT
LEE
RICHMOND
Petersburg
Appomattox Courtho.
Lynchburg
STONEMAN'S RAIDS

KENTUCKY

N. CAROLINA
Durham Sta.
Raleigh
Goldsboro
BENTONVILLE 19/3/1865
AVERASBORO 16/3/1865
SCHOFIELD 22/2/1865
Wilmington
Ft. Fisher 15/1/1865
BEAUREGARD
Salisbury
Columbia 17/2/1865
19/4/1865
SHERMAN
HARDEE
Georgetown 18/2/1865
Charleston 18/2/1865
Hilton Head Island

ATLANTIC OCEAN

UNION NAVAL BLOCKADE

S. CAR.

Jonesboro
Knoxville 20/3/1865
Chattanooga
Dalton
JOHNSTON
TENN.
FRANKLIN 30/11
HOOD
Tennessee

GEORGIA
KENESAW MTN. 27/6
1 BATTLE 22/7
Atlanta 28/7- 2/9
2 BATTLE 28/7
JONESBORO 31/8
Macon
SHERMAN
CROXTON'S RAID
WILSON'S RAID 4/1/1865
Savannah 21/12
Irwinsville
OLUSTEE
SEYMOUR
Jacksonville
FLORIDA

MISSOURI

ARKANSAS
Little Rock
Washington
Camden 15-23/5
JENKIN'S FERRY 30/4
STEELE
PRICE
Shreveport
SABINE CROSS-ROADS 8/4
PLEASANT HILL 9/4
BANKS
KIRBY SMITH

LOUISIANA
Alexandria
PORTER
New Orleans

MISSISSIPPI
Paducah 25/3
NASHVILLE 15-16/12
FORREST'S RAID
Union City
Jackson
Chickasaw Landing
SMITH 25/2/1865
TUPELO 13-15/7
Fort Pillow 13/4
Memphis
Helena
Canton
Jackson
Vicksburg
Meridian
SHERMAN'S RAID
Tuscaloosa
Citronelle
Mobile
MOBILE BAY 5/8
Mobile Fts. 23/3-12/4/1865
FARRAGUT 22/8
ALA.
Selma

Gulf of Mexico

UNION NAVAL BLOCKADE

THE BATTLES OF ULYSSES S. GRANT

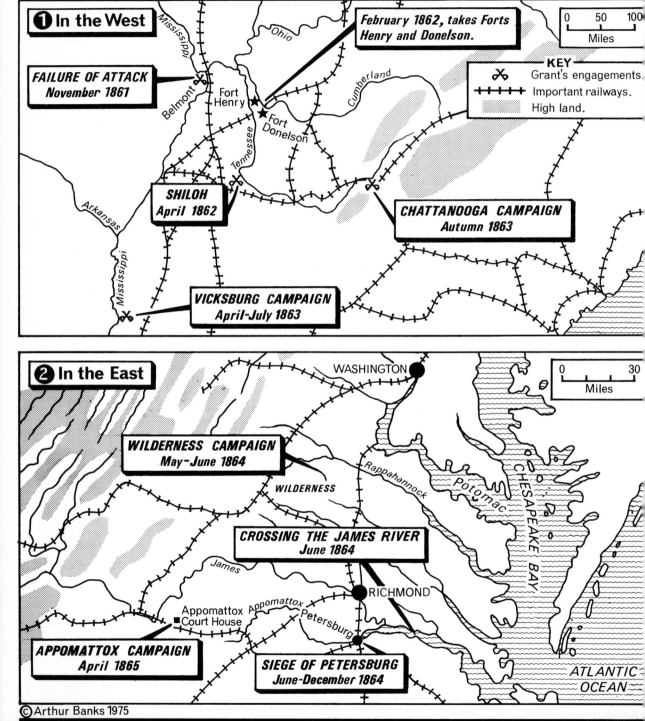

① In the West

February 1862, takes Forts Henry and Donelson.

FAILURE OF ATTACK
November 1861

Belmont

Fort Henry

Fort Donelson

KEY
✂ Grant's engagements.
╫╫╫ Important railways.
High land.

0   50   100
Miles

SHILOH
April 1862

CHATTANOOGA CAMPAIGN
Autumn 1863

VICKSBURG CAMPAIGN
April–July 1863

Mississippi

Ohio

Cumberland

Tennessee

Arkansas

Mississippi

② In the East

WASHINGTON ●

WILDERNESS CAMPAIGN
May–June 1864

WILDERNESS

Rappahannock

Potomac

CHESAPEAKE BAY

0   30
Miles

CROSSING THE JAMES RIVER
June 1864

James

Appomattox
Court House

Appomattox

Petersburg

● RICHMOND

APPOMATTOX CAMPAIGN
April 1865

SIEGE OF PETERSBURG
June–December 1864

ATLANTIC OCEAN

© Arthur Banks 1975

Ulysses Simpson Grant (1822–1885) served as an infantry officer in the Mexican War but resigned from the army in 1854 following a period of heavy drinking. He volunteered for service in the Union army in 1861, and was speedily given command of an infantry regiment. Rapidly promoted brigadier-general, he became lieutenant general in March 1864 and general-in-chief three days later. In 1868 he was elected president and served twice.

THE BATTLES OF WILLIAM T. SHERMAN

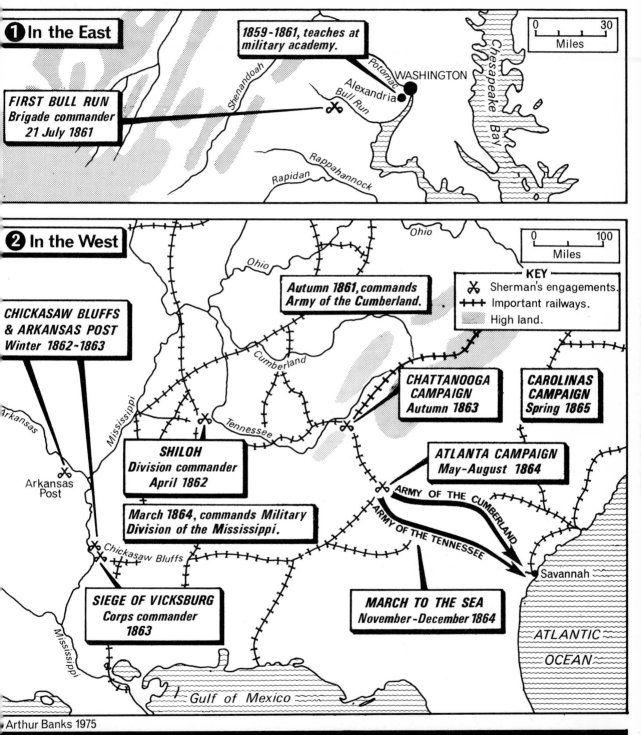

1 In the East

1859-1861, teaches at military academy.

WASHINGTON
Alexandria
Bull Run

FIRST BULL RUN
Brigade commander
21 July 1861

Shenandoah
Potomac
Rappahannock
Rapidan

Chesapeake Bay

0 — 30
Miles

2 In the West

Ohio

CHICKASAW BLUFFS & ARKANSAS POST
Winter 1862-1863

Autumn 1861, commands Army of the Cumberland.

KEY
✗ Sherman's engagements.
+++ Important railways.
▒ High land.

CHATTANOOGA CAMPAIGN
Autumn 1863

CAROLINAS CAMPAIGN
Spring 1865

Ohio
Cumberland
Tennessee
Mississippi

Arkansas

ATLANTA CAMPAIGN
May-August 1864

SHILOH
Division commander
April 1862

Arkansas Post

March 1864, commands Military Division of the Mississippi.

ARMY OF THE CUMBERLAND

ARMY OF THE TENNESSEE

Chickasaw Bluffs

Savannah

SIEGE OF VICKSBURG
Corps commander
1863

MARCH TO THE SEA
November-December 1864

Mississippi

ATLANTIC OCEAN

Gulf of Mexico

0 — 100
Miles

Arthur Banks 1975

William Tecumseh Sherman (1820-1891) resigned from the army in 1853 and, after working as a banker and practising law, became superintendent of a military academy in 1859. In 1861 he volunteered for Federal service and was promoted to brigadier-general in August, major-general in May 1862, lieutenant-general in July 1866, and, as a full general, succeeded Grant as commander-in-chief in 1869. He held this post until 1883.

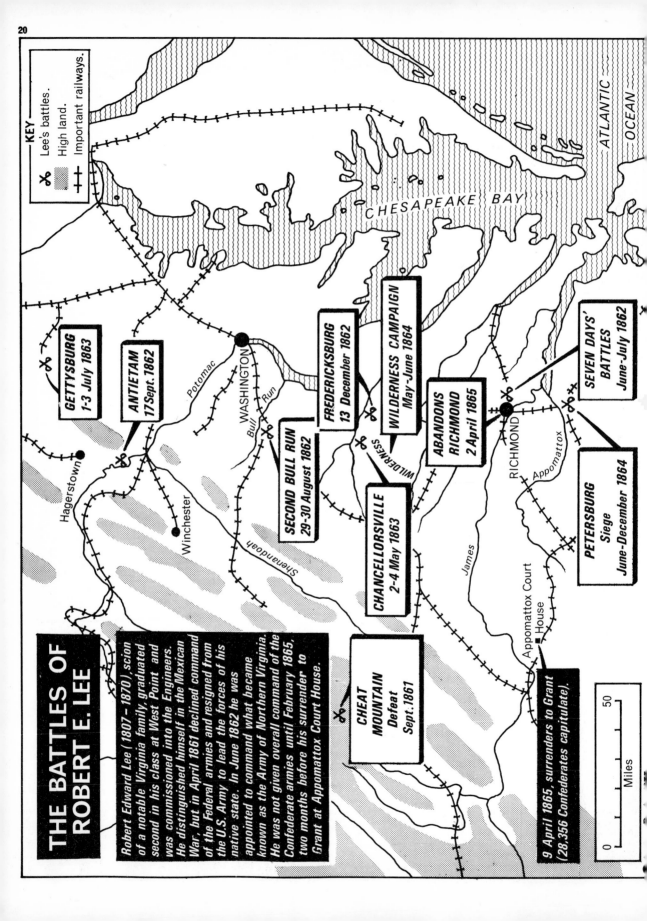

KEY
⚔ Lee's battles.
▨ High land.
╪╪ Important railways.

ATLANTIC OCEAN

CHESAPEAKE BAY

THE BATTLES OF ROBERT E. LEE

Robert Edward Lee (1807–1870), scion of a notable Virginia family, graduated second in his class at West Point and was commissioned into the Engineers. He distinguished himself in the Mexican War, but in April 1861 declined command of the Federal armies and resigned from the U.S. Army to lead the forces of his native state. In June 1862 he was appointed to command what became known as the Army of Northern Virginia. He was not given overall command of the Confederate armies until February 1865, two months before his surrender to Grant at Appomattox Court House.

GETTYSBURG
1-3 July 1863

ANTIETAM
17 Sept. 1862

FREDERICKSBURG
13 December 1862

WILDERNESS CAMPAIGN
May–June 1864

SEVEN DAYS'
BATTLES
June–July 1862

ABANDONS
RICHMOND
2 April 1865

SECOND BULL RUN
29-30 August 1862

CHANCELLORSVILLE
2-4 May 1863

PETERSBURG
Siege
June–December 1864

CHEAT
MOUNTAIN
Defeat
Sept. 1861

9 April 1865, surrenders to Grant
(28,356 Confederates capitulate).

Potomac

WASHINGTON

Bull Run

Hagerstown

Winchester

Shenandoah

WILDERNESS

RICHMOND

Appomattox

James

Appomattox Court
House

0   50
Miles

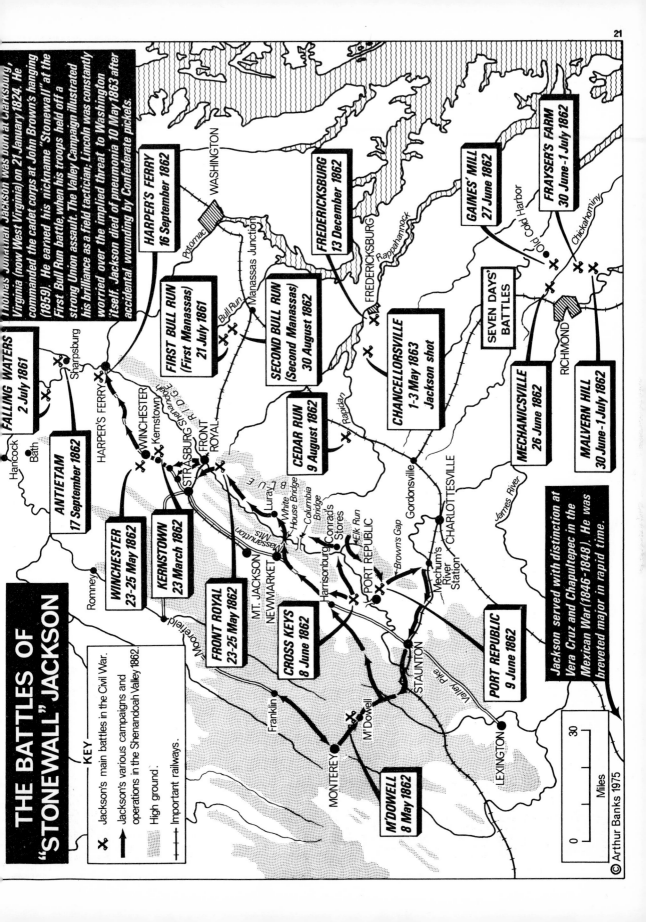

THE BATTLES OF "STONEWALL" JACKSON

KEY

- **✗** Jackson's main battles in the Civil War.
- **↑** Jackson's various campaigns and operations in the Shenandoah Valley 1862.
- High ground.
- **┼┼┼** Important railways.

Thomas Jonathan Jackson was born at Clarksburg, Virginia (now West Virginia) on 21 January 1824. He commanded the cadet corps at John Brown's hanging (1859). He earned his nickname "Stonewall" at the First Bull Run battle, when his troops held off a strong Union assault. The Valley Campaign illustrated his brilliance as a field tactician. Lincoln was constantly worried over the implied threat to Washington itself. Jackson died of pneumonia 10 May 1863 after accidental wounding by Confederate pickets.

Jackson served with distinction at Vera Cruz and Chapultepec in the Mexican War (1846-1848). He was breveted major in rapid time.

FALLING WATERS 2 July 1861

ANTIETAM 17 September 1862

WINCHESTER 23-25 May 1862

KERNSTOWN 23 March 1862

FRONT ROYAL 23-25 May 1862

CROSS KEYS 8 June 1862

M'DOWELL 8 May 1862

PORT REPUBLIC 9 June 1862

HARPER'S FERRY 16 September 1862

FIRST BULL RUN (First Manassas) 21 July 1861

SECOND BULL RUN (Second Manassas) 30 August 1862

CEDAR RUN 9 August 1862

CHANCELLORSVILLE 1-3 May 1863 Jackson shot

FREDERICKSBURG 13 December 1862

GAINES' MILL 27 June 1862

FRAYSER'S FARM 30 June-1 July 1862

SEVEN DAYS' BATTLES

MECHANICSVILLE 26 June 1862

MALVERN HILL 30 June-1 July 1862

WASHINGTON

Potomac

Manassas Junction

Bull Run

Sharpsburg

Hancock

Bath

Romney

Moorefield

HARPER'S FERRY

WINCHESTER

Kernstown

STRASBURG

FRONT ROYAL

Luray

White House Bridge

Columbia Bridge

MT. JACKSON

NEWMARKET

Harrisonburg

Conrad's Stores

Elk Run

PORT REPUBLIC

Brown's Gap

Mechum's River Station

Gordonsville

CHARLOTTESVILLE

STAUNTON

Franklin

M'Dowell

MONTEREY

LEXINGTON

FREDERICKSBURG

Rappahannock

Rapidan

Old Cold Harbor

Chickahominy

RICHMOND

James River

Valley Pike

BLUE RIDGE

MASSANUTTEN MTS

Shenandoah R.

0   30   Miles

© Arthur Banks 1975

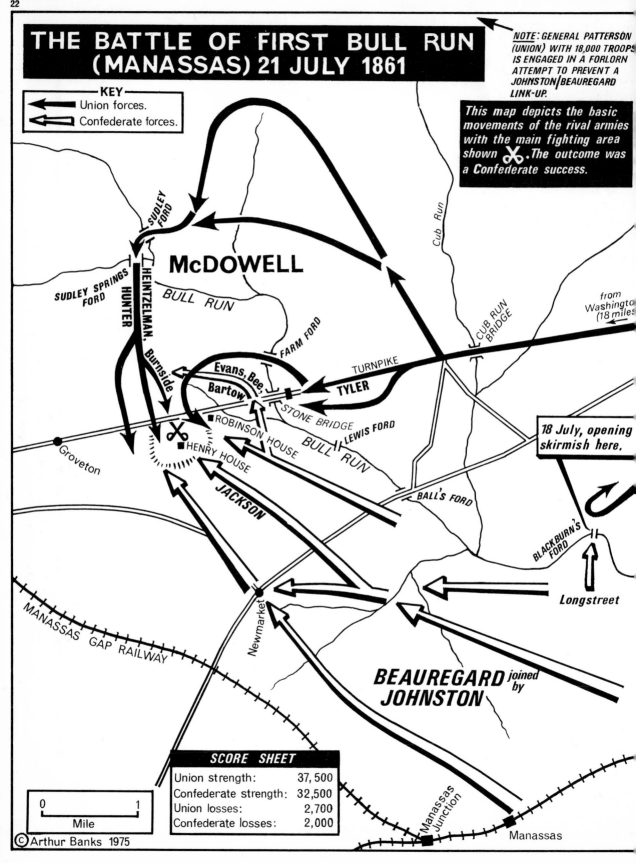

THE BATTLE OF FIRST BULL RUN (MANASSAS) 21 JULY 1861

NOTE: GENERAL PATTERSON (UNION) WITH 18,000 TROOPS IS ENGAGED IN A FORLORN ATTEMPT TO PREVENT A JOHNSTON/BEAUREGARD LINK-UP.

This map depicts the basic movements of the rival armies with the main fighting area shown ✂. The outcome was a **Confederate success.**

KEY
◀━━ Union forces.
◁══ Confederate forces.

McDOWELL

SUDLEY FORD

SUDLEY SPRINGS FORD

HUNTER

HEINTZELMAN, Burnside

BULL RUN

FARM FORD

Cub Run

CUB RUN BRIDGE

from Washington (18 miles)

TURNPIKE

Evans, Bee, Bartow

TYLER

STONE BRIDGE

LEWIS FORD

BULL RUN

Groveton

ROBINSON HOUSE

✂ HENRY HOUSE

JACKSON

BALL'S FORD

18 July, opening skirmish here.

BLACKBURN'S FORD

Longstreet

MANASSAS GAP RAILWAY

Newmarket

BEAUREGARD joined by JOHNSTON

SCORE SHEET

Union strength:	37,500
Confederate strength:	32,500
Union losses:	2,700
Confederate losses:	2,000

0 ___ 1
Mile

© Arthur Banks 1975

Manassas Junction

Manassas

THE BATTLE OF SECOND BULL RUN (MANASSAS) 30 AUGUST 1862

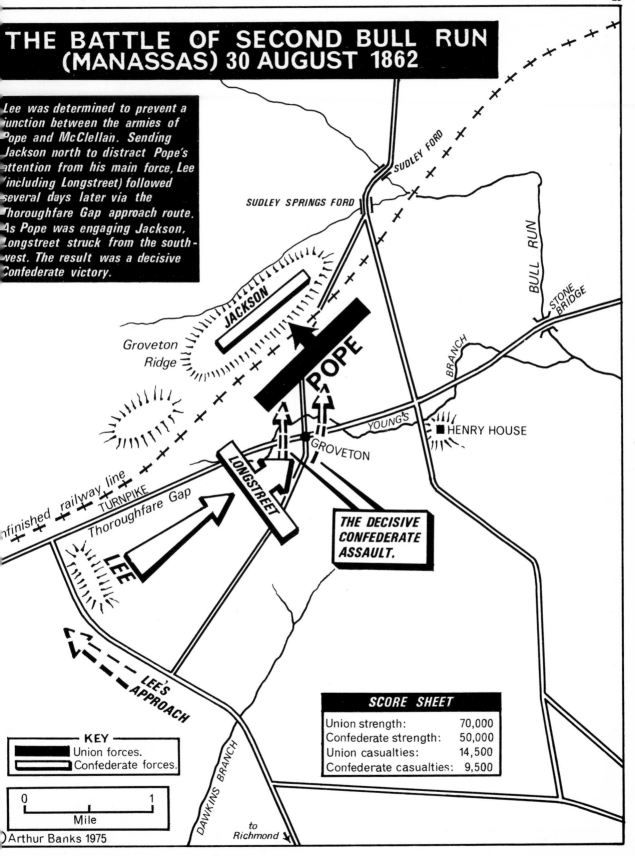

Lee was determined to prevent a junction between the armies of Pope and McClellan. Sending Jackson north to distract Pope's attention from his main force, Lee (including Longstreet) followed several days later via the Thoroughfare Gap approach route. As Pope was engaging Jackson, Longstreet struck from the south-west. The result was a decisive Confederate victory.

SUDLEY FORD

SUDLEY SPRINGS FORD

BULL RUN

STONE BRIDGE

JACKSON

Groveton Ridge

POPE

BRANCH

YOUNG'S

HENRY HOUSE

GROVETON

Unfinished railway line

TURNPIKE

Thoroughfare Gap

LONGSTREET

THE DECISIVE CONFEDERATE ASSAULT.

LEE

LEE'S APPROACH

KEY
Union forces.
Confederate forces.

0   1
Mile

DAWKINS BRANCH

to Richmond

SCORE SHEET

Union strength:	70,000
Confederate strength:	50,000
Union casualties:	14,500
Confederate casualties:	9,500

© Arthur Banks 1975

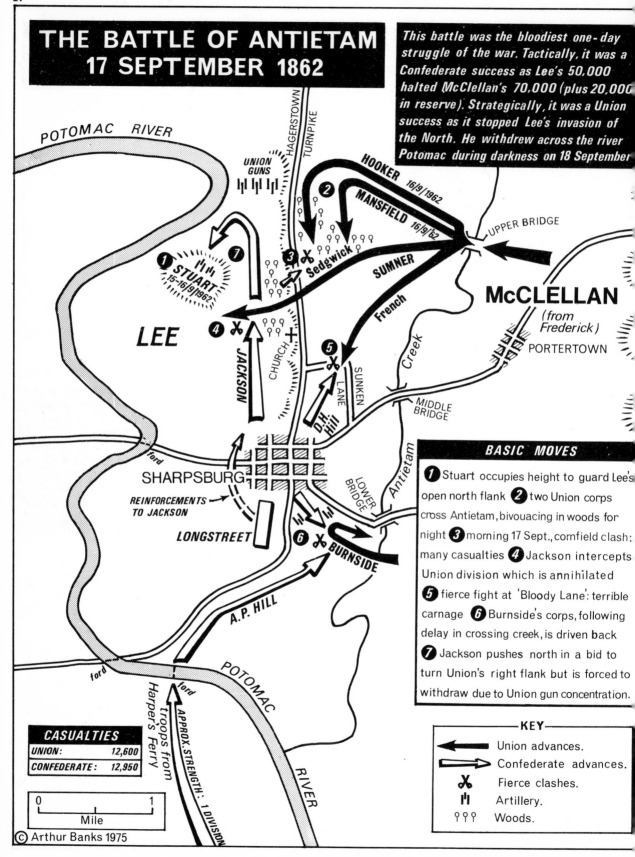

THE BATTLE OF ANTIETAM 17 SEPTEMBER 1862

This battle was the bloodiest one-day struggle of the war. Tactically, it was a Confederate success as Lee's 50,000 halted McClellan's 70,000 (plus 20,000 in reserve). Strategically, it was a Union success as it stopped Lee's invasion of the North. He withdrew across the river Potomac during darkness on 18 September

POTOMAC RIVER

HAGERSTOWN TURNPIKE

UNION GUNS

HOOKER 16/9/1962

MANSFIELD 16/9/'62

UPPER BRIDGE

2

1 STUART 15-16/9/1962

7

3 Sedgwick

SUMNER

French

McCLELLAN *(from Frederick)*

PORTERTOWN

LEE

4 JACKSON

CHURCH

5 LANE SUNKEN

Creek

MIDDLE BRIDGE

D.H. Hill

Antietam

BASIC MOVES

1 Stuart occupies height to guard Lee's open north flank **2** two Union corps cross Antietam, bivouacing in woods for night **3** morning 17 Sept., cornfield clash: many casualties **4** Jackson intercepts Union division which is annihilated **5** fierce fight at 'Bloody Lane': terrible carnage **6** Burnside's corps, following delay in crossing creek, is driven back **7** Jackson pushes north in a bid to turn Union's right flank but is forced to withdraw due to Union gun concentration.

Ford

SHARPSBURG

REINFORCEMENTS TO JACKSON

LONGSTREET

6 BURNSIDE

LOWER BRIDGE

A.P. HILL

POTOMAC

RIVER

ford

ford

ford

troops from Harper's Ferry

APPROX. STRENGTH: 1 DIVISION

CASUALTIES

UNION:	12,600
CONFEDERATE:	12,950

0 ———— 1
Mile

KEY

⬅	Union advances.
⬅	Confederate advances.
✂	Fierce clashes.
⚏	Artillery.
♀♀♀	Woods.

© Arthur Banks 1975

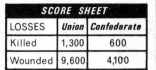
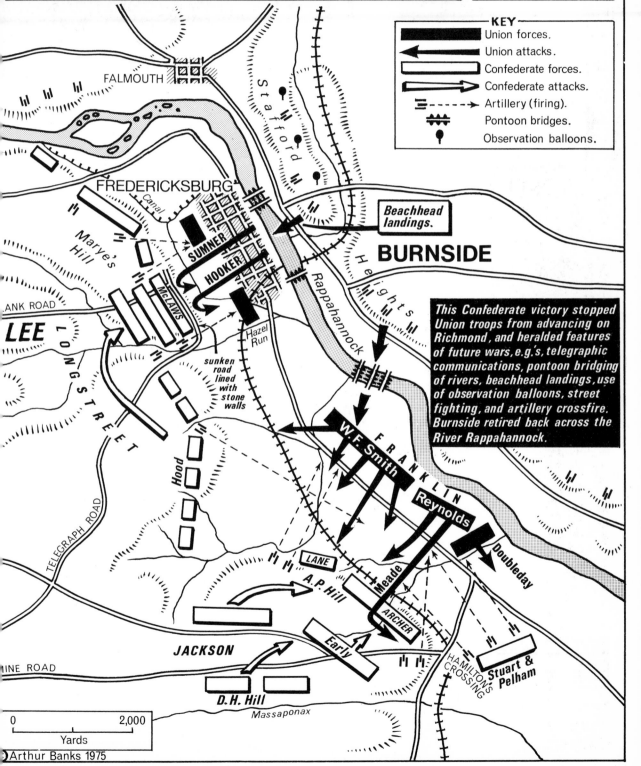

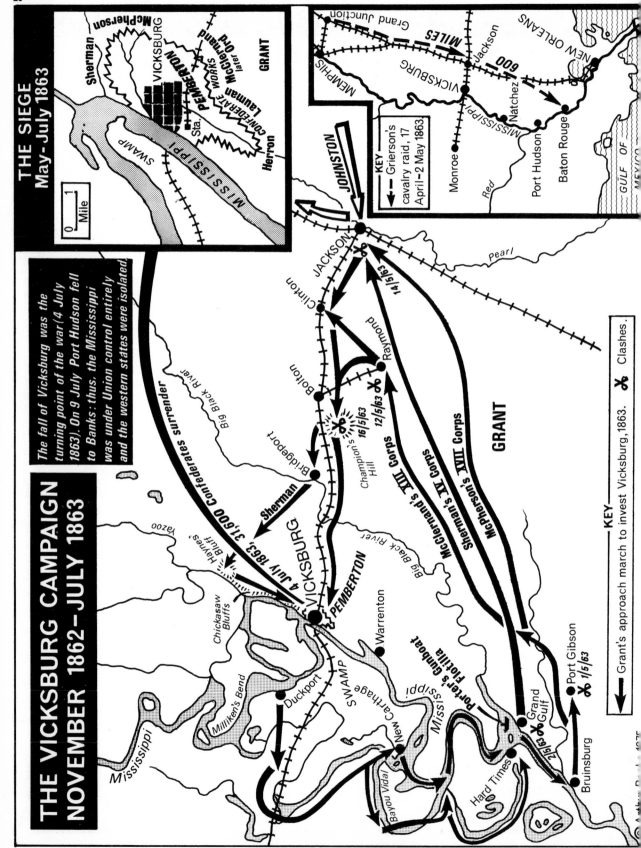

THE VICKSBURG CAMPAIGN NOVEMBER 1862–JULY 1863

THE SIEGE May–July 1863

The fall of Vicksburg was the turning point of the war (4 July 1863). On 9 July Port Hudson fell to Banks; thus, the Mississippi was under Union control entirely and the western states were isolated.

KEY

Grierson's cavalry raid, 17 April – 2 May 1863

600 MILES

McPHERSON
Sherman
VICKSBURG
PEMBERTON
CONFEDERATE WORKS
McClernand
Ord
later
Lauman
Herron
Sta.
GRANT
SWAMP
MISSISSIPPI

JOHNSTON
JACKSON
Clinton
Bolton
Raymond
Pearl
14/5/63
16/5/63
Champion's Hill
12/5/63

McClernand's XIII Corps
Sherman's XV Corps
McPherson's XVII Corps
GRANT

Bridgeport
Big Black River
Sherman
Confederates surrender
31,600
4 July 1863
Haynes' Bluff
Chickasaw Bluffs
Yazoo
VICKSBURG
PEMBERTON
Warrenton
Big Black River

Duckport
Milliken's Bend
Mississippi
SWAMP
New Carthage
Bayou Vidal
Porter's Gunboat Flotilla
Mississippi
Hard Times
Grand Gulf
2/5/63
Port Gibson
1/5/63
Bruinsburg

Grand Junction
Jackson
MEMPHIS
VICKSBURG
MISSISSIPPI
Monroe
Natchez
Red
Port Hudson
Baton Rouge
NEW ORLEANS
GULF OF MEXICO

KEY
Grant's approach march to invest Vicksburg, 1863.
Clashes.

THE BATTLE OF CHANCELLORSVILLE 1-6 MAY 1863

1 Opening Moves 1-2 May

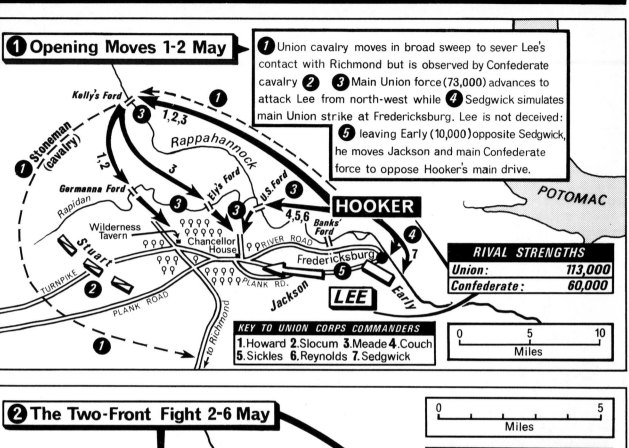

1 Union cavalry moves in broad sweep to sever Lee's contact with Richmond but is observed by Confederate cavalry 2 3 Main Union force (73,000) advances to attack Lee from north-west while 4 Sedgwick simulates main Union strike at Fredericksburg. Lee is not deceived: 5 leaving Early (10,000) opposite Sedgwick, he moves Jackson and main Confederate force to oppose Hooker's main drive.

RIVAL STRENGTHS	
Union:	113,000
Confederate:	60,000

KEY TO UNION CORPS COMMANDERS
1. Howard 2. Slocum 3. Meade 4. Couch
5. Sickles 6. Reynolds 7. Sedgwick

0 ___ 5 ___ 10
Miles

2 The Two-Front Fight 2-6 May

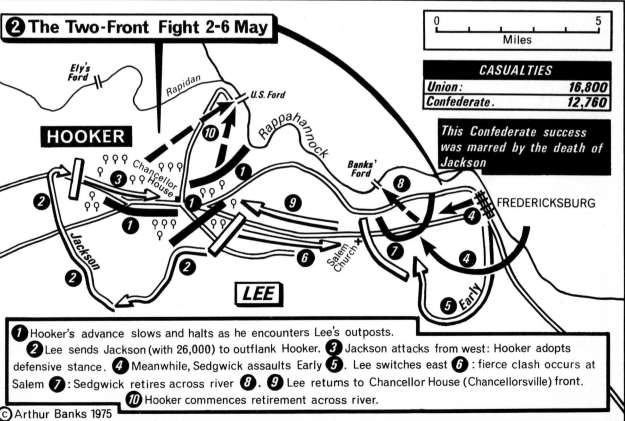

0 ___ 5
Miles

CASUALTIES	
Union:	16,800
Confederate.	12,760

This Confederate success was marred by the death of Jackson

1 Hooker's advance slows and halts as he encounters Lee's outposts. 2 Lee sends Jackson (with 26,000) to outflank Hooker. 3 Jackson attacks from west: Hooker adopts defensive stance. 4 Meanwhile, Sedgwick assaults Early 5. Lee switches east 6: fierce clash occurs at Salem 7: Sedgwick retires across river 8. 9 Lee returns to Chancellor House (Chancellorsville) front. 10 Hooker commences retirement across river.

© Arthur Banks 1975

THE BATTLE OF GETTYSBURG 1-3 JULY 1863

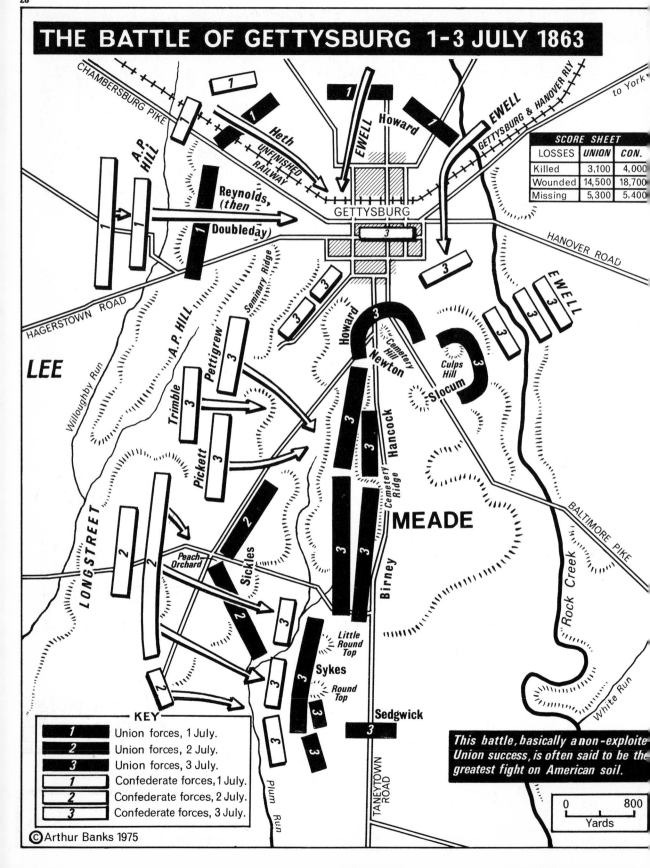

CHAMBERSBURG PIKE

A.P. HILL

Heth

UNFINISHED RAILWAY

Reynolds, (then Doubleday)

EWELL

Howard

EWELL

GETTYSBURG & HANOVER RLY

to York

GETTYSBURG

HANOVER ROAD

EWELL

HAGERSTOWN ROAD

LEE

Willoughby Run

A.P. HILL

Seminary Ridge

Pettigrew

Trimble

Pickett

Howard

Newton

Cemetery Hill

Culps Hill

Slocum

Hancock

Cemetery Ridge

MEADE

BALTIMORE PIKE

Rock Creek

LONGSTREET

Peach Orchard

Sickles

Birney

Little Round Top

Sykes

Round Top

Sedgwick

White Run

Plum Run

SCORE SHEET

LOSSES	UNION	CON.
Killed	3,100	4,000
Wounded	14,500	18,700
Missing	5,300	5,400

KEY

1	Union forces, 1 July.
2	Union forces, 2 July.
3	Union forces, 3 July.
1	Confederate forces, 1 July.
2	Confederate forces, 2 July.
3	Confederate forces, 3 July.

This battle, basically a non-exploite Union success, is often said to be the greatest fight on American soil.

0	800

Yards

TANEYTOWN ROAD

© Arthur Banks 1975

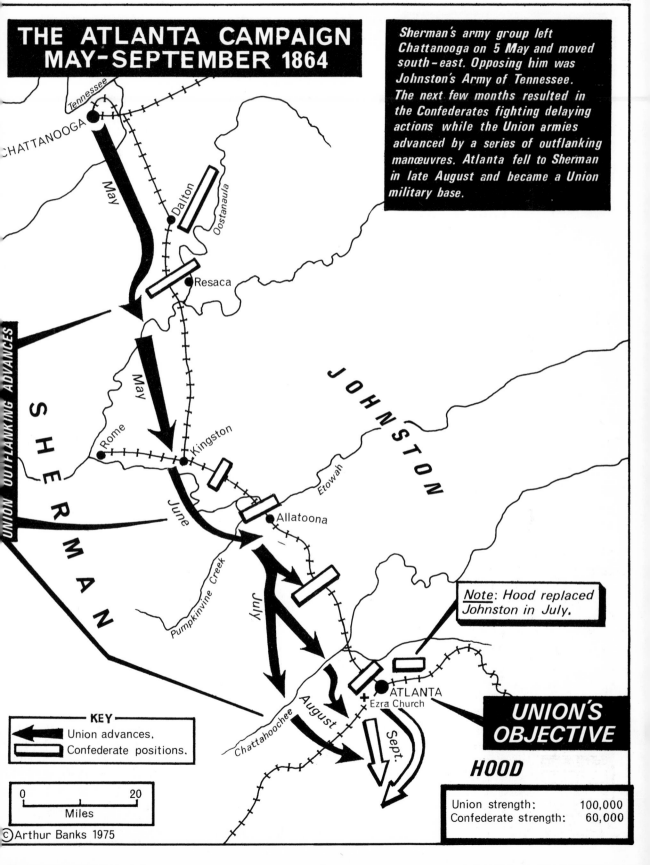

THE ATLANTA CAMPAIGN MAY–SEPTEMBER 1864

Sherman's army group left Chattanooga on 5 May and moved south-east. Opposing him was Johnston's Army of Tennessee. The next few months resulted in the Confederates fighting delaying actions while the Union armies advanced by a series of outflanking manœuvres. Atlanta fell to Sherman in late August and became a Union military base.

CHATTANOOGA

Tennessee

May

Dalton

Oostanaula

Resaca

SHERMAN

May

Rome

Kingston

Etowah

June

Allatoona

JOHNSTON

Pumpkinvine Creek

July

Note: Hood replaced Johnston in July.

ATLANTA
Ezra Church

Chattahoochee

August

Sept.

UNION'S OBJECTIVE

HOOD

KEY
← Union advances.
▭ Confederate positions.

UNION OUTFLANKING ADVANCES

0   20
Miles

© Arthur Banks 1975

Union strength:	100,000
Confederate strength:	60,000

LEE'S RETREAT FROM RICHMOND–PETERSBURG TO APPOMATTOX 31 MARCH–9 APRIL 1865

Miles
0 5 10 15

→ to West Point

2 April, realising the significance of the fall of Petersburg, Lee abandons the Confederate capital which is sacked and burnt by its own inhabitants. Union forces are hailed as liberators.

Weitzel 3 April

RICHMOND

4 April, Lincoln arrives by ship.

City Point

Ft. Stedman
PETERSBURG

GRANT

2 April

These Union attacks prove to be decisive. Confederate lines are breached: Petersburg falls.

EWELL

LEE

GORDON 2–4 April

LONGSTREET

2 April

2 April

Five Forks

2 April

1 April

PICKETT'S COUNTER-ATTACK

31 March

Dinwiddie Court House

Hatcher's Run

2–4 April

2–4 April

James

ANDERSON 2–4 April

SHERIDAN

SOUTHSIDE RAILROAD

5 April, Lee arrives here to learn that Union forces have reached Jetersville ahead of him, thus severing the railway to the south. Lee detours to the north-west.

Appomattox

Amelia Court House

5–6 April

Jetersville

Burke's Station

Burkesville

DANVILLE RAILROAD

James

9 April, recognizing the hopelessness of his situation, Lee surrenders to Grant. Terms are generous: Lee's men can return home on parole and officers retain their swords for prestige purposes. The war ended officially on 29 May.

6 April. Union forces catch up with Confederate rearguard at Sailor's (or Sayler's) Creek. In fierce action, Union take 8,000 prisoners including Ewell, thus depleting Lee's force.

7 April

7 April

Grant's aim is to control these railway lines to prevent Lee from joining with Johnston's forces to the south.

7 April

Farmville

SHERIDAN

7 April

CAVALRY

7 April

This Union advance seals fate of Lee's march-weary army.

Appomattox Court House

to Lynchburg & mountainous terrain

James

KEY

∧∧∧	Confederate siege lines.
⇨	Confederate retreats.
⊓⊓	Union siege lines.
➡	Union advances.
+++	Important railways.

© Arthur Banks 1975

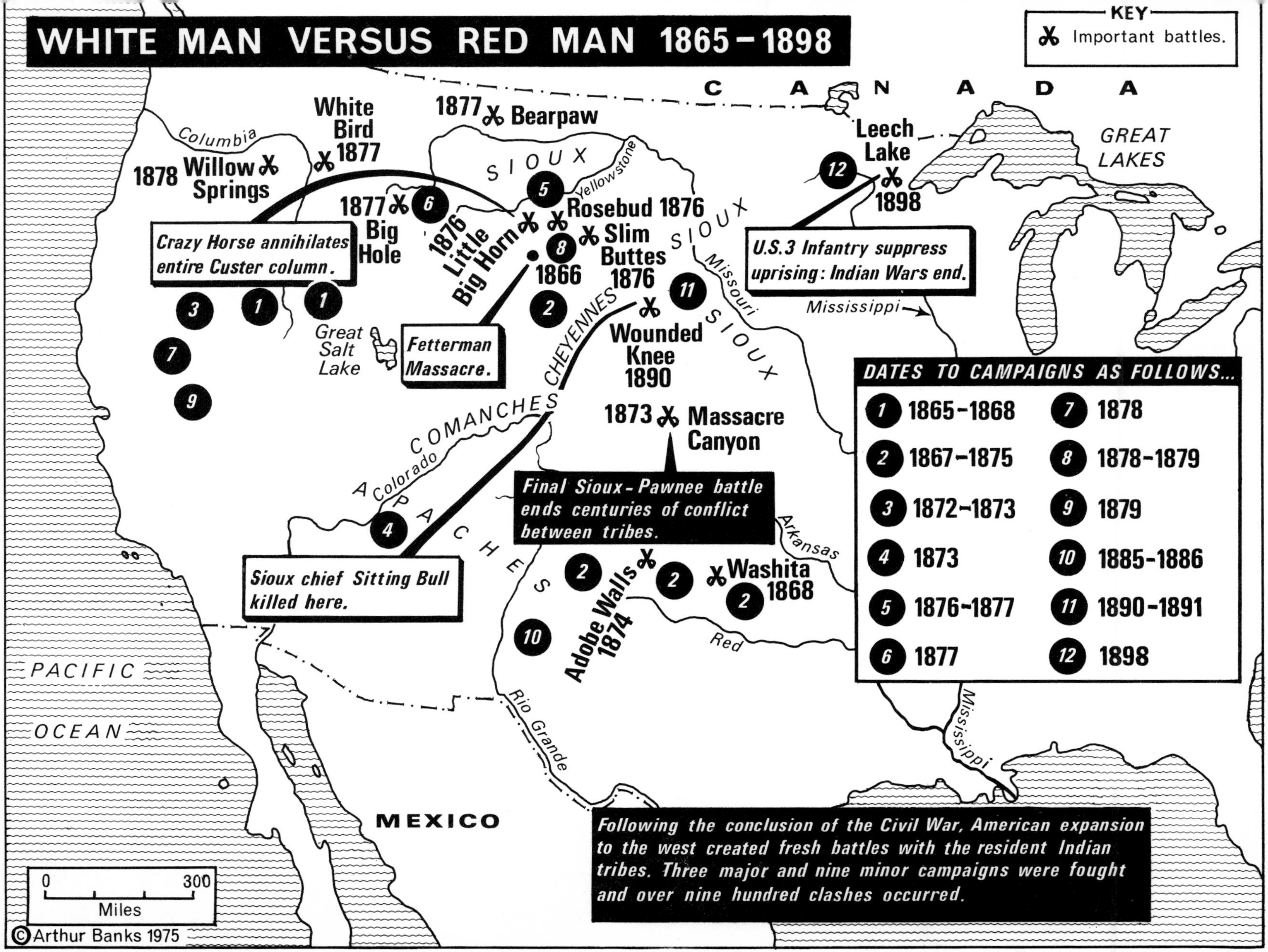
WHITE MAN VERSUS RED MAN 1865–1898
KEY
Important battles.
CANADA
GREAT LAKES
Columbia
1878 Willow Springs
White Bird 1877
1877 Big Hole
1877 Bearpaw
1876 Little Big Horn
Rosebud 1876
Slim Buttes 1876
1866
SIOUX
Yellowstone
Missouri
Leech Lake 1898
U.S.3 Infantry suppress uprising: Indian Wars end.
Mississippi
Crazy Horse annihilates entire Custer column.
Great Salt Lake
Fetterman Massacre.
CHEYENNES
Wounded Knee 1890
COMANCHES
1873 Massacre Canyon
Colorado
APACHES
Final Sioux-Pawnee battle ends centuries of conflict between tribes.
Arkansas
Sioux chief Sitting Bull killed here.
Adobe Walls 1874
Washita 1868
Red
Rio Grande
PACIFIC OCEAN
MEXICO
DATES TO CAMPAIGNS AS FOLLOWS...
1 1865–1868
2 1867–1875
3 1872–1873
4 1873
5 1876–1877
6 1877
7 1878
8 1878–1879
9 1879
10 1885–1886
11 1890–1891
12 1898
Following the conclusion of the Civil War, American expansion to the west created fresh battles with the resident Indian tribes. Three major and nine minor campaigns were fought and over nine hundred clashes occurred.
0 300 Miles
©Arthur Banks 1975

III
STRIFE & ALIGNMENTS

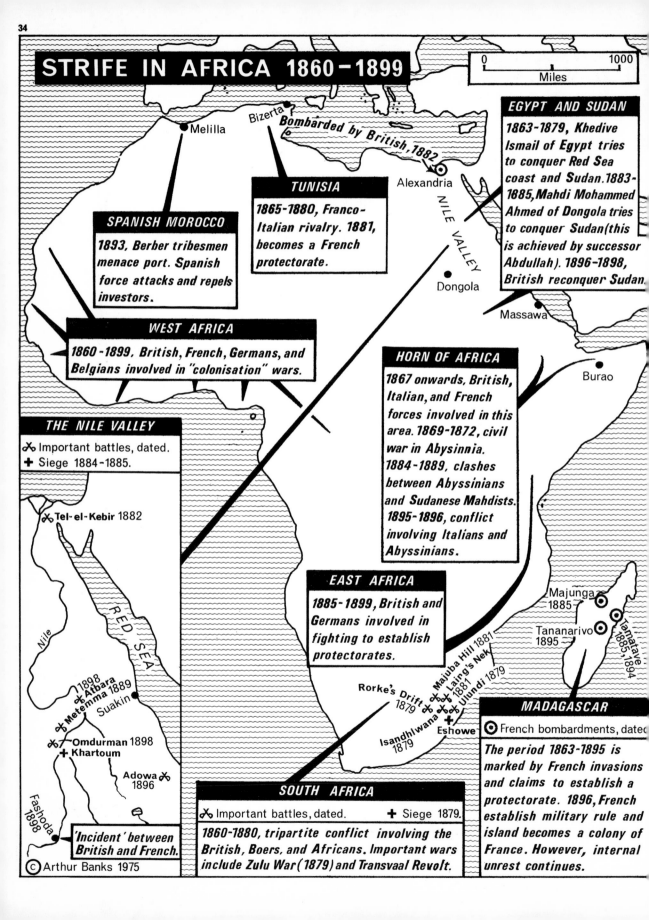

STRIFE IN AFRICA 1860-1899

0   1000

Miles

Melilla

Bizerta

Bombarded by British, 1882

Alexandria

EGYPT AND SUDAN

1863-1879, Khedive Ismail of Egypt tries to conquer Red Sea coast and Sudan. 1883-1885, Mahdi Mohammed Ahmed of Dongola tries to conquer Sudan (this is achieved by successor Abdullah). 1896-1898, British reconquer Sudan.

TUNISIA

1865-1880, Franco-Italian rivalry. 1881, becomes a French protectorate.

SPANISH MOROCCO

1893, Berber tribesmen menace port. Spanish force attacks and repels investors.

Dongola

NILE VALLEY

Massawa

WEST AFRICA

1860-1899, British, French, Germans, and Belgians involved in "colonisation" wars.

HORN OF AFRICA

1867 onwards, British, Italian, and French forces involved in this area. 1869-1872, civil war in Abysinnia. 1884-1889, clashes between Abyssinians and Sudanese Mahdists. 1895-1896, conflict involving Italians and Abyssinians.

Burao

THE NILE VALLEY

⚔ Important battles, dated.
✝ Siege 1884-1885.

⚔ **Tel-el-Kebir** 1882

Nile

RED SEA

1898
⚔**Atbara**
⚔**Metemma** 1889
Suakin

⚔7 **Omdurman** 1898
✝ **Khartoum**

Adowa ⚔
1896

Fashoda
1898

'Incident' between British and French.

EAST AFRICA

1885-1899, British and Germans involved in fighting to establish protectorates.

Majunga
1885

Tananarivo
1895

Tamatave
1885, 1894

Majuba Hill 1881
Laing's Nek
1881

Rorke's Drift
1879
Ulundi 1879

Isandhlwana
1879
✝
Eshowe

MADAGASCAR

◉ French bombardments, dated

The period 1863-1895 is marked by French invasions and claims to establish a protectorate. 1896, French establish military rule and island becomes a colony of France. However, internal unrest continues.

SOUTH AFRICA

⚔ Important battles, dated.   ✝ Siege 1879.

1860-1880, tripartite conflict involving the British, Boers, and Africans. Important wars include Zulu War (1879) and Transvaal Revolt.

© Arthur Banks 1975

34

STRIFE IN AFRICA 1899-1914

0 1000
Miles

This map shows areas of local conflict numbered in chronological sequence.

Tripoli

Agadir

5

NORTHERN SAHARA
1900, French establish their authority in desert areas (e.g. oases).

WADAI
1909-11, conquered by French.

MAURETANIA
1908-9, conquered by French.

NORTHERN NIGERIA
1900-3, British conquer area.

16

N.W. NIGERIA
1906, insurrection in Sokoto.

BAGIRMI
1900, French defeat R. Zobeir.

14 **6** **17** **4**

3

SOMALILAND
1899-1900, Mohammed ben Abdullah clashes with British, Italians, Ethiopians.

1

9

12

GOLD COAST
1900, uprising: British suppress Ushantis.

FRENCH CONGO
1905, uprising.

10

13

SOUTHERN NIGERIA
1904, insurrection.

CAMEROON
1904-5, Germans suppress insurrection.

ANGOLA
1907, uprising (inspired by Herero uprising in German S.W. Africa).

15

ANGOLA
1902, uprising suppressed by Portuguese.

7

8

GERMAN S.W. AFRICA
1903, Hottentot uprising.

11

2

18

GERMAN EAST AFRICA
1905, insurrection.

GERMAN S.W. AFRICA
1904-8, uprising (Herero tribe plus Hottentots).

SOUTH AFRICA
1914, Boer uprising.

SOUTH AFRICA
1899-1902, Boer War (see page).

© Arthur Banks 1975

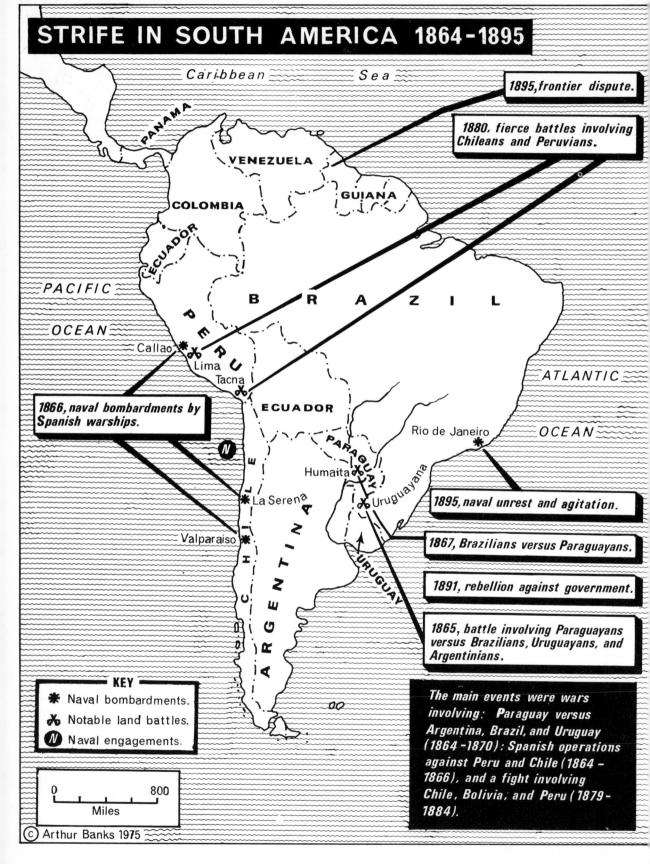

36

STRIFE IN SOUTH AMERICA 1864-1895

Caribbean ~ *Sea*

PANAMA

VENEZUELA

COLOMBIA

GUIANA

ECUADOR

PACIFIC

OCEAN

B R A Z I L

P E R U

Callao

Lima

Tacna

ECUADOR

ATLANTIC

Rio de Janeiro

OCEAN

PARAGUAY

Humaita

Uruguayana

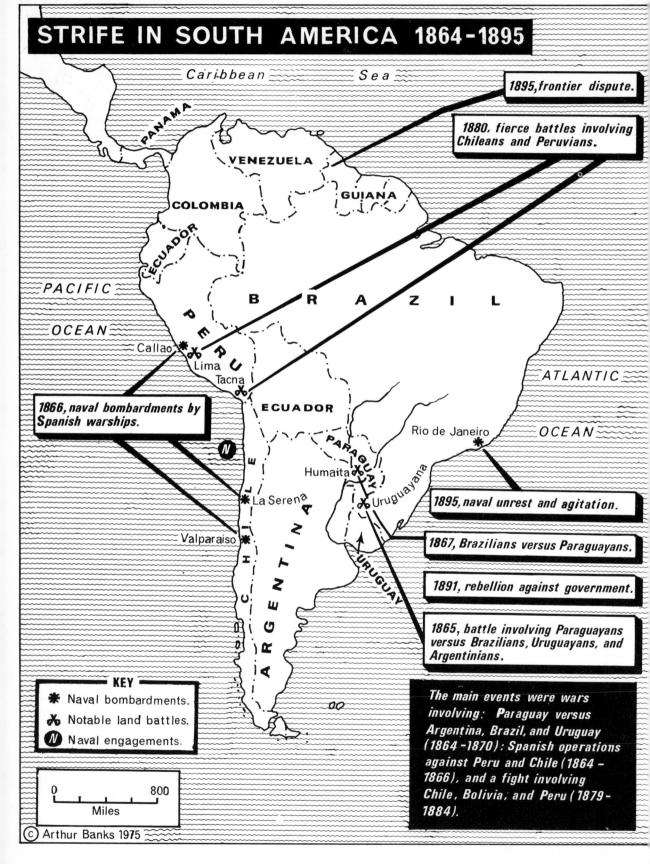

La Serena

C H I L E

Valparaiso

A R G E N T I N A

URUGUAY

1895, frontier dispute.

1880, fierce battles involving Chileans and Peruvians.

1866, naval bombardments by Spanish warships.

1895, naval unrest and agitation.

1867, Brazilians versus Paraguayans.

1891, rebellion against government.

1865, battle involving Paraguayans versus Brazilians, Uruguayans, and Argentinians.

KEY
* **Naval bombardments.**
* **Notable land battles.**
* **N** **Naval engagements.**

The main events were wars involving: Paraguay versus Argentina, Brazil, and Uruguay (1864-1870): Spanish operations against Peru and Chile (1864-1866), and a fight involving Chile, Bolivia, and Peru (1879-1884).

0 ———————— 800
Miles

© Arthur Banks 1975

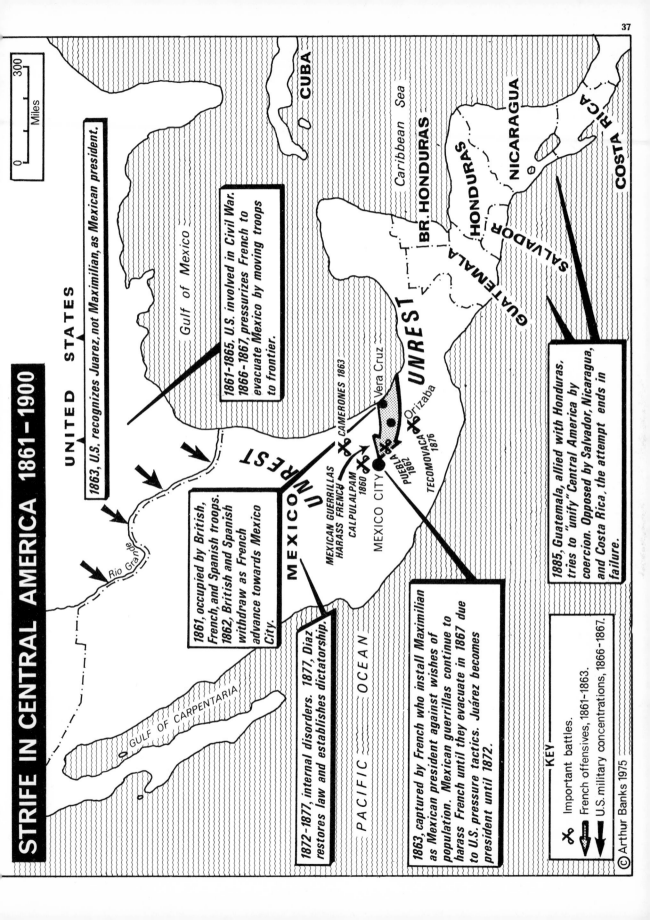

STRIFE IN CENTRAL AMERICA 1861–1900

UNITED STATES

1863, U.S. recognizes Juarez, not Maximilian, as Mexican president.

Gulf of Mexico

1861–1865, U.S. involved in Civil War. 1866–1867, pressurizes French to evacuate Mexico by moving troops to frontier.

1861, occupied by British, French, and Spanish troops. 1862, British and Spanish withdraw as French advance towards Mexico City.

1872–1877, internal disorders. 1877, Diaz restores law and establishes dictatorship.

1863, captured by French who install Maximilian as Mexican president against wishes of population. Mexican guerrillas continue to harass French until they evacuate in 1867 due to U.S. pressure tactics. Juárez becomes president until 1872.

MEXICAN UNREST

MEXICAN GUERRILLAS HARASS FRENCH

CALPULALPAM 1860

CAMERONES 1863

Vera Cruz

Orizaba

PUEBLA 1862

TECOMOVACA 1876

MEXICO CITY

UNREST

Rio Grande

GULF OF CARPENTARIA

PACIFIC OCEAN

Caribbean Sea

CUBA

BR. HONDURAS

HONDURAS

HONDURAS

GUATEMALA

SALVADOR

NICARAGUA

COSTA RICA

1885, Guatemala, allied with Honduras, tries to "unify" Central America by coercion. Opposed by Salvador, Nicaragua, and Costa Rica, the attempt ends in failure.

Miles
0   300

— KEY —

⚔ Important battles.

▸ French offensives, 1861–1863.

⬇ U.S. military concentrations, 1866–1867.

© Arthur Banks 1975

THE UNIFICATION OF ITALY

KEY

- ✗ Important battles.
- ▬▬ Northern extent of Kingdom of Italy, 1866–1914.
- ⋯⋯ States joined with Kingdom of Italy.

0   Miles   300

In 1859, the Kingdom of Sardinia, supported by France, went to war to drive Austria out of Italy. Victories at Magenta and Solferino and Garibaldi's successes in the south encouraged revolutionary activities and these were followed by the collapse of most governments south of the River Po. In 1861, the Kingdom of Italy was proclaimed under Savoy, excluding Venetia and Rome: these were annexed to Italy in 1866 and 1870 respectively.

© Arthur Banks 1975

1859, allied with France.

1860, Garibaldi and the Thousand 'land here.

KINGDOM OF SARDINIA

GARIBALDI

PIEDMONT

SAVOY

NICE

Genoa

LOMBARDY

MAGENTA 1859

PARMA 1859

MODENA

LUCCA

TUSCANY

VENETIA

SOLFERINO 1859

Po

PAPAL STATES

ABRUZZI

ROME 1862

PONTECORVO

VOLTURNO 1860

BENEVENTO

CAMPANIA

APULIA

KINGDOM OF THE TWO SICILIES

CALABRIA

ASPROMONTE 1862

MILAZZO 1860

SICILY

Marsala

SARDINIA

CORSICA

ADRIATIC SEA

MEDITERRANEAN SEA

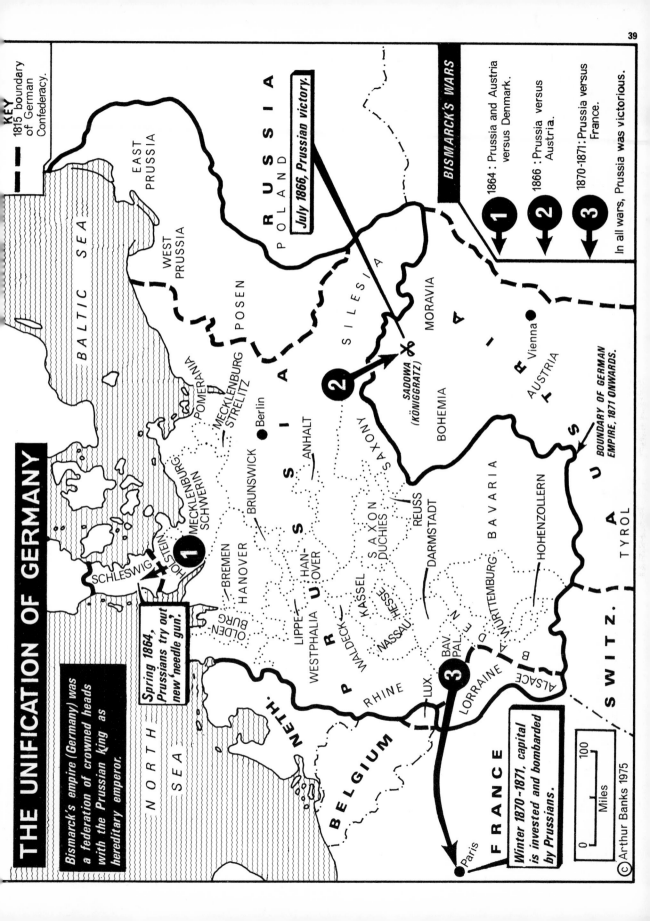

THE UNIFICATION OF GERMANY

Bismarck's empire (Germany) was a federation of crowned heads with the Prussian king as hereditary emperor.

KEY
1815 boundary of German Confederacy.

July 1866, Prussian victory.

BISMARCK'S WARS

1 1864 : Prussia and Austria versus Denmark.

2 1866 : Prussia versus Austria.

3 1870-1871: Prussia versus France.

In all wars, Prussia was victorious.

Spring 1864, Prussians try out new 'needle gun'.

Winter 1870-1871, capital is invested and bombarded by Prussians.

BOUNDARY OF GERMAN EMPIRE, 1871 ONWARDS.

RUSSIA
POLAND
EAST PRUSSIA
WEST PRUSSIA
BALTIC SEA
POSEN
SILESIA
MORAVIA
BOHEMIA
Vienna
AUSTRIA
SADOWA (KÖNIGGRATZ)
MECKLENBURG STRELITZ
MECKLENBURG SCHWERIN
POMERANIA
Berlin
ANHALT
SAXONY
SAXON DUCHIES
REUSS
DARMSTADT
BRUNSWICK
HANOVER
BREMEN
OLDENBURG
LIPPE
WESTPHALIA
WALDECK
KASSEL
HESSE
NASSAU
HOHENZOLLERN
BAVARIA
WÜRTTEMBURG
BAV. PAL.
TYROL
SWITZ.
ALSACE
LORRAINE
LUX.
RHINE
NETH.
BELGIUM
FRANCE
Paris
SCHLESWIG
HOLSTEIN
NORTH SEA
HANOVER

0   100
Miles

© Arthur Banks 1975

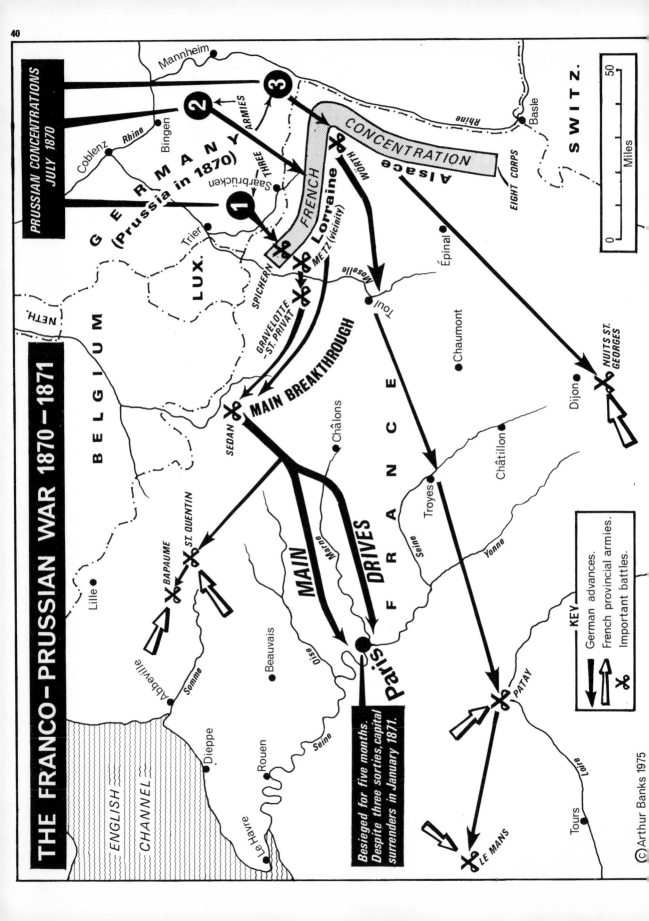

THE FRANCO-PRUSSIAN WAR 1870-1871

PRUSSIAN CONCENTRATIONS JULY 1870

Mannheim

SWITZ.

Basle

Rhine

Coblenz

Rhine

Bingen

GERMANY (Prussia in 1870)

THREE ARMIES

Saarbrucken

Trier

LUX.

WÖRTH

CONCENTRATION

Alsace

EIGHT CORPS

Épinal

NETH.

BELGIUM

SPICHERN

FRENCH

Lorraine

METZ (vicinity)

GRAVELOTTE – ST. PRIVAT

Moselle

Toul

Chaumont

Châtillon

Dijon

NUITS ST. GEORGES

MAIN BREAKTHROUGH

SEDAN

Châlons

Troyes

Seine

Yonne

F R A N C E

MAIN

DRIVES

Marne

Oise

Lille

ST. QUENTIN

BAPAUME

Beauvais

Somme

Abbeville

Dieppe

Rouen

Seine

Paris

Besieged for five months.
Despite three sorties, capital
surrenders in January 1871.

KEY
German advances.
French provincial armies.
Important battles.

PATAY

Le Havre

ENGLISH CHANNEL

Loire

Tours

LE MANS

© Arthur Banks 1975

50
Miles
0

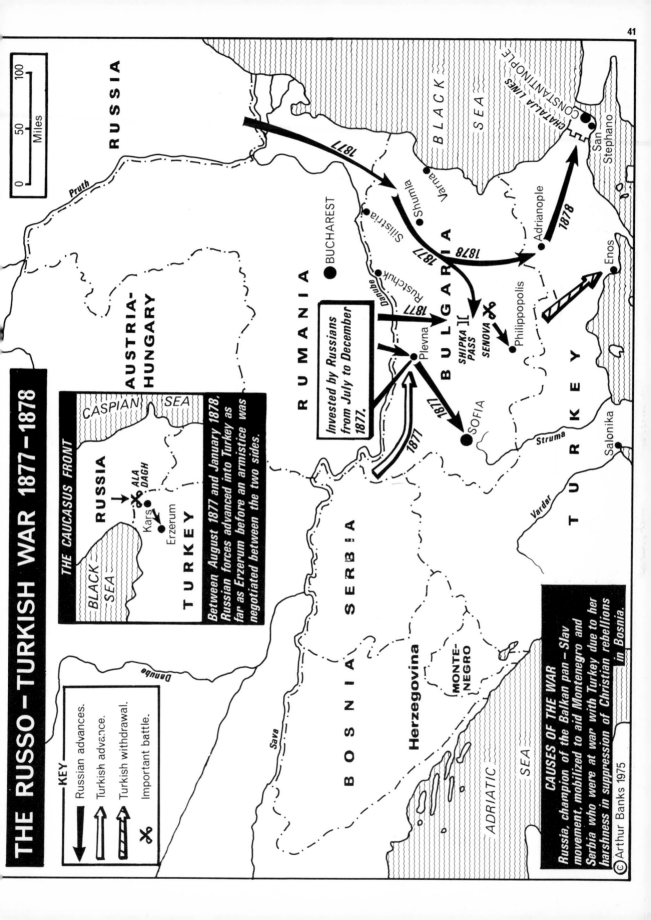

THE RUSSO–TURKISH WAR 1877–1878

KEY
- → Russian advances.
- ⇧ Turkish advance.
- ⇨ Turkish withdrawal.
- ✕ Important battle.

RUSSIA

100
50
0
Miles

Pruth

Danube

AUSTRIA-HUNGARY

BUCHAREST

R U M A N I A

Danube

Silistria

Rustchuk

1877

1877

Plevna

Invested by Russians from July to December 1877.

B U L G A R I A

Shumla

Varna

1877

1878

1878

Adrianople

Enos

SHIPKA PASS

SENOVA ✕

Philippopolis

SOFIA

Struma

T U R K E Y

Salonika

Vardar

B L A C K   S E A

CHATALJA LINES

CONSTANTINOPLE

San Stephano

1878

THE CAUCASUS FRONT

CASPIAN SEA

RUSSIA

ALA DAGH
→ ✕
Kars
Erzerum
T U R K E Y

BLACK SEA

Between August 1877 and January 1878, Russian forces advanced into Turkey as far as Erzerum before an armistice was negotiated between the two sides.

B O S N I A
S E R B I A

Herzegovina

MONTE-NEGRO

Sava

ADRIATIC SEA

CAUSES OF THE WAR

Russia, champion of the Balkan pan–Slav movement, mobilized to aid Montenegro and Serbia who were at war with Turkey due to her harshness in suppression of Christian rebellions in Bosnia.

© Arthur Banks 1975

AUSTRIA–HUNGARY 1867–1918

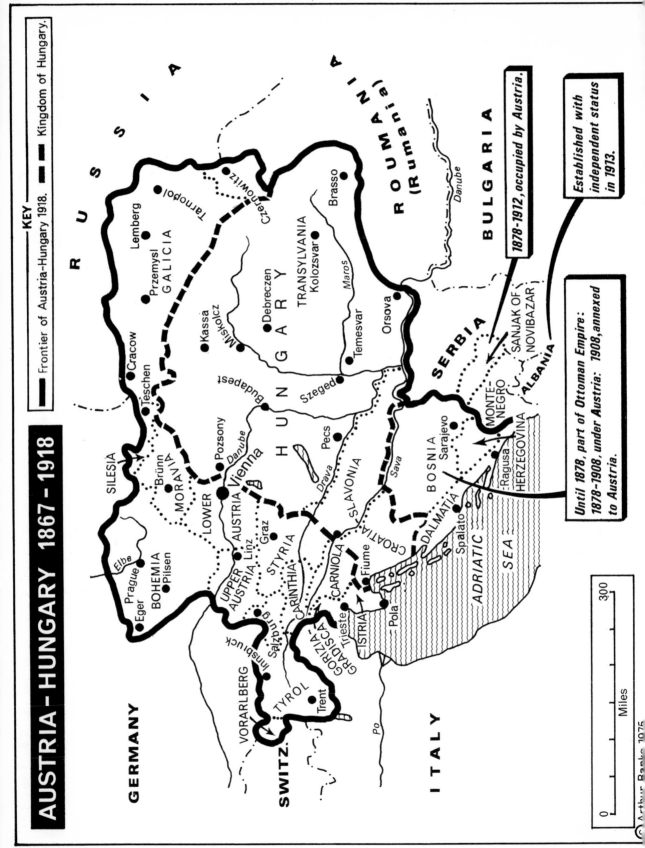

KEY

—— Frontier of Austria-Hungary 1918.

- - - Kingdom of Hungary.

GERMANY

SWITZ.

ITALY

R U S S I A

R O U M A N I A
(Rumania)

BULGARIA

SERBIA

SILESIA

BOHEMIA

Prague
Eger
Pilsen
Elbe

MORAVIA

Brünn

Cracow
Teschen

GALICIA

Przemysl
Lemberg

Tarnopol

Czernowitz

Kassá
Miskolcz

Debreczen

TRANSYLVANIA

Kolozsvar

Brasso

LOWER
AUSTRIA

Vienna

Linz

Pozsony

Danube

Budapest

H U N G A R Y

Szeged

Temesvar

Maros

Orsova

Danube

UPPER
AUSTRIA

Salzburg

Graz

STYRIA

Pecs

Drava

Sava

BOSNIA

Sarajevo

MONTE-
NEGRO

SANJAK OF
NOVIBAZAR

ALBANIA

CARINTHIA

CARNIOLA

SLAVONIA

CROATIA

Fiume

HERZEGOVINA

Ragusa

DALMATIA

Spalato

VORARLBERG

Innsbruck

TYROL

Trent

GORIZIA
GRADISCA

Trieste

ISTRIA

Pola

ADRIATIC   SEA

Po

Miles

0   300

1878-1912, occupied by Austria.

Established with
independent status
in 1913.

Until 1878, part of Ottoman Empire:
1878-1908, under Austria: 1908, annexed
to Austria.

© Arthur Banks 1975

THE WORLD FOLLOWING THE CONGRESS OF BERLIN 1878

KEY

- ■ British territories.
- Russian territories.
- Turkish (Ottoman Empire) territories.
- United States' territories.
- French territories.
- Dutch territories.
- Danish territories.
- Spanish territories.
- Portuguese territories.

Note how Germany (growing in power in Europe) has no imperialist ambitions at this period.

PACIFIC OCEAN

ATLANTIC OCEAN

INDIAN OCEAN

PACIFIC OCEAN

RUSSIA

TURKEY

INDIA

CHINA

FR. INDO CHINA

PHILIPPINE IS. (S)

DUTCH EAST INDIES

AUSTRALIA

Tasmania

NEW ZEALAND

Chatham I. (B)

Norfolk I. (B)

New Caledonia (F)

Fiji Is. (B)

Caroline Is. (S)

Mariana Is. (S)

Hong Kong (B)

Singapore

Andaman Is. (B)

CEYLON

Laccadives (B)

Maldives (B)

Seychelles (B)

MADAGASCAR

Mauritius (F)

Reunion (F)

DENMARK

BRITAIN

FRANCE

SPAIN

PORTUGAL

HOLLAND

ICELAND

GREENLAND

Malta (B)

Gibraltar (B)

Azores (P)

Madeira (P)

Canary Is. (S)

ALGERIA

EGYPT

SENEGAL

S. LEONE

GOLD COAST

ANGOLA

MOZAM-BIQUE

SOUTH AFRICA

Walvisch Bay (B)

Ascension (B)

St. Helena I. (B)

Tristan da Cunha (B)

CANADA

ALASKA

UNITED STATES

MEXICO

BRITISH HONDURAS

Bermuda (B)

Bahama Is. (B)

Porto Rico (S)

Cuba (S)

Jamaica (B)

Leeward Is. (B)

Windward Is. (B)

Trinidad (B)

FR. GUIANA

BR. GUIANA

BRAZIL

PERU

EQUADOR

URUGUAY

ARGENTINA

CHILE

Falkland Is. (B)

Malden I. (B)

Marquesas Is. (F)

Paumotu Is. (F)

Pitcairn I. (B)

Society Is. (F)

0   2000

Miles

© Arthur Banks 1975

THE ZULU WAR 1879

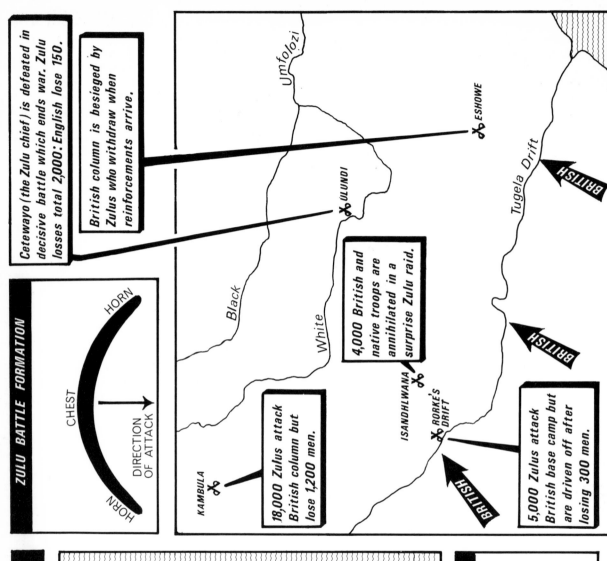

ZULU BATTLE FORMATION

HORN

CHEST

DIRECTION
OF ATTACK

HORN

Cetewayo (the Zulu chief) is defeated in decisive battle which ends war. Zulu losses total 2,000: English lose 150.

British column is besieged by Zulus who withdraw when reinforcements arrive.

4,000 British and native troops are annihilated in a surprise Zulu raid.

18,000 Zulus attack British column but lose 1,200 men.

5,000 Zulus attack British base camp but are driven off after losing 300 men.

Umfolozi

ESHOWE

ULUNDI

Black

White

ISANDHLWANA

RORKE'S DRIFT

KAMBULA

Tugela Drift

BRITISH

BRITISH

BRITISH

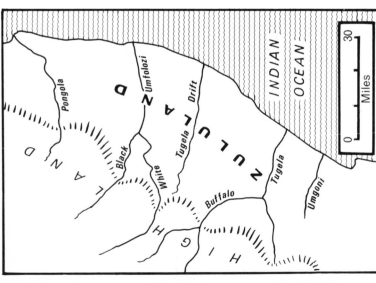

Pongola

Umfolozi

Drift

Z U L U L A N D

Black

White

Tugela

Buffalo

Tugela

Umgeni

H I G H L A N D

INDIAN
OCEAN

0   30
Miles

MAIN EVENTS

1 22 JANUARY: Battle of Isandhlwana.

2 22/23 JANUARY: Battle of Rorke's Drift.

3 JANUARY–APRIL: Siege of Eshowe.

4 29 MARCH: Battle of Kambula.

5 4 JULY: Battle of Ulundi.

© Arthur Banks 1975

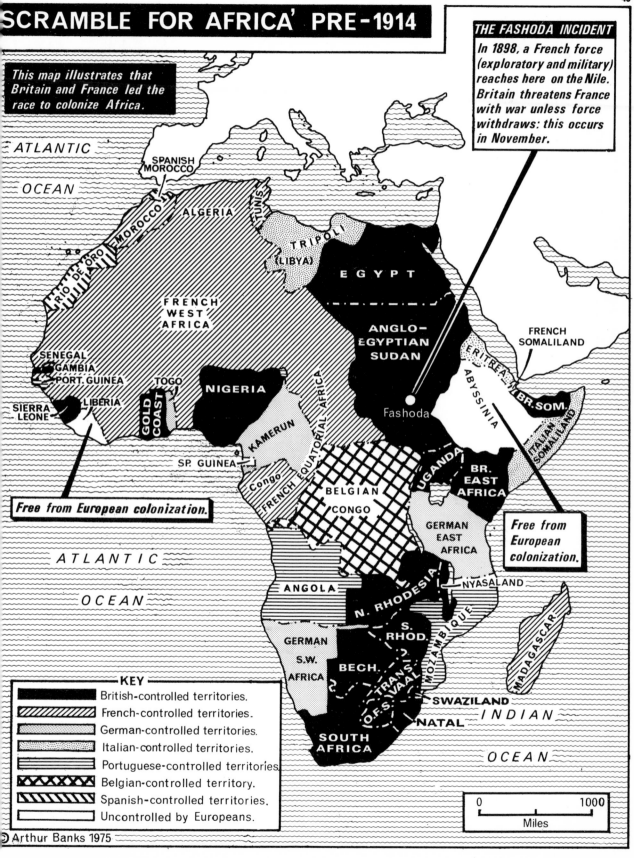

SCRAMBLE FOR AFRICA' PRE-1914

This map illustrates that Britain and France led the race to colonize Africa.

THE FASHODA INCIDENT

In 1898, a French force (exploratory and military) reaches here on the Nile. Britain threatens France with war unless force withdraws: this occurs in November.

ATLANTIC OCEAN

SPANISH MOROCCO

ALGERIA

TUNIS

RIO DE ORO

MOROCCO

TRIPOLI (LIBYA)

EGYPT

FRENCH WEST AFRICA

ANGLO-EGYPTIAN SUDAN

FRENCH SOMALILAND

ERITREA

BR. SOM.

ABYSSINIA

SENEGAL
GAMBIA
PORT. GUINEA
LIBERIA
SIERRA LEONE

TOGO

GOLD COAST

NIGERIA

KAMERUN

SP. GUINEA

Congo

FRENCH EQUATORIAL AFRICA

Fashoda

ITALIAN SOMALILAND

BELGIAN CONGO

UGANDA

BR. EAST AFRICA

Free from European colonization.

GERMAN EAST AFRICA

Free from European colonization.

ATLANTIC OCEAN

ANGOLA

N. RHODESIA

NYASALAND

S. RHOD.

MOZAMBIQUE

MADAGASCAR

GERMAN S.W. AFRICA

BECH.

TRANS-VAAL

O.F.S.

SWAZILAND

NATAL

INDIAN OCEAN

SOUTH AFRICA

KEY

- British-controlled territories.
- French-controlled territories.
- German-controlled territories.
- Italian-controlled territories.
- Portuguese-controlled territories.
- Belgian-controlled territory.
- Spanish-controlled territories.
- Uncontrolled by Europeans.

0   1000
Miles

© Arthur Banks 1975

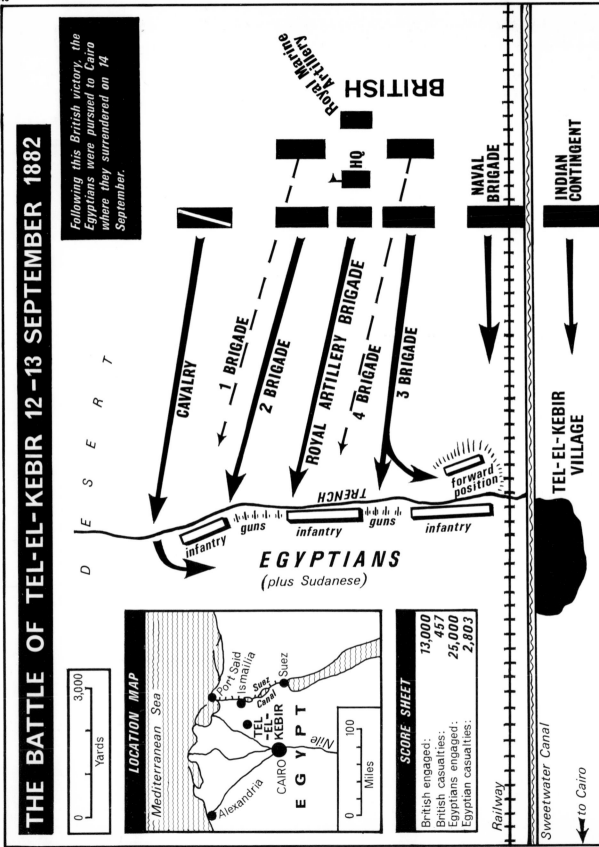

THE BATTLE OF TEL-EL-KEBIR 12–13 SEPTEMBER 1882

Following this British victory, the Egyptians were pursued to Cairo where they surrendered on 14 September.

BRITISH

Royal Marine
Royal Artillery

HQ

CAVALRY
1 BRIGADE
2 BRIGADE
ROYAL ARTILLERY BRIGADE
4 BRIGADE
3 BRIGADE

NAVAL BRIGADE
INDIAN CONTINGENT

TEL-EL-KEBIR VILLAGE

D E S E R T

forward position

TRENCH

infantry   guns   infantry   guns   infantry

EGYPTIANS
(plus Sudanese)

Railway
Sweetwater Canal
to Cairo

LOCATION MAP

Mediterranean Sea
Port Said
Ismailia
Suez Canal
Suez
TEL-EL-KEBIR
CAIRO
E G Y P T
Nile
Alexandria

0   3,000
Yards

0   100
Miles

SCORE SHEET

British engaged: 13,000
British casualties: 457
Egyptians engaged: 25,000
Egyptian casualties: 2,803

© Arthur Banks 1975

46

THE BATTLE OF OMDURMAN 2 SEPTEMBER 1898

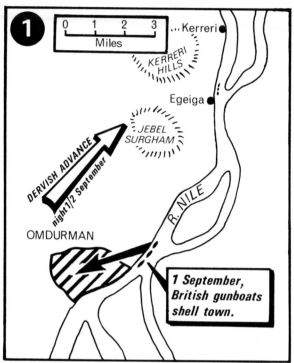

1

0 1 2 3
Miles

...Kerreri

KERRERI HILLS

Egeiga

JEBEL SURGHAM

DERVISH ADVANCE night 1/2 September

R. NILE

OMDURMAN

1 September, British gunboats shell town.

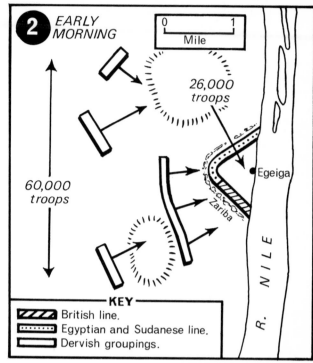

2 *EARLY MORNING*

0 1
Mile

26,000 troops

60,000 troops

Egeiga

Zariba

R. NILE

KEY
- British line.
- Egyptian and Sudanese line.
- Dervish groupings.

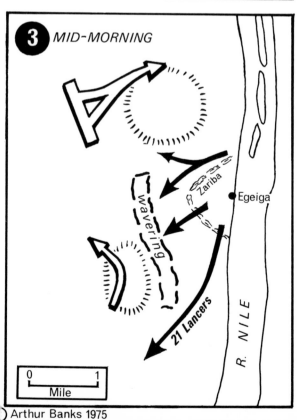

3 *MID-MORNING*

Zariba

wavering

Egeiga

21 Lancers

R. NILE

0 1
Mile

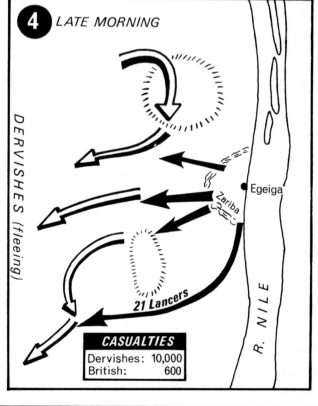

4 *LATE MORNING*

DERVISHES (fleeing)

Zariba

Egeiga

21 Lancers

R. NILE

CASUALTIES
Dervishes: 10,000
British: 600

Arthur Banks 1975

48

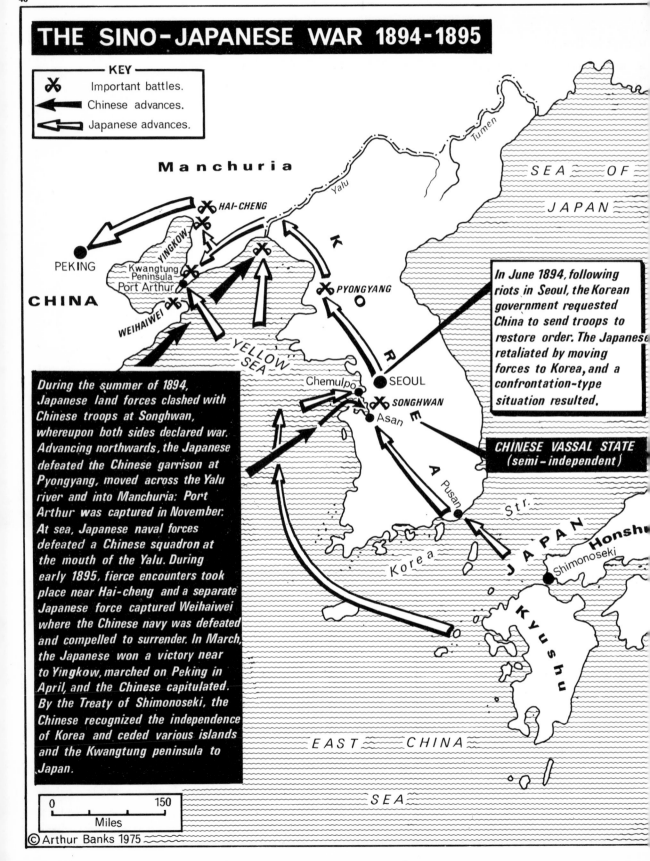

THE SINO-JAPANESE WAR 1894-1895

KEY
Important battles.
Chinese advances.
Japanese advances.

Manchuria

HAI-CHENG

PEKING

YINGKOW

Kwangtung Peninsula
Port Arthur

CHINA

WEIHAIWEI

PYONGYANG

YELLOW SEA

K O R E A

SEA OF JAPAN

Yalu

Tumen

In June 1894, following riots in Seoul, the Korean government requested China to send troops to restore order. The Japanese retaliated by moving forces to Korea, and a confrontation-type situation resulted.

Chemulpo

SEOUL

SONGHWAN

Asan

CHINESE VASSAL STATE
(semi-independent)

During the summer of 1894, Japanese land forces clashed with Chinese troops at Songhwan, whereupon both sides declared war. Advancing northwards, the Japanese defeated the Chinese garrison at Pyongyang, moved across the Yalu river and into Manchuria: Port Arthur was captured in November. At sea, Japanese naval forces defeated a Chinese squadron at the mouth of the Yalu. During early 1895, fierce encounters took place near Hai-cheng and a separate Japanese force captured Weihaiwei where the Chinese navy was defeated and compelled to surrender. In March, the Japanese won a victory near to Yingkow, marched on Peking in April, and the Chinese capitulated. By the Treaty of Shimonoseki, the Chinese recognized the independence of Korea and ceded various islands and the Kwangtung peninsula to Japan.

Pusan

Str.

J A P A N

Shimonoseki

Honshu

Korea

Kyushu

EAST CHINA

SEA

0   150
Miles

© Arthur Banks 1975

THE BOER (or SOUTH AFRICAN) WAR 1899-1902

The war was in two phases: the first (1899–1902) was an active open fight between Boers and British Empire troops which seemed to end with the victorious British advance of 1900. The second (1900-1902) was a guerrilla-style campaign by the Boers which caused the British to raid farms and homes and to force Boer women and children into concentration camps.

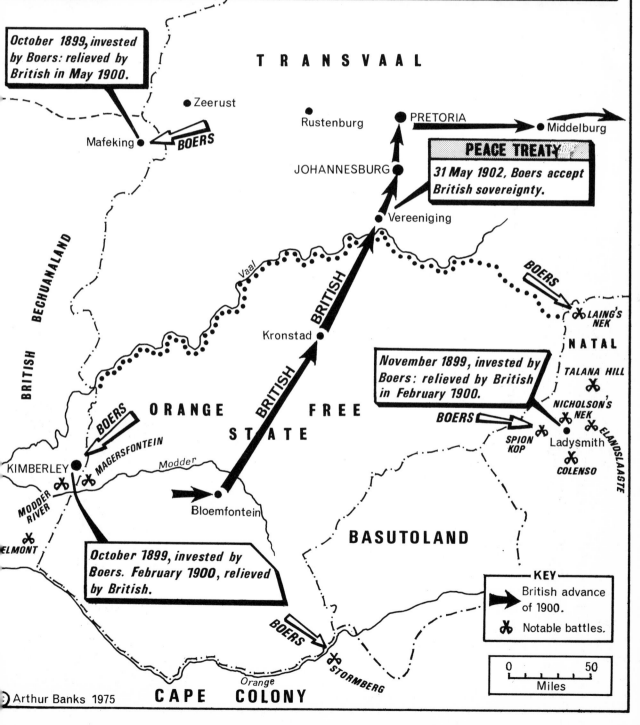

October 1899, invested by Boers: relieved by British in May 1900.

T R A N S V A A L

• Zeerust

• Rustenburg

• PRETORIA → • Middelburg

• JOHANNESBURG

BOERS → Mafeking

PEACE TREATY

31 May 1902, Boers accept British sovereignty.

Vereeniging

Vaal

BRITISH

Kronstad

November 1899, invested by Boers: relieved by British in February 1900.

BOERS →

LAING'S NEK

N A T A L

TALANA HILL

NICHOLSON'S NEK

BRITISH

O R A N G E   F R E E

BOERS →

S T A T E

SPION KOP

Ladysmith

ELANDSLAAGTE

MAGERSFONTEIN

KIMBERLEY

Modder

COLENSO

MODDER RIVER

ELMONT

Bloemfontein

October 1899, invested by Boers. February 1900, relieved by British.

B A S U T O L A N D

KEY

→ British advance of 1900.

✖ Notable battles.

BOERS →

STORMBERG

0   50

Miles

Orange

© Arthur Banks 1975

C A P E   C O L O N Y

BRITISH BECHUANALAND

THE "BOXER" REBELLION 1900

THE TWO ALLIED ATTEMPTS TO RELIEVE PEKING

2

August, Allied relief force arrives here.

Peking

Pei Ho

Yang Tsun

Pietsang

TIENTSIN

Hun Ho

1

Peking

Tungchow

Pei Ho

Anping

June, Allied relief force repulsed by Boxers.

Yang Tsun

TIENTSIN

Taku

Hun Ho

0   30
Miles

↓ Allied relief forces.

✕ Important battles.

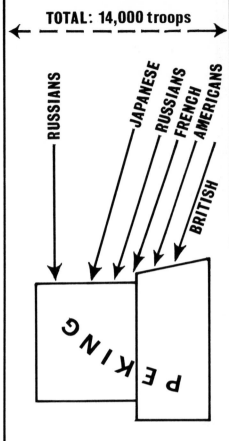

TOTAL: 14,000 troops

RUSSIANS

JAPANESE
RUSSIANS
FRENCH
AMERICANS

BRITISH

PEKING

PLAN OF PEKING

WALL

TARTAR CITY   Imperial City

Forbidden City

Palace

North Cathedral

South Cathedral

LEGATION AREA

BESIEGED DIPLOMATS AND FAMILIES

WALL

CHINESE CITY

WALL

For fifty-five days during the summer of 1900, some two thousand Europeans and Chinese Christians were besieged in Peking by a peasant army known as "Boxers" (Society of Righteous Harmonious Fists). Two attempts were made to relieve them by Allied (British, French, American, Russian, and Japanese) forces, the first (in June) being unsuccessful, the second (in August) succeeding.

© Arthur Renie 1975

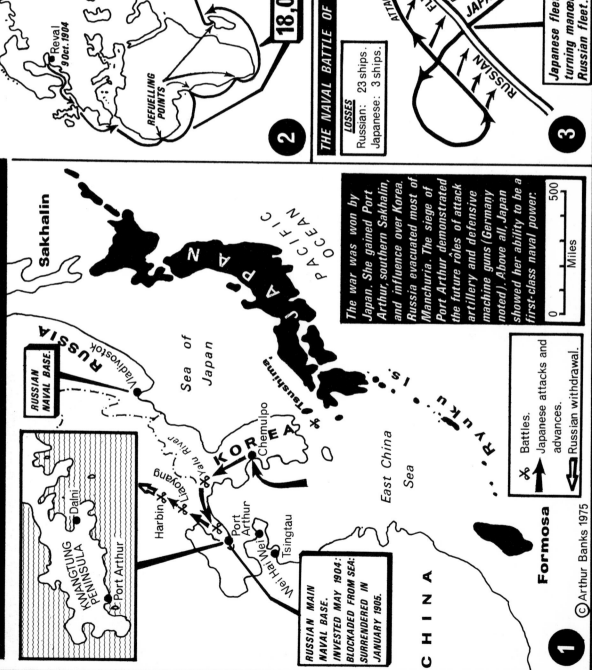

THE RUSSO–JAPANESE WAR 1904–1905

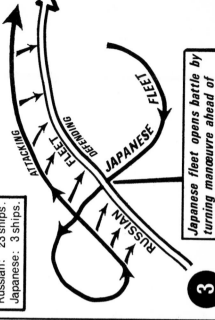

THE LONG VOYAGE OF RUSSIA'S BALTIC FLEET

Tsushima 27 May 1905

Reval 9 Oct. 1904

18,000 miles

REFUELLING POINTS

2

THE NAVAL BATTLE OF TSUSHIMA 27 MAY 1905

LOSSES
Russian: 23 ships.
Japanese: 3 ships.

ATTACKING

RUSSIAN FLEET

DEFENDING

JAPANESE FLEET

Japanese fleet opens battle by turning manoeuvre ahead of Russian fleet.

3

Sakhalin

J A P A N

P A C I F I C   O C E A N

Sea of Japan

Vladivostok

RUSSIAN NAVAL BASE.

RUSSIA

Harbin

Liaoyang

Yalu River

K O R E A

Chemulpo

Port Arthur

Wei Hai Wei

Tsingtau

KWANGTUNG PENINSULA

Dalni

Port Arthur

RUSSIAN MAIN NAVAL BASE.
INVESTED MAY 1904:
BLOCKADED FROM SEA:
SURRENDERED IN JANUARY 1905.

Tsushima

R Y U K Y U   I s.

East China Sea

Formosa

C H I N A

The war was won by Japan. She gained Port Arthur, southern Sakhalin, and influence over Korea. Russia evacuated most of Manchuria. The siege of Port Arthur demonstrated the future rôles of attack artillery and defensive machine guns (Germany noted). Above all, Japan showed her ability to be a first-class naval power.

0 ⊢——————⊣ 500
Miles

✳ Battles.
➡ Japanese attacks and advances.
⇨ Russian withdrawal.

© Arthur Banks 1975

1

CHIEF ARMIES OF THE WORLD 1906

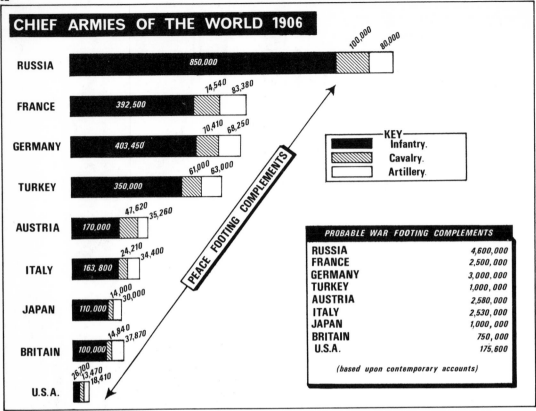

RUSSIA	850,000	100,000	80,000
FRANCE	392,500	74,540	83,380
GERMANY	403,450	70,410	68,250
TURKEY	350,000	61,000	63,000
AUSTRIA	170,000	47,620	35,260
ITALY	163,800	24,210	34,400
JAPAN	110,000	14,000	30,000
BRITAIN	100,000	14,840	37,870
U.S.A.	26,100	13,470	18,410

PEACE FOOTING COMPLEMENTS

KEY
- Infantry.
- Cavalry.
- Artillery.

PROBABLE WAR FOOTING COMPLEMENTS

RUSSIA	4,600,000
FRANCE	2,500,000
GERMANY	3,000,000
TURKEY	1,000,000
AUSTRIA	2,580,000
ITALY	2,530,000
JAPAN	1,000,000
BRITAIN	750,000
U.S.A.	175,600

(based upon contemporary accounts)

CHIEF NAVIES OF THE WORLD 1906

This was the year when the British 'Dreadnought' battleship was launched.

COUNTRY	BATTLESHIPS (first class)	BATTLESHIPS (other classes)	CRUISERS (first class)	CRUISERS (other classes)	DESTROYERS, SUBMARINES, M.T.B.'s	OFFICERS & MEN
BRITAIN	45	15	38	87	232	129,000
U.S.A.	15	11	7	14	47	37,000
FRANCE	11	19	10	37	271	29,500
GERMANY	18	13	6	24	103	33,500
RUSSIA	4	7	2	10	145	60,000
ITALY	4	9	3	17	61	26,800
JAPAN	10	4	9	17	72	36,000

Note: it was the axiom of British naval policy that her navy should roughly equal in strength the combined fleets of the next two largest naval powers.

THE ITALO-TURKISH WAR 1911-1912

BLACK SEA

TURKEY

TURKEY

April 1912, Italian naval units attack straits which are closed by Turks.

Dardanelles

Dodecanese

Rhodes

May 1912, occupied by Italian naval forces.

SPAIN

ITALY

TURKEY

MEDITERRANEAN SEA

TUNISIA

ALGERIA

MOROCCO

FRENCH EMPIRE

TRIPOLI

MAIN CAUSE OF THE WAR. Italy wished to counterbalance the French empire in North Africa by conquering the Turkish colony of Tripoli (Libya).

ALGERIA

TUNISIA

MEDITERRANEAN SEA

1911-1912, bombarded and occupied by Italians.

Tripoli

Homs

Benghazi

Derna

Tobruk

TRIPOLI

EGYPT

Due to the outbreak of the Balkan War, Turkey sued for peace in October 1912.

0 200 Miles

© Arthur Banks 1975

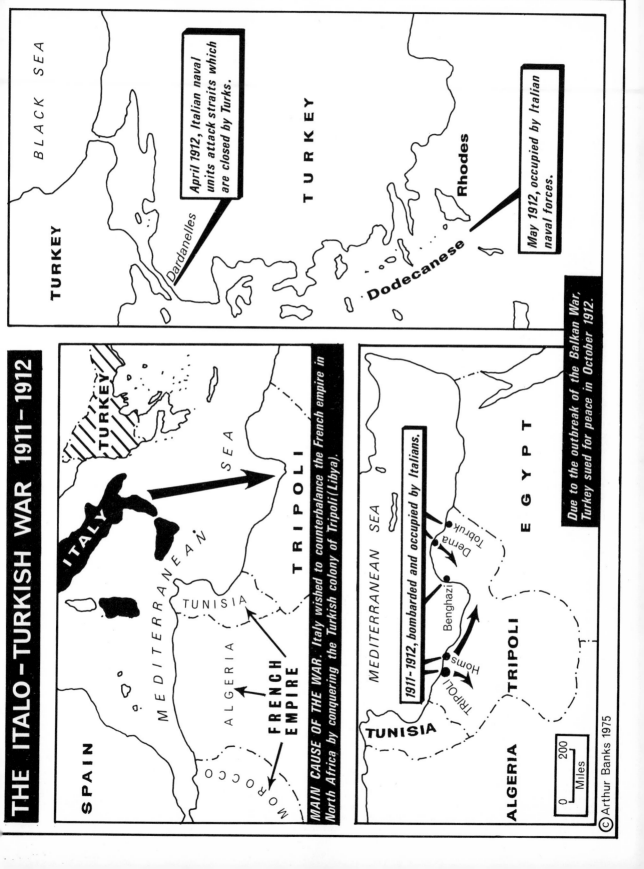

CRISES IN NORTH AFRICA AND THE BALKANS 1905-1912

0 [____] 300
Miles

RUSSIA

GERMANY

AUSTRIA-HUNGARY

SWITZ.

FRANCE

SPAIN

ITALY

BRITAIN

closer links

BULGARIA

Constantinople

Black Sea

O T T O M A N

E M P I R E

(T U R K E Y)

Salonika

REVOLT SPREADS

Herzegovina

Bosnia

GREECE

union

Crete

Sea

Rhodes

Mediterranean Sea

Tunis (French)

Tripolitania

TRIPOLI (LIBYA)

F E Z Z A N

Cyrenaica

Ouchy

Algeciras

Tangier

Fez

Agadir

M O R O C C O

ATLANTIC OCEAN

1 *1905-1906 CRISIS IN MOROCCO*
31 March 1905, Kaiser Wilhelm II visits Tangier and claims equal rights for Germany in Morocco and the maintenance of the Moorish Empire; this is a challenge to the position of France in Morocco. Britain supports France. The Algeciras Conference of 1906 avoids a Franco-German clash.

2 *1908 YOUNG TURK REVOLT*
Young Turkey Party demands constitutional government; this is conceded by Sultan of Turkey. Bulgaria violates Treaty of Berlin 1878 (Article One) by proclaiming herself an independent kingdom. Greece-Crete union.

3 *1908 CRISIS IN BOSNIA*
Austria annexes Bosnia and Herzegovina (mainly Serb-populated). Germany supports Austria. Slavs look to Russia for support, but latter is still weak after Russo-Japanese war (1904-1905). Faced by the Austro-German combination, Russia backs out.

4 *1911 CRISIS IN MOROCCO*
French army units occupy Fez to assist Sultan in maintaining control against rebels. Germany views this action as a breach of the 1906 Algeciras Treaty and despatches warship SMS "Panther" to Agadir to safeguard German interests. 5 November 1911, Germany recognizes French protectorate in return for territorial adjustments in her favour in West Africa.

5 *1911-1912 TURCO-ITALIAN WAR*
Having lost Tunis to France in 1881, Italy views activity in Morocco with suspicion. Fearful of eventually losing Tripoli also, she declares war on Turkey (29 September 1911) and her troops occupy Tripoli's coastal zone (shaded ▨ on map). Turkey fears an attack by the Balkan League and concludes peace with Italy at Ouchy (15 October 1912). Italy virtually (not formally) annexes the whole area.

After the Bosnian crisis, Russia saw Germany as her future main foe, not Austria.

1912, Italy seizes the Dodecanese and Rhodes.

As a result of the crisis in Bosnia, Italy distrusted Austria, thus weakening the Triple Alliance.

The crises in Morocco caused France to draw closer to Britain.

Britain was worried over development of Agadir; future 'naval base' for Germany?

Italian occupation of the interior hampered by both Arab and

WORLD EMPIRES OF BRITAIN, FRANCE, AND GERMANY 1914

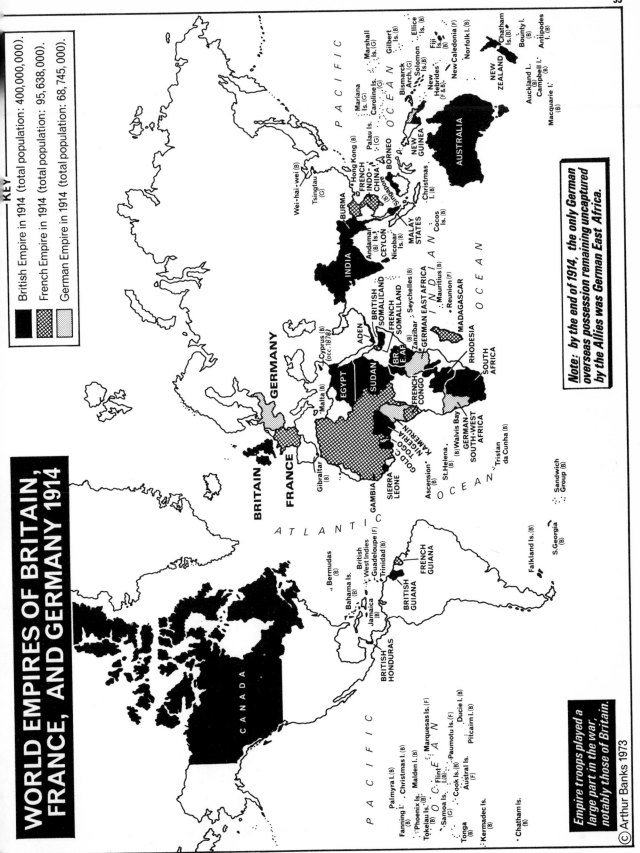

KEY

■	British Empire in 1914 (total population: 400,000,000).
▨	French Empire in 1914 (total population: 95,638,000).
▧	German Empire in 1914 (total population: 68,745,000).

Note: *by the end of 1914, the only German overseas possession remaining uncaptured by the Allies was German East Africa.*

Empire troops played a large part in the war, notably those of Britain.

© Arthur Banks 1973

PACIFIC OCEAN

Marshall Is. (G)
Mariana Is. (G)
Caroline Is. (G)
Palau Is. (G)
Gilbert Is. (B)
Ellice Is. (B)
Bismarck Arch.(G)
Solomon Is.(G)
New Hebrides (F & B)
New Caledonia (F)
Fiji Is. (B)
Norfolk I. (B)
Chatham Is. (B)
Bounty I. (B)
Antipodes I. (B)
Auckland I. (B)
Campbell I. (B)
Macquarie I. (B)
NEW ZEALAND
AUSTRALIA

Wei-hai-wei (B)
Tsingtau
Hong Kong (B)
FRENCH INDO-CHINA
BORNEO
NEW GUINEA
BURMA
Andaman Is. (B)
Nicobar Is. (B)
CEYLON
MALAY STATES
Singapore (B)
Christmas I. (B)
Cocos Is. (B)
INDIA
INDIAN OCEAN

BRITISH SOMALILAND
FRENCH SOMALILAND
Seychelles (B)
Zanzibar (B)
GERMAN EAST AFRICA
BR. E. AF.
Mauritius (F)
Reunion (F)
MADAGASCAR
RHODESIA
SOUTH AFRICA
ADEN
Cyprus (B) (occ. 1878)
Malta (B)
EGYPT
SUDAN
FRENCH CONGO
GERMANY
GERMAN SOUTH-WEST AFRICA
Walvis Bay (B)
CAMERUN
TOGO
NIGERIA
GOLD COAST
SIERRA LEONE
GAMBIA
Gibraltar (B)
BRITAIN
FRANCE
St. Helena (B)
Ascension (B)
Tristan da Cunha (B)

ATLANTIC OCEAN

Bermudas (B)
Bahama Is. (B)
British West Indies (B)
Guadeloupe (F)
Jamaica (B)
Trinidad (B)
BRITISH HONDURAS
CANADA
BRITISH GUIANA
FRENCH GUIANA
Falkland Is. (B)
S. Georgia (B)
Sandwich Group (B)

PACIFIC OCEAN

Palmyra I. (B)
Christmas I. (B)
Malden I. (B)
Marquesas Is. (F)
Fanning I. (B)
Phoenix Is. (B)
Tokelau Is. (B)
Flint I. (B)
Ducie I. (B)
Pitcairn I. (B)
Samoa I. (G)
Cook Is. (B)
Paumotu Is. (F)
Tonga (B)
Austral Is. (F)
Kermadec Is. (B)
Chatham Is. (B)

THE FIRST BALKAN WAR 1912-1913*

❶ The General Situation

*Note: in two parts, viz.,
1. 18 Oct.– 3 Dec. 1912.
2. 3 Feb.– 10 May 1913.

Russia supports Serbia's demand for a port on the Adriatic coast.

Austria opposes Serbia's demand for a port on Adriatic coast

Rumania does not join Balkan allies but is keen to share in their gains.

Bulgaria is anxious to obtain territory to her south, most of which has been promised to her

Greece occupies and wishes to retain Salonika, which is claimed by Bulgaria.

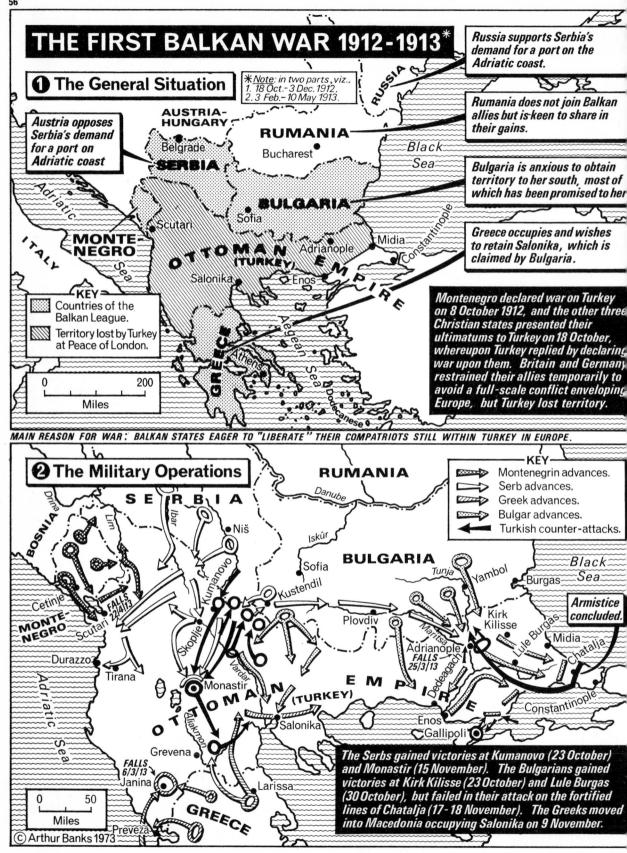

AUSTRIA-HUNGARY

RUMANIA

Belgrade

Bucharest

Black Sea

SERBIA

BULGARIA

Scutari

Sofia

MONTE-NEGRO

OTTOMAN (TURKEY)

Midia

Adrianople

Constantinople

ITALY

Adriatic Sea

Salonika

Enos

EMPIRE

KEY
- Countries of the Balkan League.
- Territory lost by Turkey at Peace of London.

GREECE

Athens

Aegean Sea

Dodecanese

0   200
Miles

Montenegro declared war on Turkey on 8 October 1912, and the other three Christian states presented their ultimatums to Turkey on 18 October, whereupon Turkey replied by declaring war upon them. Britain and Germany restrained their allies temporarily to avoid a full-scale conflict enveloping Europe, but Turkey lost territory.

MAIN REASON FOR WAR: BALKAN STATES EAGER TO "LIBERATE" THEIR COMPATRIOTS STILL WITHIN TURKEY IN EUROPE.

❷ The Military Operations

RUMANIA

KEY
- Montenegrin advances.
- Serb advances.
- Greek advances.
- Bulgar advances.
- Turkish counter-attacks.

SERBIA

Drina

Lim

Ibar

Danube

BOSNIA

Niš

Iskûr

BULGARIA

Sofia

Tunja

Yambol

Black Sea

Burgas

Cetinje

Kumanovo

Kustendil

Plovdiv

Kirk Kilisse

Armistice concluded.

MONTE-NEGRO

Scutari
FALLS 22/4/13

Skoplje

Maritsa

Adrianople
FALLS 25/3/13

Lule Burgas

Midia

Durazzo

Vardar

Dedeagach

Chatalja

Tirana

Monastir

OTTOMAN

EMPIRE

Constantinople

Adriatic Sea

Aliakmon

(TURKEY)

Salonika

Enos

Gallipoli

Grevena

FALLS 6/3/13

Janina

Larissa

The Serbs gained victories at Kumanovo (23 October) and Monastir (15 November). The Bulgarians gained victories at Kirk Kilisse (23 October) and Lule Burgas (30 October), but failed in their attack on the fortified lines of Chatalja (17-18 November). The Greeks moved into Macedonia occupying Salonika on 9 November.

0   50
Miles

© Arthur Banks 1973

Preveza

GREECE

THE SECOND BALKAN WAR 1913*

© Arthur Banks 1973

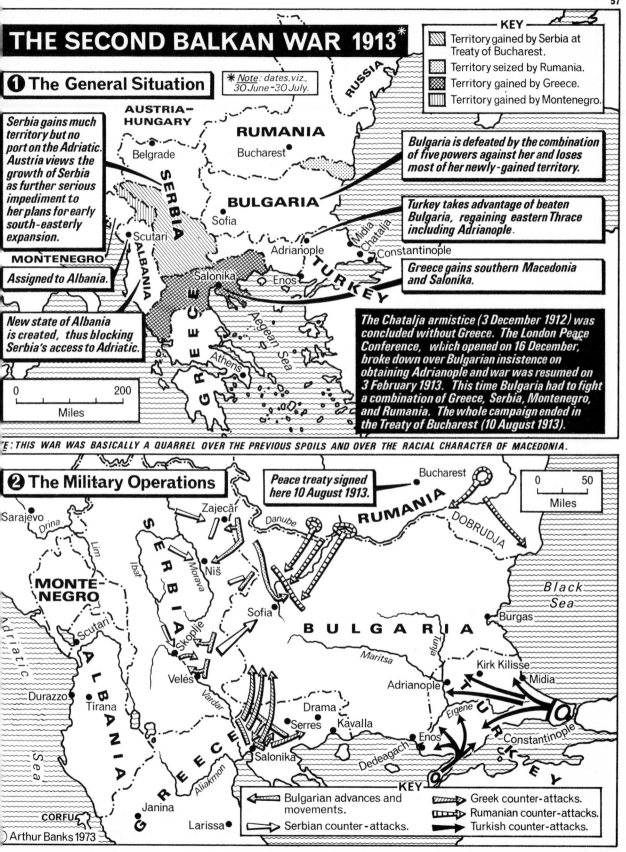

❶ The General Situation

✱ Note: dates, viz., 30 June – 30 July.

KEY
- Territory gained by Serbia at Treaty of Bucharest.
- Territory seized by Rumania.
- Territory gained by Greece.
- Territory gained by Montenegro.

Serbia gains much territory but no port on the Adriatic. Austria views the growth of Serbia as further serious impediment to her plans for early south-easterly expansion.

Bulgaria is defeated by the combination of five powers against her and loses most of her newly-gained territory.

Turkey takes advantage of beaten Bulgaria, regaining eastern Thrace including Adrianople.

MONTENEGRO
Assigned to Albania.

Greece gains southern Macedonia and Salonika.

New state of Albania is created, thus blocking Serbia's access to Adriatic.

The Chatalja armistice (3 December 1912) was concluded without Greece. The London Peace Conference, which opened on 16 December, broke down over Bulgarian insistence on obtaining Adrianople and war was resumed on 3 February 1913. This time Bulgaria had to fight a combination of Greece, Serbia, Montenegro, and Rumania. The whole campaign ended in the Treaty of Bucharest (10 August 1913).

NOTE: THIS WAR WAS BASICALLY A QUARREL OVER THE PREVIOUS SPOILS AND OVER THE RACIAL CHARACTER OF MACEDONIA.

❷ The Military Operations

Peace treaty signed here 10 August 1913.

KEY
- Bulgarian advances and movements.
- Serbian counter-attacks.
- Greek counter-attacks.
- Rumanian counter-attacks.
- Turkish counter-attacks.

THE GROWTH OF THE RUSSIAN EMPIRE IN EUROPE PRE - 1914

0   200

Miles

KOLA

Baltic Sea

Uleaborg

Archangel

G   O   R   O   D

FINLAND

Dvina

Helsingfors

St. Petersburg

Ustiug

N   O   V

Vologda

Perm

Novgorod

Riga

Pskov

Nizhni Novgorod

Kazan

Memel

Rzhev

Tver

Moscow

Ufa

Duna

LITHUANIA

Vilna

Smolensk

Orel

BULGARIANS OF KAZAN

Samara

Niemen

Minsk

Samara

Ural

Warsaw

Pripet

Novgorod Severski

Voronezh

Saratov

Uralsk

POLAND

VOLHYNIA

A   S   T   R   A   K   H   A   N

Kiev

UKRAINE

T   A   R   T   A   R   S

Dniester

Kharkov

GOLDEN

BESSARABIA

Dnieper

HORDE

Volga

Pruth

Odessa

Kherson

DON COSSACKS

Don

Astrakhan

Danube

KRIM

Azov

Kuban

Sevastopol

Terek

Caspian Sea

Black Sea

Batum

Kars

Tiflis

Baku

Krasnovodsk

Aras

Atre

KEY

■	Principality of Moscow 1462.
	Acquisitions 1462 - 1505.
	Acquisitions 1505 - 1584.
	Acquisitions 1584 - 1689.
	Acquisitions 1689 - 1762.
	Acquisitions 1762 - 1801.
	Acquisitions 1801 - 1914.

© Arthur Banks 1975

THE GROWTH OF BRITISH AND RUSSIAN INFLUENCE IN ASIA PRE–1914

KEY

- British possessions 1805.
- British acquisitions 1805–1858.
- British acquisitions 1858–1914.
- British dependent states in India 1914.
- Russian Empire 1725.
- Russian acquisitions 1725–1815.
- Russian acquisitions 1815–1855.
- Russian acquisitions 1855–1914.
- Important railways.
- Important canals.
- ⦿ Treaty ports in China (opening dates).

Bering Sea

Sea of Okhotsk

PACIFIC OCEAN

JAPAN

Verkhoyansk

Turukhansk

RUSSIAN EMPIRE

EUROPE

North Sea

St. Petersburg
Moscow
Warsaw
Kiev
Angora
Black Sea
Kars
Mediterranean Sea
Baghdad
Caspian Sea
Tehran
PERSIA
Kuwait
Omsk
Tashkent
TURKESTAN
AFGHANISTAN
Quetta
Karachi
Arabian Sea
Aden
Red Sea
Cairo
EGYPT
ANGLO EGYPTIAN-SUDAN

MONGOLIA

SINKIANG

TIBET

CHINA

Lahore
Delhi
Lucknow
INDIA
Calcutta
Bay of Bengal
Madras
Colombo
INDIAN OCEAN

Vladivostok 1858
Newchwang 1858
Port Arthur
Weihaiwei
Chefoo 1858
Tungchow 1858
Peking
Nanking 1842
Chinkiang 1861
Shanghai 1842
Ningpo 1842
Wenchow 1876
Foochow 1842
Wuhu 1899
Hankow 1876
Ichang 1876
Shashi 1895
1895
Hangchow
Amoy 1842
Swatow 1858
Canton 1842
Hongkong
Pakhoi 1876
South China Sea
Singapore

1000

0   Miles

© Arthur Banks 1975

THE MIDDLE EAST PRE – 1914

Russian Zone (1907 onwards).

British Zone (1907 onwards).

Neutral Zone (1907 onwards).

800

0

Miles

CHINA

INDIA

Bombay

Indus

RUSSIA

TURKESTAN

Tashkent

Samarkand

Merv

Aral Sea

Caspian Sea

AFGHANISTAN

Kabul

Herat

BALUCHISTAN

Karachi

PERSIA

Meshed

Tehran

Isfahan

Batum

Constantinople

Smyrna

Mediterranean Sea

OTTOMAN

EMPIRE

Aleppo

Damascus

Jerusalem

Tigris

Euphrates

Cairo

Nile

EGYPT

ANGLO-EGYPTIAN SUDAN

HEJAZ

Medina

Jiddah

Mecca

Red Sea

ASSIR

NEJD

YEMEN

Hodeida

Aden

HADRAMAUT

Persian Gulf

QATAR

OMAN

Muscat

ARABIAN GULF

FRENCH SOMALILAND

ERITREA

BRITISH SOMALI

ITALIAN SOMALILAND

ABYSSINIA

POSSESSIONS OF THE UNITED STATES PRE–1914

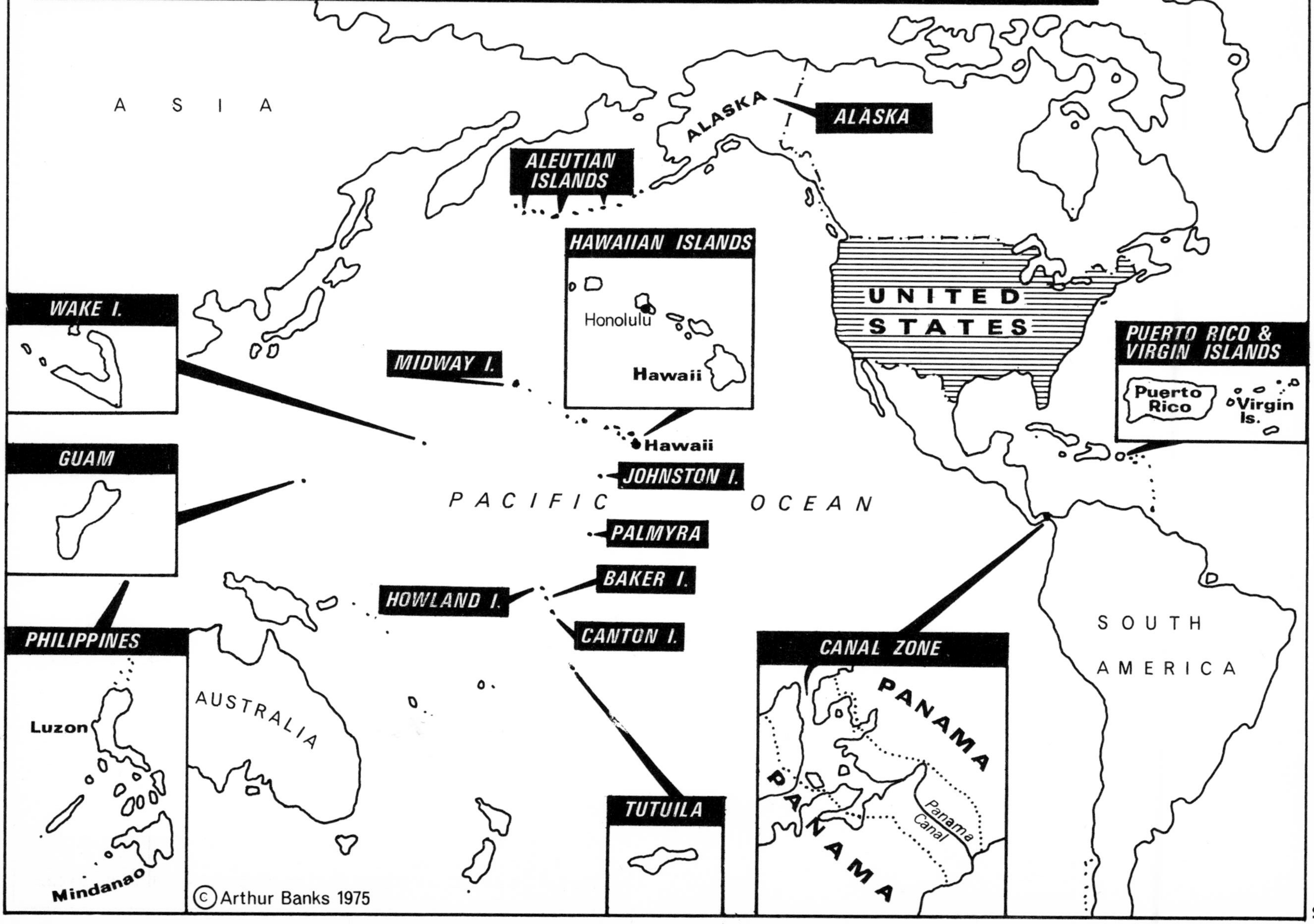

61

PUERTO RICO & VIRGIN ISLANDS

Puerto Rico
Virgin Is.

SOUTH AMERICA

UNITED STATES

ALASKA

ALASKA

PANAMA

Panama Canal

CANAL ZONE

PANAMA

PANAMA

HAWAIIAN ISLANDS

Honolulu
Hawaii

Hawaii

JOHNSTON I.

PALMYRA

BAKER I.

CANTON I.

TUTUILA

ALEUTIAN ISLANDS

PACIFIC OCEAN

MIDWAY I.

HOWLAND I.

ASIA

AUSTRALIA

WAKE I.

GUAM

PHILIPPINES

Luzon

Mindanao

© Arthur Banks 1975

IV
THE FIRST WORLD WAR

EUROPE IN 1914

Note the extents of Germany and Austria-Hungary.

RUSSIA

Finland

SWEDEN

NORWAY

Baltic Sea

DEN.

North Sea

BRITAIN

IRELAND

ATLANTIC OCEAN

GERMANY

Poland

NETH.

BELG.

LUX.

FRANCE

SWITZ.

AUSTRIA-HUNGARY

ITALY

RUMANIA

SERBIA

BULGARIA

MONTE-NEGRO

ALB.

GRECE

Black Sea

TURKEY

SPAIN

PORTUGAL

Mediterranean Sea

Sea

TUNISIA

ALGERIA

MOROCCO

TRIPOLI

EGYPT

© Arthur Banks 1975

Miles
0   400

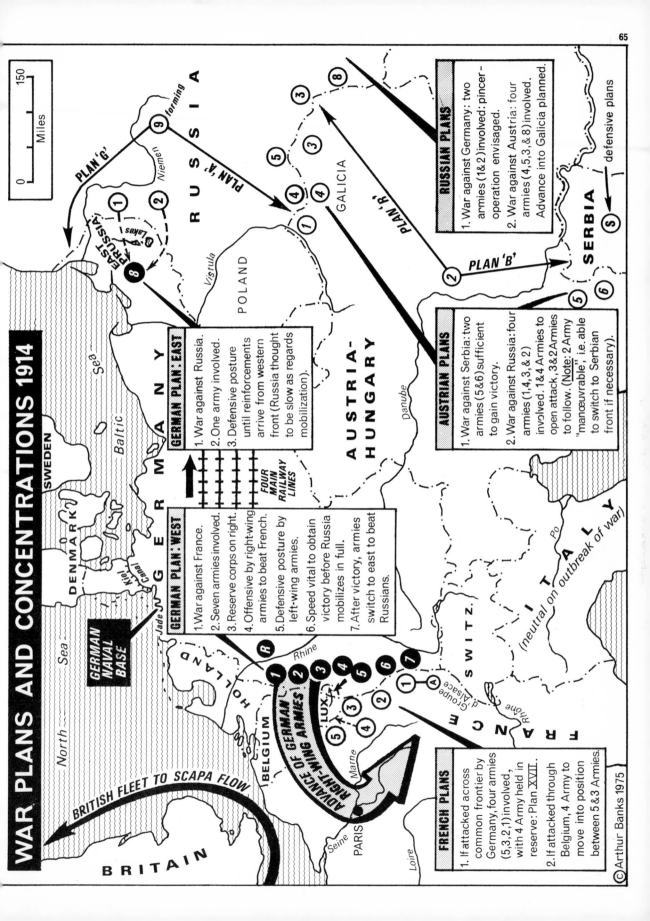

WAR PLANS AND CONCENTRATIONS 1914

150
Miles
0

PLAN 'G'

PLAN 'A'

forming

⑨

① ②

Niemen

EAST PRUSSIA

Lakes

❽

Vistula

R U S S I A

P O L A N D

④ ①

④

⑤

③

③

⑧

GALICIA

PLAN 'R'

RUSSIAN PLANS

1. War against Germany: two armies (1&2) involved: pincer-operation envisaged.
2. War against Austria: four armies (4,5,3, & 8) involved. Advance into Galicia planned.

PLAN 'B'

②

S E R B I A

Ⓢ → defensive plans

⑥

⑤

GERMAN PLAN: EAST

1. War against Russia.
2. One army involved.
3. Defensive posture until reinforcements arrive from western front (Russia thought to be slow as regards mobilization).

FOUR MAIN RAILWAY LINES

AUSTRIAN PLANS

1. War against Serbia: two armies (5&6) sufficient to gain victory.
2. War against Russia: four armies (1,4,3, & 2) involved. 1&4 Armies to open attack, 3&2 Armies to follow. (Note: 2 Army "manoeuvrable", i.e. able to switch to Serbian front if necessary).

GERMAN PLAN: WEST

1. War against France.
2. Seven armies involved.
3. Reserve corps on right.
4. Offensive by right-wing armies to beat French.
5. Defensive posture by left-wing armies.
6. Speed vital to obtain victory before Russia mobilizes in full.
7. After victory, armies switch to east to beat Russians.

SWEDEN

Baltic Sea

G E R M A N Y

DENMARK

Kiel Canal

Jade

GERMAN NAVAL BASE

North Sea

HOLLAND

BELGIUM

Rhine

Ⓡ
① ② ③ ④ ⑤ ⑥ ⑦

ADVANCE OF GERMAN RIGHT-WING ARMIES

LUX.

⑤ ③ ② ①
④ ②
⑤ ③

Ⓐ
Groupe d'Alsace

Rhône

S W I T Z.

A U S T R I A - H U N G A R Y

Danube

I T A L Y

Po

(neutral on outbreak of war)

F R A N C E

Marne

PARIS

Seine

Loire

FRENCH PLANS

1. If attacked across common frontier by Germany, four armies (5,3,2,1) involved, with 4 Army held in reserve: Plan XVII.
2. If attacked through Belgium, 4 Army to move into position between 5 & 3 Armies.

B R I T A I N

BRITISH FLEET TO SCAPA FLOW

© Arthur Banks 1975

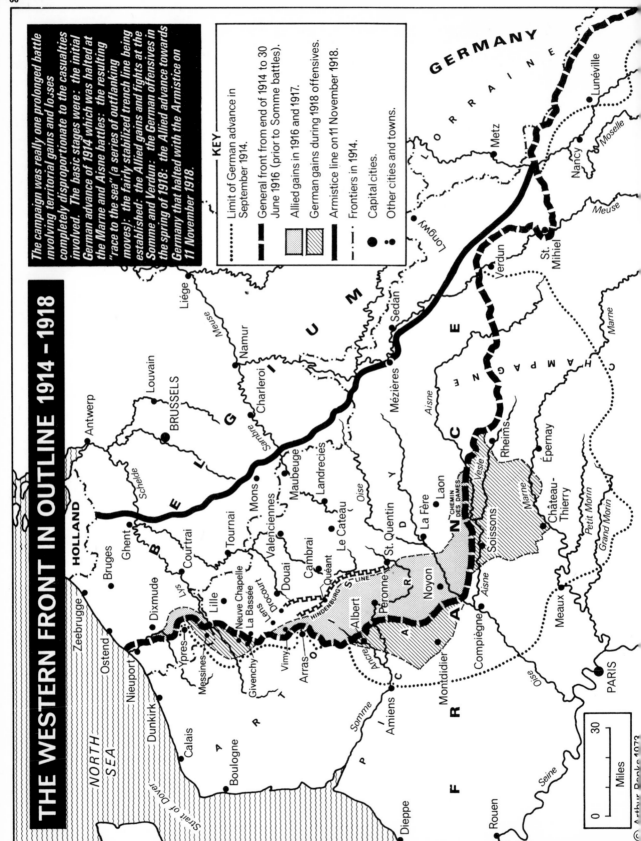

THE WESTERN FRONT IN OUTLINE 1914–1918

The campaign was really one prolonged battle involving territorial gains and losses completely disproportionate to the casualties involved. The basic stages were: the initial German advance of 1914 which was halted at the Marne and Aisne battles: the resulting "race to the sea" (a series of outflanking moves): the fairly stabilized trench line being established: the Allied gains and fights at the Somme and Verdun: the German offensives in the spring of 1918: the Allied advance towards Germany that halted with the Armistice on 11 November 1918.

KEY

- .... Limit of German advance in September 1914.
- ▮▮▮ General front from end of 1914 to 30 June 1916 (prior to Somme battles).
- ▨ Allied gains in 1916 and 1917.
- ▨ German gains during 1918 offensives.
- ▮ Armistice line on 11 November 1918.
- –·–·– Frontiers in 1914.
- ● Capital cities.
- • Other cities and towns.

GERMANY

LORRAINE

Lunéville

Metz

Nancy

Moselle

Meuse

Longwy

Verdun

St. Mihiel

Liège

Namur

Sedan

Mézières

BELGIUM

Louvain

Antwerp

BRUSSELS

Charleroi

Sambre

Schelde

Aisne

ARDENNE

CHAMPAGNE

Rheims

Épernay

Château-Thierry

Marne

Vesle

Soissons

Laon

La Fère

Marne

Petit Morin

Grand Morin

HOLLAND

Ghent

Bruges

Zeebrugge

Ostend

Nieuport

Dunkirk

Calais

Boulogne

Dieppe

Rouen

Dixmude

Ypres

Messines

Courtrai

Lille

Tournai

Mons

Valenciennes

Maubeuge

Landrecies

Le Cateau

Cambrai

Douai

Quéant

St. Quentin

Péronne

Noyon

Albert

Ancre

Somme

Amiens

Montdidier

Compiègne

Oise

Aisne

Meaux

PARIS

Seine

Neuve Chapelle

La Bassée

Givenchy

Lens

Drocourt

Vimy

Arras

HINDENBURG'S LINE

CHEMIN DES DAMES

NORTH SEA

Strait of Dover

Lys

FRANCE

ARTOIS

PICARDY

Scale: Miles 0 — 30

© Arthur Banks 1973

THE EASTERN FRONT IN OUTLINE
1914 – 1918

The battle fronts were not continuous and therefore, the lines on map are generalized. The trench system was not so detailed as on the Western Front and the limits of advances or retreats were not contemporaneous. For example, the Russian advance into East Prussia in 1914 was ended at Tannenberg before their large gains in Galicia were achieved.

KEY
- — · — Frontiers in 1914.
- ● Capital cities.
- • Other cities and towns.

0   200
Miles

Gulf of Finland
Revel
ST. PETERSBURG (Petrograd)
Narva
Pskov
Moscow
Gulf of Riga
Riga
Baltic Sea
Libau
Dvinsk
Dvina
Memel
Kovno
Smolensk
Königsberg
Danzig
Vilna
EAST PRUSSIA
Masuria
Grodno
Tannenberg
Narew
Niemen
Minsk
Prasnysz
Vistula
R U S S I A
Warsaw
Brest-Litovsk
Pinsk
Pripet
POLAND
Lodz
Pripet Marshes
Desna
Radom
Lublin
Vorskha
Cracow
Lemberg
Lutsk
Rovno
Jaroslav
San
GALICIA
Brody
Kiev
Przemysl
Tarnopol
Dnieper
AUSTRIA-HUNGARY
Carpathian Mountains
Stanislau
Bug
Budapest
Dniester
Nikolaiev
HUNGARY
Czernovitz
BUKOVINA
Kishinev
Drava
Danube
Tisza
TRANSYLVANIA
MOLDAVIA
Pruth
BESS-ARABIA
Odessa
Sava
R U M A N I A
DOBRUDJA
MONTE-NEGRO
BELGRADE
WALLACHIA
BUCHAREST
SERBIA
Danube
BULGARIA

KEY
- ▬ ▬ ▬ Limit of Russian advances 1914 - 1915.
- · · · · · · Limit of German advances 1915 - 1916.
- ▨ Territory regained by Brusilov, June - August 1916.
- ▧ German gains in September 1917.
- ▬▬▬ Extent of German penetration into Russia by 3 March 1918 (Treaty of Brest-Litovsk).

©Arthur Banks 1973

OPENING MOVES INVOLVING GERMANY

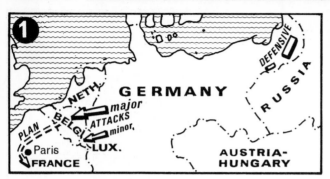

1 GERMANY — RUSSIA — DEFENSIVE — NETH. — PLAN — BELGIUM — *major* ATTACKS — *minor* — LUX. — Paris — FRANCE — AUSTRIA-HUNGARY

2 BRITAIN — GERMANY — NETH. — BEL. — AID — RAPID MOBILISATION — RUSSIA — FRANCE — APPEAL FOR DIVERSIONARY ACTION — AUSTRIA-HUNGARY

3 Antwerp ★ DELAY — NETH. — GERMANY — BELGIUM — FRANCE — Maubeuge ★ DELAY — Liége DELAY ★ — Namur DELAY — LUX. — to Paris — FIRST ARMY — DIVERGING — SECOND ARMY — FRANCE

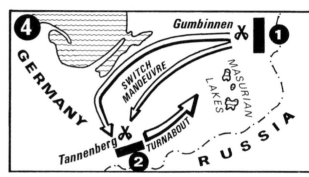

4 Gumbinnen ✂ **1** — GERMANY — SWITCH MANOEUVRE — MASURIAN LAKES — Tannenberg ✂ TURNABOUT **2** — RUSSIA

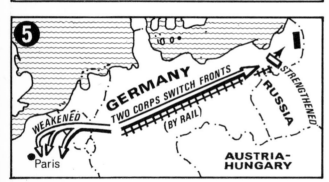

6 SEVENTH ARMY — AISNE — GAP BETWEEN ARMIES — AISNE — FIRST ARMY — FRANCE — SECOND ARMY — BRITISH — VESLE — FRENCH FIFTH ARMY — MARNE

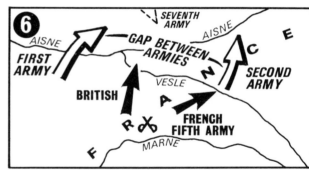

5 GERMANY — TWO CORPS SWITCH FRONTS — STRENGTHENED — RUSSIA — WEAKENED — (BY RAIL) — Paris — AUSTRIA-HUNGARY

7 Kovno ★ — Königsberg ★ — Vilna — RUSSIAN FIRST ARMY — GERMANY — Niemen — EIGHTH ARMY — Masurian Lakes — RUSSIA — Grodno ★

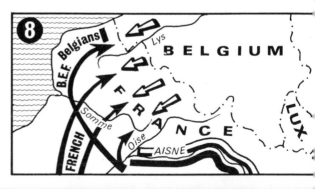

8 Belgians — B.E.F. — Lys — BELGIUM — FRANCE — Somme — FRENCH — Oise — LUX. — AISNE

© Arthur Banks 1975

These sections depict basic military moves involving Germany in the first weeks of the European campaign and illustrate how events and situations on her western and eastern fronts affected and reacted upon each other. In brief, her overall effort was split and she rapidly became involved in an active two-front war situation, the very position for which her detailed pre-war plans had been designed to avoid. These moves are shown in more detail on following pages.

OPENING MOVES INVOLVING OTHER POWERS

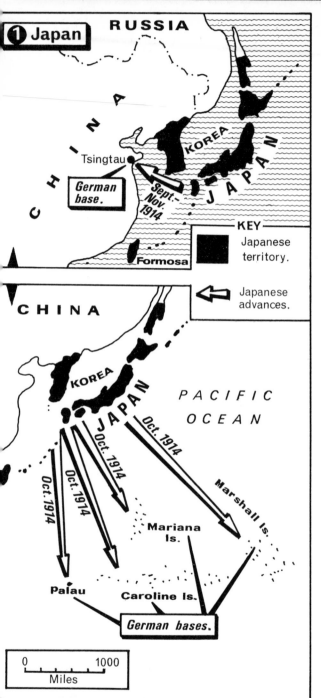

① Japan

RUSSIA

CHINA

KOREA

JAPAN

Tsingtau

German base.

Sept.-Nov. 1914

Formosa

KEY

Japanese territory.

Japanese advances.

CHINA

KOREA

JAPAN

PACIFIC OCEAN

Oct. 1914

Oct. 1914

Oct. 1914

Oct. 1914

Oct. 1914

Marshall Is.

Mariana Is.

Palau

Caroline Is.

German bases.

0   1000
Miles

② Austria-Hungary

RUSSIA

GERMANY

Russians

AUSTRIA-HUNGARY

SWITZ.

ITALY

MONTENEGRO

SERBIA

ALB.

GREECE

RUMANIA

BULGARIA

KEY
Austrian attacks.

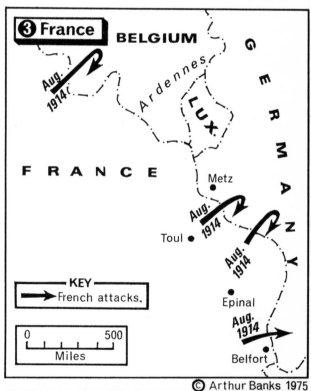

③ France

BELGIUM

Aug. 1914

Ardennes

LUX.

G E R M A N Y

FRANCE

Metz

Aug. 1914

Toul

Aug. 1914

Aug. 1914

Epinal

Aug. 1914

Belfort

KEY
French attacks.

0   500
Miles

© Arthur Banks 1975

These sections depict basic moves involving Japan, Austria Hungary, and France during the opening months of the war. In the Far East, Japan attacked and captured the German mainland base at Tsingtau plus a number of German Pacific islands. In Europe, Austria–Hungary met with rebuffs in clashes with Russia and Serbia: France attempted operations against Germany, but these moves came to naught. Consequently, with Russia and Britain involved also, the conflict rapidly engulfed hundreds of millions of people.

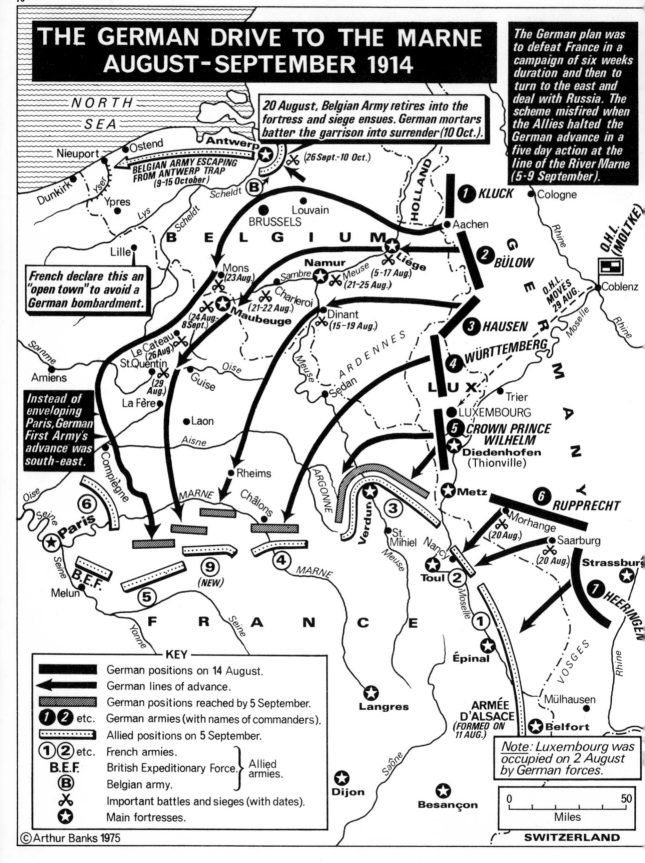

THE GERMAN DRIVE TO THE MARNE AUGUST-SEPTEMBER 1914

The German plan was to defeat France in a campaign of six weeks duration and then to turn to the east and deal with Russia. The scheme misfired when the Allies halted the German advance in a five day action at the line of the River Marne (5-9 September).

NORTH SEA

20 August, Belgian Army retires into the fortress and siege ensues. German mortars batter the garrison into surrender (10 Oct.).

Nieuport
Ostend
Antwerp
BELGIAN ARMY ESCAPING FROM ANTWERP TRAP (9-15 October) (26 Sept.-10 Oct.)
Dunkirk
Ypres
Yser
Lys
Scheldt
(B)
Scheldt
HOLLAND

① **KLUCK** · Cologne
② **BÜLOW**

Louvain
BRUSSELS
BELGIUM
Lille
Mons (23 Aug.)
Namur
Liége (5-17 Aug.) (21-25 Aug.)
Aachen

O.H.L. (MOLTKE)
Coblenz

French declare this an "open town" to avoid a German bombardment.

Maubeuge (24 Aug.- 8 Sept.)
Sambre
Charleroi (21-22 Aug.)
Dinant (15-19 Aug.)
Meuse
ARDENNES
Sedan

G E R M A N Y
O.H.L. MOVES 29 AUG.
Rhine
Moselle
Rhine

③ **HAUSEN**
④ **WÜRTTEMBERG**

Somme
Amiens
Le Cateau (26 Aug.)
St.Quentin (29 Aug.)
Oise
Guise
La Fère

LUX.
Trier
LUXEMBOURG

⑤ **CROWN PRINCE WILHELM**
Diedenhofen (Thionville)

Instead of enveloping Paris, German First Army's advance was south-east.

Laon
Aisne
Rheims
MARNE
Châlons
ARGONNE
Verdun
Metz

⑥ **RUPPRECHT**
Morhange (20 Aug.)
Saarburg (20 Aug.)
Strassburg

Compiègne
Oise
Seine
⑥
Paris
B.E.F.
Melun
⑤
⑨ (NEW)
④
MARNE
③
St. Mihiel
Meuse
Nancy
Toul ②
①
Épinal
⑦ **HEERINGEN**
VOSGES
Rhine

F R A N C E
Seine
Yonne

Langres

ARMÉE D'ALSACE (FORMED ON 11 AUG.)
Mülhausen
Belfort

Note: Luxembourg was occupied on 2 August by German forces.

Saône
Dijon
Besançon

KEY

▬▬►	German positions on 14 August.
◄▬▬	German lines of advance.
▨▨▨	German positions reached by 5 September.
①② etc.	German armies (with names of commanders).
··········	Allied positions on 5 September.
①② etc.	French armies.
B.E.F.	British Expeditionary Force. } Allied armies.
Ⓑ	Belgian army.
✂	Important battles and sieges (with dates).
✪	Main fortresses.

0 ——————— 50
Miles

© Arthur Banks 1975

SWITZERLAND

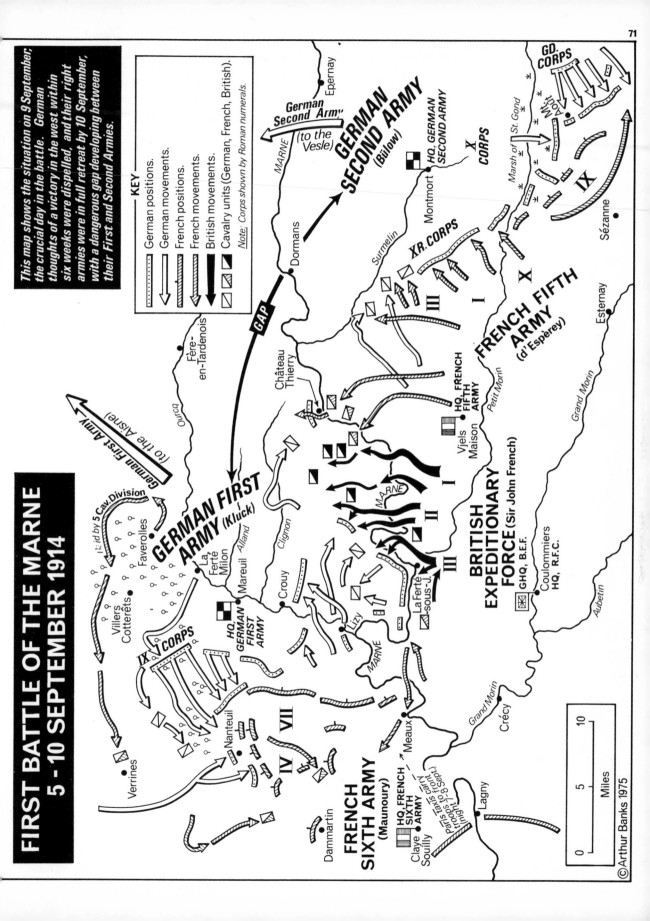

FIRST BATTLE OF THE MARNE 5 - 10 SEPTEMBER 1914

This map shows the situation on 9 September, the crucial day in the battle. German thoughts of a victory in the west within six weeks were dispelled, and their right armies were in full retreat by 10 September, with a dangerous gap developing between their First and Second Armies.

KEY

- German positions.
- German movements.
- French positions.
- French movements.
- British movements (German, French, British).
- Cavalry units (German, French, British).

Note: Corps shown by Roman numerals.

German Second Army (to the Vesle)

GERMAN SECOND ARMY (Bülow)

HQ. GERMAN SECOND ARMY

X CORPS

GD. CORPS

Mt. St. Gond

Marsh of St. Gond

IX

Epernay

Montmort

Sézanne

XR. CORPS

III   I   X

FRENCH FIFTH ARMY (d'Espèrey)

Esternay

HQ. FRENCH FIFTH ARMY

Vjels Maison

Petit Morin

Grand Morin

Dormans

Surmelin

Château Thierry

MARNE

I

II

III

BRITISH EXPEDITIONARY FORCE (Sir John French)

GHQ. B.E.F.

Coulommiers HQ. R.F.C.

Fère-en-Tardenois

Ourcq

GAP

German First Army (to the Aisne)

GERMAN FIRST ARMY (Kluck)

La Ferté Milon

Mareuil   Alland

Clignon

Crouy

Lizy

La Ferté -sous-J.

MARNE

HQ. GERMAN FIRST ARMY

IX CORPS

Villers Cotterêts

Faverolles

:id by 5 Cav.Division

Verrines

Nanteuil

IV   VII   I

Meaux

Crécy

Lagny

Grand Morin

Aubetin

Dammartin

FRENCH SIXTH ARMY (Maunoury)

Claye Souilly

HQ. FRENCH SIXTH ARMY

Paris Taxis carry troops 7-8 Sept. (night 7-8 Sept.)

0   5   10

Miles

© Arthur Banks 1975

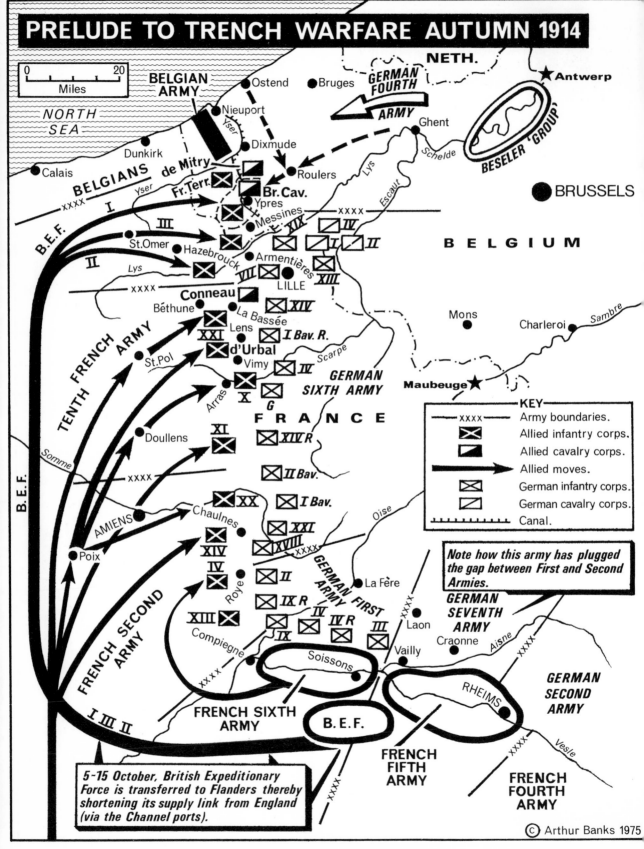

PRELUDE TO TRENCH WARFARE AUTUMN 1914

NETH.

GERMAN FOURTH ARMY

★ **Antwerp**

BESELER 'GROUP'

0 20
Miles

BELGIAN ARMY

Ostend   ● Bruges   Ghent

NORTH SEA

Nieuport

Dunkirk   Dixmude   Roulers

● Calais   de Mitry   Schelde

BELGIANS   Fr.Terr.   **Br. Cav.**

Yser   Ypres

B.E.F.   Messines   XIX   IV   ● **BRUSSELS**

I   St.Omer   Hazebrouck   Armentières   **BELGIUM**

III   VII   XIII

II   Lys   **Conneau**   LILLE

XXXX

Béthune   La Bassée   XIV   Mons   Charleroi   Sambre

XXI   Lens   I Bav. R.

St.Pol   **d'Urbal**   Vimy   **Maubeuge** ★

Arras   X   IV   Scarpe

G   **GERMAN SIXTH ARMY**

F R A N C E

Doullens   XI   XIV R

KEY

── xxxx Army boundaries.

Allied infantry corps.

Allied cavalry corps.

Allied moves.

German infantry corps.

German cavalry corps.

Canal.

II Bav.

AMIENS   XX   I Bav.

Poix   Chaulnes   XXI

XIV   XVIII   XXXX

Note how this army has plugged the gap between First and Second Armies.

Somme

II   La Fère   **GERMAN SEVENTH ARMY**

Roye   IX R   Laon

XIII   IV   IV R   III   Craonne   Aisne

Compiegne   IX   Vailly   **GERMAN SECOND ARMY**

Soissons   RHEIMS

I III II   **FRENCH SIXTH ARMY**   **B.E.F.**   Vesle

FRENCH SECOND ARMY   **FRENCH FIFTH ARMY**   **FRENCH FOURTH ARMY**

5-15 October, British Expeditionary Force is transferred to Flanders thereby shortening its supply link from England (via the Channel ports).

© Arthur Banks 1975

TENTH FRENCH ARMY

GERMAN FIRST ARMY

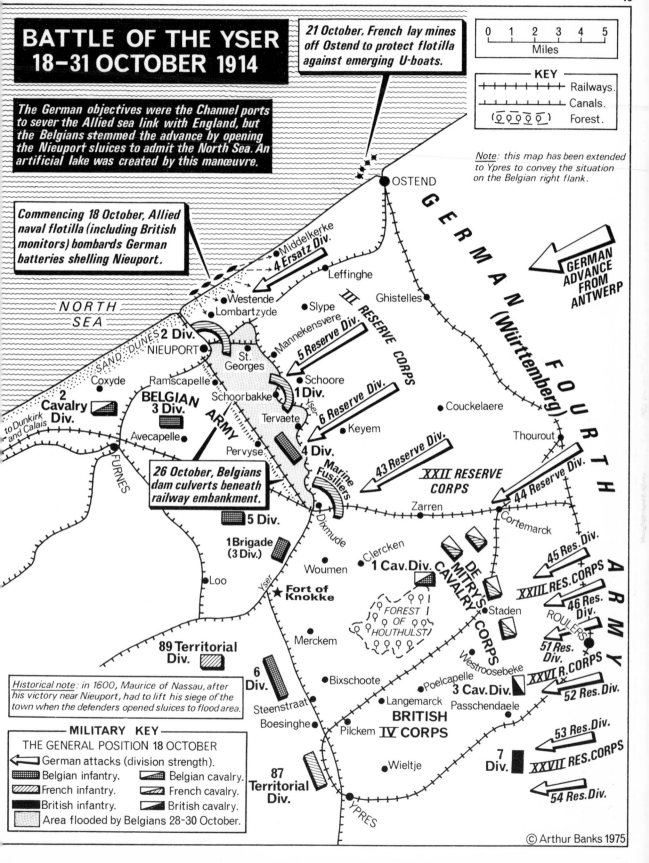

BATTLE OF THE YSER 18–31 OCTOBER 1914

21 October, French lay mines off Ostend to protect flotilla against emerging U-boats.

The German objectives were the Channel ports to sever the Allied sea link with England, but the Belgians stemmed the advance by opening the Nieuport sluices to admit the North Sea. An artificial lake was created by this manœuvre.

0 1 2 3 4 5
Miles

KEY
Railways.
Canals.
Forest.

Note: this map has been extended to Ypres to convey the situation on the Belgian right flank.

Commencing 18 October, Allied naval flotilla (including British monitors) bombards German batteries shelling Nieuport.

OSTEND

G E R M A N   F O U R T H   A R M Y   (Württemberg)

GERMAN ADVANCE FROM ANTWERP

NORTH SEA

Middelkerke
4 Ersatz Div.
Leffinghe
Westende
Ghistelles
Lombartzyde
Slype
Mannekensvere
III RESERVE CORPS
5 Reserve Div.
SAND DUNES
2 Div.
NIEUPORT
St. Georges
Schoore
1 Div.
6 Reserve Div.
Couckelaere
Coxyde
Ramscapelle
Schoorbakke
2 Cavalry Div.
BELGIAN 3 Div.
Tervaete
Keyem
Thourout
Avecapelle
Pervyse
4 Div.
ARMY
Marine Fusiliers
43 Reserve Div.
XXII RESERVE CORPS
44 Reserve Div.

FURNES

26 October, Belgians dam culverts beneath railway embankment.

5 Div.
Zarren
Cortemarck

1 Brigade (3 Div.)
Dixmude
Clercken
1 Cav. Div.
DE MITRY'S CAVALRY CORPS
45 Res. Div.
Loo
Woumen
Staden
XXIII RES. CORPS
46 Res. Div.
ROULERS
FOREST OF HOUTHULST
51 Res. Div.

89 Territorial Div.
Merckem
Westroosebeke
XXVI R. CORPS
52 Res. Div.

Historical note: in 1600, Maurice of Nassau, after his victory near Nieuport, had to lift his siege of the town when the defenders opened sluices to flood area.

6 Div.
Bixschoote
Poelcapelle
3 Cav. Div.
Langemarck
Passchendaele
Steenstraat
BRITISH IV CORPS
53 Res. Div.
Boesinghe
Pilckem

MILITARY KEY
THE GENERAL POSITION 18 OCTOBER
German attacks (division strength).
Belgian infantry.   Belgian cavalry.
French infantry.   French cavalry.
British infantry.   British cavalry.
Area flooded by Belgians 28-30 October.

87 Territorial Div.
Wieltje
7 Div.
XXVII RES. CORPS
54 Res. Div.
YPRES

to Dunkirk and Calais

© Arthur Banks 1975

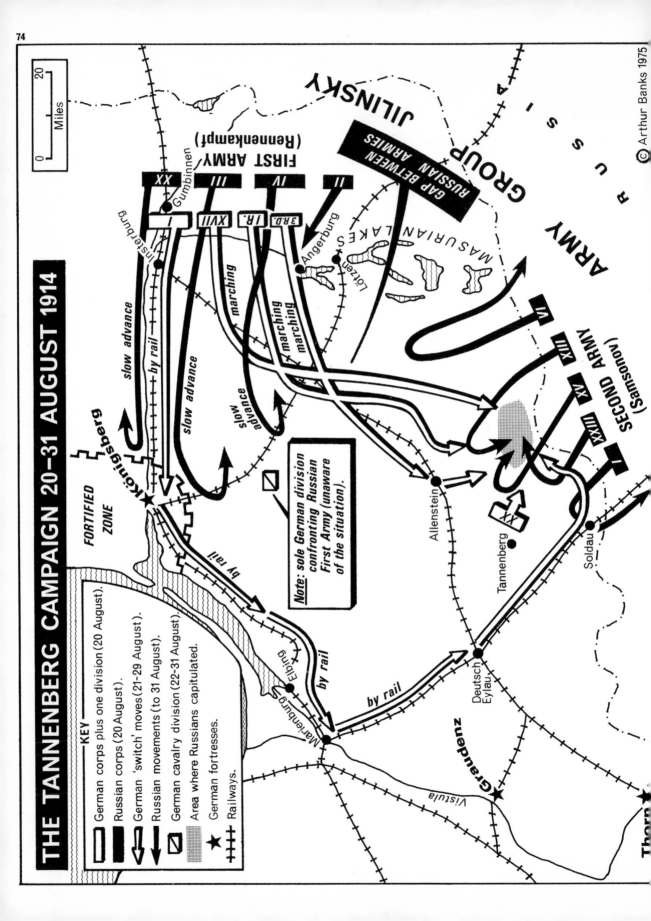

THE TANNENBERG CAMPAIGN 20-31 AUGUST 1914

© Arthur Banks 1975

0 20
Miles

KEY

⬜ German corps plus one division (20 August).
⬛ Russian corps (20 August).
⇩ German 'switch' moves (21-29 August).
⬇ Russian movements (to 31 August).
◻ German cavalry division (22-31 August).
▦ Area where Russians capitulated.
★ German fortresses.
+++ Railways.

Note: sole German division confronting Russian First Army (unaware of the situation).

JILINSKY

ARMY GROUP

GAP BETWEEN RUSSIAN ARMIES

RUSSIA

FIRST ARMY (Rennenkampf)

XX I III XVII IV IR. II 3RD.

Gumbinnen
Insterburg

slow advance
by rail
slow advance
slow advance
marching
marching
marching

Angerburg
Lötzen
MASURIAN LAKES

Königsberg
FORTIFIED ZONE

by rail
Elbing
by rail
Marienburg

Allenstein
Tannenberg

XX

VI
XIII
XV
XXIII
SECOND ARMY (Samsonov)

Soldau

by rail
Deutsch Eylau

Graudenz
Vistula

Thorn

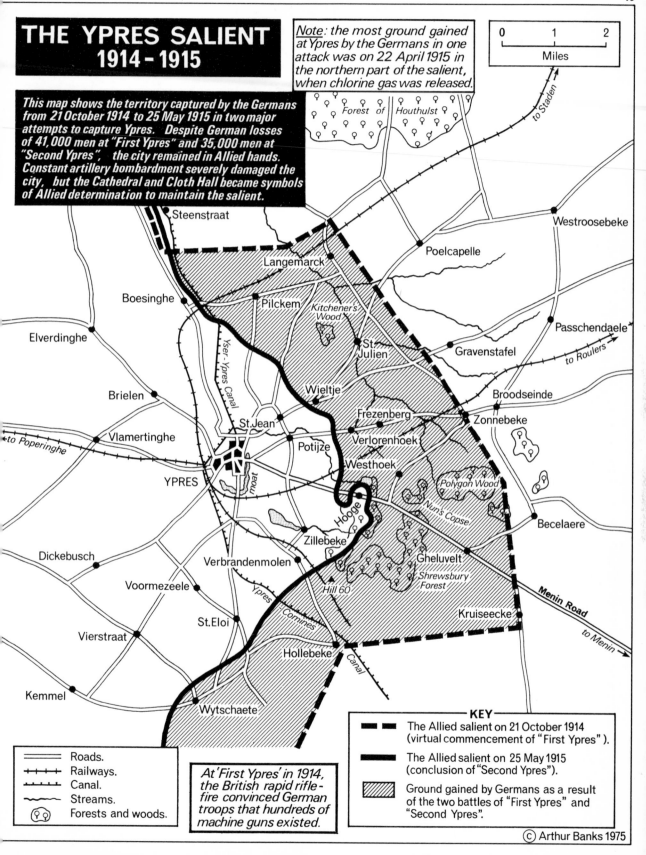

THE YPRES SALIENT 1914-1915

This map shows the territory captured by the Germans from 21 October 1914 to 25 May 1915 in two major attempts to capture Ypres. Despite German losses of 41,000 men at "First Ypres" and 35,000 men at "Second Ypres", the city remained in Allied hands. Constant artillery bombardment severely damaged the city, but the Cathedral and Cloth Hall became symbols of Allied determination to maintain the salient.

Note: the most ground gained at Ypres by the Germans in one attack was on 22 April 1915 in the northern part of the salient, when chlorine gas was released.

0   1   2
Miles

Forest of Houthulst

to Staden

Steenstraat

Westroosebeke

Langemarck

Poelcapelle

Boesinghe

Pilckem

Kitcheners' Wood

St. Julien

Gravenstafel

Passchendaele

Elverdinghe

to Roulers

Wieltje

Broodseinde

Brielen

Frezenberg

Zonnebeke

St.Jean

Verlorenhoek

to Poperinghe

Vlamertinghe

Potijze

Westhoek

Polygon Wood

YPRES

Nun's Copse

Becelaere

Hooge

Zillebeke

Gheluvelt

Dickebusch

Verbrandenmolen

Shrewsbury Forest

Voormezeele

Hill 60

Kruiseecke

Menin Road

St.Eloi

Vierstraat

to Menin

Hollebeke

Kemmel

Wytschaete

At 'First Ypres' in 1914, the British rapid rifle-fire convinced German troops that hundreds of machine guns existed.

── KEY ──

▄▄ ▄▄ ▄▄ The Allied salient on 21 October 1914 (virtual commencement of "First Ypres").

━━━━ The Allied salient on 25 May 1915 (conclusion of "Second Ypres").

▨▨▨ Ground gained by Germans as a result of the two battles of "First Ypres" and "Second Ypres".

═══ Roads.
+++++ Railways.
·─·─· Canal.
∼∼∼ Streams.
🌳🌳 Forests and woods.

Ⓒ Arthur Banks 1975

THE STATIC WESTERN FRONT 1915

0   40
Miles

Bruges
Antwerp
Düsseldorf
Ghent
Cologne
Ypres
BRUSSELS
Bonn
Lille
Liége
N.Chapelle
B E L G I U M
Festubert
Loos
Lens
Mons
Namur
Douai
ARTOIS
Arras
Cambrai
ARDENNES
G E R M A N Y
Péronne
LUXEMBOURG
St.Quentin
Hirson
Noyon
Méziéres
Laon
Sedan
Compiègne
Soissons
Perthes
ARGONNE
Verdun
Metz
F R A N C E
Rheims
CHAMPAGNE
St.
Mihiel
LORRAINE
© Arthur Banks 1973
Châlons

THIS GERMAN SALIENT EXISTED (WITH VARIATIONS) UNTIL SEPTEMBER 1918.

Toul   Nancy

Despite Allied efforts to achieve a breakthrough, the basic shape of the front line remained virtually unaltered on small scale maps. Note the important rail network under German control.

Épinal

VOSGES

Belfort

JOFFRE'S PLANS IN EARLY 1915

BRUSSELS
HOLLAND
Cologne
Rhine
Lille
B E L G I U M
Douai
GERMANY
Hirson
LUX.
trench
Noyon
Méziéres
F R A N C E
Rheims
warfare
Metz
St.Mihiel
0   60
Miles
Nancy

KEY
→ Opening attacks.
⇨ Subsequent advances.

KEY
▬ Front line in February.
➤ Allied offensives.
⇦ German offensives.

THE MOBILE EASTERN FRONT 1915

0   50   100
Miles

Riga

Libau

Fell on 8 May.

Memel

Not captured by Germans.

Dvinsk

Dvina

BALTIC SEA

Stormed by Germans 17-18 August.

Kovno

Königsberg

Danzig

EAST PRUSSIA

MASURIAN LAKES

Niemen

Germany's aim was to make the Eastern Front safe and passive so that she could switch her main assault to the Western Front (she did not hope to completely defeat Russia). Rather than instituting an "enveloping" operation, she decided to attempt a "breakthrough" attack between Gorlice and Tarnow. This commenced on 2 May 1915, in concert with the Austrians. This front contrasts sharply with the Western Front during 1915.

Graudenz

Vistula

Grodno

Narew

Fell on 2 September.

R U S S I A

Thorn

Vistula

Capitulated on 20 August.

Entered by Germans on 5 August.

Novo-Georgievsk

Warsaw

Bug

Brest-Litovsk

North of this position, the front line remained as shown (with minor variations) until the end of 1917.

P O L A N D

Vistula

Ivangorod

Surrendered on 26 August.

Pripet

Fell on 5 August.

South of this position, the front line remained as shown (with minor variations) until June 1916.

San

Evacuated by Russians on 22 June.

Cracow

Tarnow

Vistula

G A L I C I A

Lemberg

Przemysl

GERMAN ELEVENTH ARMY

2 MAY 1915

Gorlice

Fell on 3 June.

CARPATHIAN MOUNTAINS

Dniester

Tisza

Pruth

KEY

⇨ Opening assault by German and Austrian armies.

⇨ Advances by German and Austrian armies.

········· Front line, 2 May.

———— Front line, 1 June.

▬▬▬ Front line, 16 July.

▭▭▭ Front line, 15 August.

– – – Front line, 1 September.

▲▲▲ Front line, winter 1915.

© Arthur Banks 1973

OCEANIC WARFARE: THE WORLD SCENE 1914

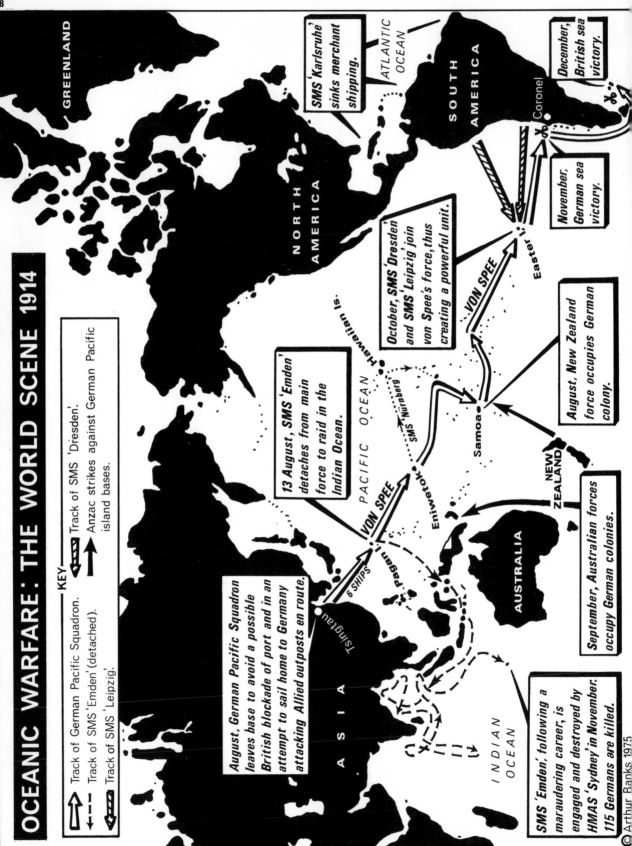

KEY

- Track of German Pacific Squadron.
- Track of SMS 'Emden' (detached).
- Track of SMS 'Leipzig'.
- Track of SMS 'Dresden'.
- Anzac strikes against German Pacific island bases.

GREENLAND

NORTH AMERICA

SOUTH AMERICA

ASIA

AUSTRALIA

NEW ZEALAND

ATLANTIC OCEAN

PACIFIC OCEAN

INDIAN OCEAN

Hawaiian Is.

Eniwetok

Samoa

Easter I.

Coronel

Tsingtau

Pagan

SMS 'Nürnberg'

VON SPEE

6 SHIPS

SMS 'Karlsruhe' sinks merchant shipping.

December, British sea victory.

November, German sea victory.

October, SMS 'Dresden' and SMS 'Leipzig' join von Spee's force, thus creating a powerful unit.

13 August, SMS 'Emden' detaches from main force to raid in the Indian Ocean.

August, German Pacific Squadron leaves base to avoid a possible British blockade of port and in an attempt to sail home to Germany attacking Allied outposts en route.

August, New Zealand force occupies German colony.

September, Australian forces occupy German colonies.

SMS 'Emden', following a marauding career, is engaged and destroyed by HMAS 'Sydney' in November. 115 Germans are killed.

FIRST BATTLE OF THE ATLANTIC 1915-1918

ICELAND

GREENLAND

BRITISH ISLES

NEWFOUNDLAND

NORTH ATLANTIC OCEAN

EUROPE

NORTH AMERICA

Azores

Gulf of Mexico

Bahama Is.

> British passenger liner "Lusitania" is torpedoed by German submarine on 7 May 1915. 1,198 lives are lost (including 124 Americans, affecting U.S.-German relations).

Canary Is.

AFRICA

Caribbean Sea

West Indies

PACIFIC OCEAN

Cape Verde Is.

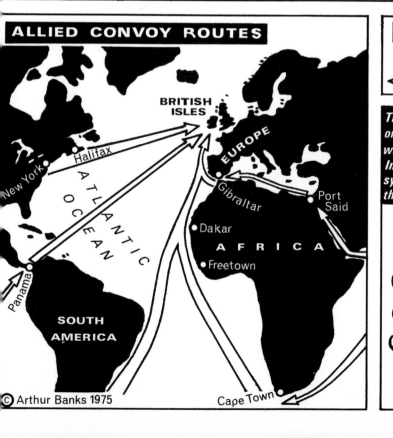

ALLIED CONVOY ROUTES

BRITISH ISLES

EUROPE

Halifax

New York

ATLANTIC OCEAN

Gibraltar

Port Said

Dakar

AFRICA

Freetown

Panama

SOUTH AMERICA

Cape Town

© Arthur Banks 1975

KEY

Areas where German U-boats sank large numbers of Allied and neutral merchant ships.

← Allied convoy routes.

The heaviest German submarine assault on Allied merchant shipping was in 1917 when over two million tons was sunk. In May, the Allies introduced the convoy system (see below) which gradually reduced their losses.

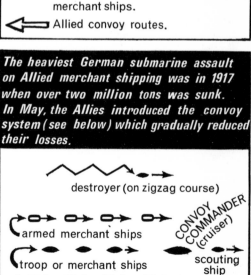

destroyer (on zigzag course)

armed merchant ships

CONVOY COMMANDER (cruiser)

troop or merchant ships

scouting ship

armed merchant ships

destroyer (on zigzag course)

EUROPE : THE MIDDLE YEARS 1915-1917

① Land Events (1915)

The Eastern Front is very active: Germans advance up to 250 miles into Russia. The onset of winter halts their advance.

Serbia is overwhelmed as a result of a combined Austro-German-Bulgarian invasion.

Allies land on Gallipoli peninsula but operation ends in failure due to determined Turkish resistance.

The Western Front is basically unaltered. The main actions occur at Festubert, Aubers Ridge, Neuve Chapelle, Loos, Ypres, in Artois, and Champagne. Trench warfare sets in.

The Italian Front is the scene of offensives by both Italians and Austro-Hungarians. Small inroads into each other's territory results.

RUSSIA

GERMANY

AUSTRIA-HUNGARY

FRANCE

SPAIN

PORTUGAL

BRITAIN

NETH.

BEL.

DEN.

SWITZ.

ITALY

RUMANIA

BULGARIA

SERBIA

MONTENEGRO

GREECE

ALB.

TURKEY

Black Sea

Mediterranean Sea

North Sea

ATLANTIC OCEAN

0   500
Miles

© Arthur Banks 1975

EUROPE: THE MIDDLE YEARS 1915–1917

② Land Events (1916)

On the Eastern Front, Russia launches major offensive which distracts Central Powers' attention from the west. It terminates after some three months.

Rumania is eliminated from the war following advances by Central Powers.

On the Italian Front, the main actions take place in the Trentino and Isonzo areas.

On the Western Front, the main actions occur at Verdun and the Somme.

RUSSIA

TURKEY

BLACK SEA

BULGARIA

RUMANIA

GREECE

SERBIA

MONTENEGRO

ALB.

AUSTRIA-HUNGARY

GERMANY

SWEDEN

NORWAY

BALTIC SEA

NORTH SEA

BRITAIN

ATLANTIC OCEAN

NETH.

BEL.

FRANCE

SWITZ.

ITALY

SPAIN

PORTUGAL

MEDITERRANEAN SEA

0   500
Miles

© Arthur Banks 1975

EUROPE: THE MIDDLE YEARS 1915-1917

③ Land Events (1917)

500

Miles

0

On the Eastern Front, Russians launch their final offensive which ends in failure. Lenin's rise to power is followed by Russian bids to end the war.

In the Balkans, the Allies are engaged in clashes with Bulgarian forces.

On the Italian Front, the main event is the Austro-German attack at Caporetto which pushes Italians back to the River Piave.

On the Western Front, a French offensive gains little ground but leads to widespread unrest among the front line units. British forces attempt breakthroughs at Ypres and Cambrai. Canadians gain local success at Vimy Ridge.

R U S S I A

Black Sea

T U R K E Y

RUMANIA

BULGARIA

SERBIA

MONTENEGRO

ALB.

SWEDEN

NORWAY

DEN.

G E R M A N Y (short of food and goods)

AUSTRIA-HUNGARY

SWITZ.

FRANCE

ITALY

BRITAIN

North Sea

ATLANTIC OCEAN

Mediterranean Sea

SPAIN

PORT.

© Arthur Banks 1975

EUROPE: THE MIDDLE YEARS 1915–1917

④ Naval Events (1915–1917)

BLACK SEA

DARDANELLES

Odessa

1915, Allied fleet fails to force passage.

1915, bombarded by Turco-German warships.

1916, battle of Jutland.

1915, battle of Dogger Bank.

BALTIC SEA

EUROPE

Adriatic Sea

U-BOATS

U-BOATS

MEDITERRANEAN SEA

U-BOAT

ROUTE

NORTH SEA

1917, destroyer clash.

Yarmouth

Lowestoft

U-BOAT

ROUTE

1916, bombarded by German warships.

ATLANTIC OCEAN

0   500

Miles

© Arthur Banks 1975

THE DARDANELLES FIASCO IN 1915

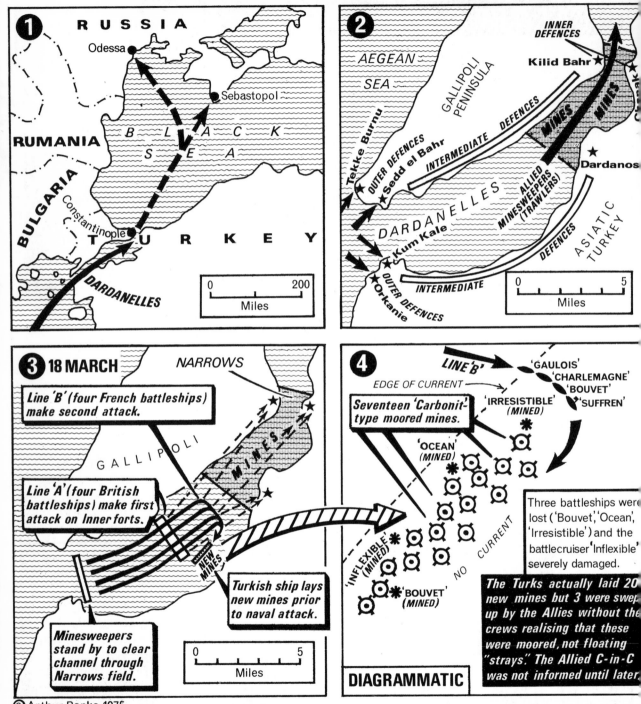

1

RUSSIA

Odessa

Sebastopol

BLACK SEA

RUMANIA

BULGARIA

Constantinople

DARDANELLES

TURKEY

0 — 200
Miles

2

AEGEAN SEA

GALLIPOLI PENINSULA

INNER DEFENCES

Kilid Bahr ★

Tekke Burnu

OUTER DEFENCES

Sedd el Bahr ★

INTERMEDIATE DEFENCES

MINES

Dardanos ★

ALLIED MINESWEEPERS (TRAWLERS)

DARDANELLES

Kum Kale ★

INTERMEDIATE DEFENCES

ASIATIC TURKEY

OUTER DEFENCES

Orkanie ★

0 — 5
Miles

3 18 MARCH

NARROWS

Line 'B' (four French battleships) make second attack.

GALLIPOLI

MINES

Line 'A' (four British battleships) make first attack on Inner forts.

NEW MINES

Turkish ship lays new mines prior to naval attack.

Minesweepers stand by to clear channel through Narrows field.

0 — 5
Miles

4

LINE 'B'

EDGE OF CURRENT

'GAULOIS'
'CHARLEMAGNE'
'BOUVET'
'SUFFREN'

'IRRESISTIBLE' (MINED)

Seventeen 'Carbonit'-type moored mines.

'OCEAN' (MINED)

NO CURRENT

'INFLEXIBLE' (MINED)

'BOUVET' (MINED)

Three battleships were lost ('Bouvet','Ocean', 'Irresistible') and the battlecruiser 'Inflexible' severely damaged.

The Turks actually laid 20 new mines but 3 were swept up by the Allies without the crews realising that these were moored, not floating "strays." The Allied C-in-C was not informed until later.

DIAGRAMMATIC

© Arthur Banks 1975

— KEY TO SECTIONS —

1 The Allied plan: fleet to steam through Dardanelles to threaten Constantinople and thence on to Russian ports.

2 Stages of plan: (a) destruction of outer defences (b) bombardment of other defences to cover minesweeping phase.

3 Allied fleet enters Dardanelles: bombardment proceeds: disaster overtakes plan when explosions rend warships.

4 Operation abandoned. Diagram illustrates cause of the mystery: group of mines laid at night unknown to Allies.

THE MINESWEEPING PROBLEM AT THE DARDANELLES

1

Note: during these events, the tenacity of the Turkish shore gunners has not always been acknowledged by Western historians.

Current runs at rate of some 4/5 knots.

Little or no current between dashed line and shore.

GALLIPOLI PENINSULA

TURKISH GUNS

MINES

MINES

TURKISH GUNS

DARDANELLES

ASIATIC COAST

The Allied minesweepers (actually fishing trawlers) were slow-speed vessels with their rate of progress retarded by the adverse current. Their crews were mainly civilians who were unaccustomed to working under shellfire and hostile conditions.

Current runs at rate of some 2 knots.

Minesweeper (steaming against current)

```
0                              12,000
         Yards
```

2

SURFACE

DEPTH 15 FEET

SEA BED

The mines were laid in rows across the Dardanelles, usually at depths of about 15 feet below the surface in calm weather, but these varied in choppy conditions.

© Arthur Banks 1975

3

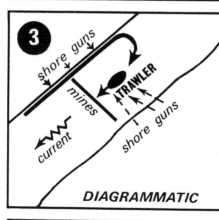

shore guns

mines

TRAWLER

shore guns

current

DIAGRAMMATIC

The trawlers needed to steam above the row of mines, turn, spread sweeps, and then come downstream with the current to increase their slow speeds.

4

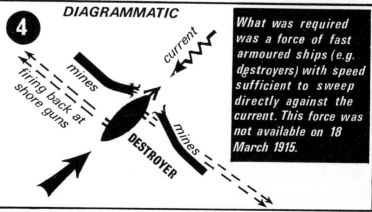

DIAGRAMMATIC

current

mines

firing back at shore guns

mines

DESTROYER

What was required was a force of fast armoured ships (e.g. destroyers) with speed sufficient to sweep directly against the current. This force was not available on 18 March 1915.

THE GALLIPOLI FIASCO IN 1915

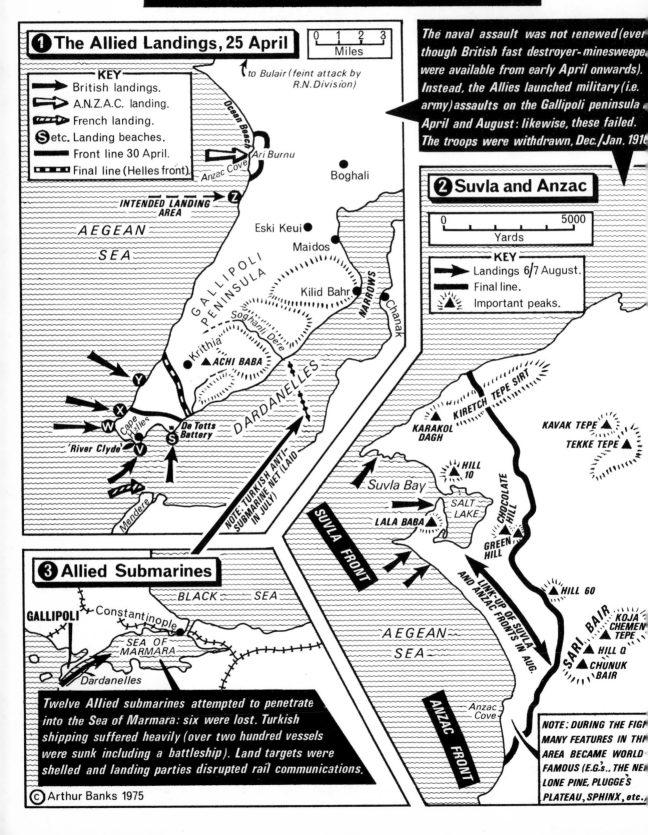

① The Allied Landings, 25 April

0 1 2 3
Miles

KEY
- ➡ British landings.
- ⇨ A.N.Z.A.C. landing.
- ⟫ French landing.
- Ⓢ etc. Landing beaches.
- ▬ Front line 30 April.
- ▭▭ Final line (Helles front).

to Bulair (feint attack by R.N. Division)

Ocean Beach

Ⓩ Ari Burnu
Anzac Cove

● Boghali

INTENDED LANDING AREA

AEGEAN SEA

● Eski Keui

Maidos

GALLIPOLI PENINSULA

Soghanli Dere

Kilid Bahr ●

MARROWS

Chanak ●

Krithia ●
▲ ACHI BABA

Ⓨ
Ⓧ
Ⓦ Cape Helles
'River Clyde'
Ⓥ
Ⓢ De Totts Battery

DARDANELLES

Mendere

NOTE: TURKISH ANTI-SUBMARINE NET (LAID IN JULY)

The naval assault was not renewed (even though British fast destroyer-minesweepers were available from early April onwards). Instead, the Allies launched military (i.e. army) assaults on the Gallipoli peninsula April and August: likewise, these failed. The troops were withdrawn, Dec./Jan. 1916.

② Suvla and Anzac

0 5000
Yards

KEY
- ➡ Landings 6/7 August.
- ▬ Final line.
- ▲ Important peaks.

KIRETCH TEPE SIRT

KARAKOL DAGH

KAVAK TEPE ▲
TEKKE TEPE ▲

HILL 10 ▲

CHOCOLATE HILL

Suvla Bay

SALT LAKE

LALA BABA ▲

GREEN HILL

SUVLA FRONT

LINK-UP OF SUVLA AND ANZAC FRONTS IN AUG.

▲ HILL 60

AEGEAN SEA

SARI BAIR

KOJA CHEMEN TEPE ▲
HILL Q ▲
CHUNUK BAIR ▲

Anzac Cove

ANZAC FRONT

③ Allied Submarines

BLACK SEA

GALLIPOLI Constantinople

SEA OF MARMARA

Dardanelles

Twelve Allied submarines attempted to penetrate into the Sea of Marmara: six were lost. Turkish shipping suffered heavily (over two hundred vessels were sunk including a battleship). Land targets were shelled and landing parties disrupted rail communications.

NOTE: DURING THE FIGHT MANY FEATURES IN THE AREA BECAME WORLD FAMOUS (E.G.'s., THE NEK, LONE PINE, PLUGGE'S PLATEAU, SPHINX, etc.)

© Arthur Banks 1975

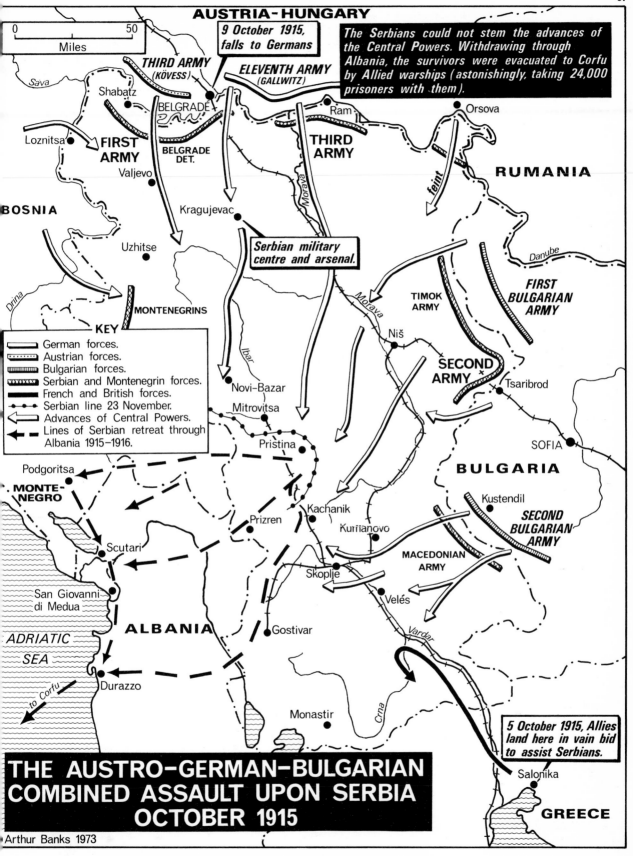

AUSTRIA-HUNGARY

9 October 1915, falls to Germans

THIRD ARMY (KÖVESS)

ELEVENTH ARMY (GALLWITZ)

The Serbians could not stem the advances of the Central Powers. Withdrawing through Albania, the survivors were evacuated to Corfu by Allied warships (astonishingly, taking 24,000 prisoners with them).

Sava

Shabatz

BELGRADE

Ram

Orsova

Loznitsa

FIRST ARMY

BELGRADE DET.

THIRD ARMY

feint

RUMANIA

Valjevo

Morava

BOSNIA

Kragujevac

Danube

Drina

Uzhitse

Serbian military centre and arsenal.

FIRST BULGARIAN ARMY

Morava

MONTENEGRINS

TIMOK ARMY

Niš

KEY

Ibar

SECOND ARMY

Tsaribrod

- German forces.
- Austrian forces.
- Bulgarian forces.
- Serbian and Montenegrin forces.
- French and British forces.
- Serbian line 23 November.
- Advances of Central Powers.
- Lines of Serbian retreat through Albania 1915–1916.

Novi-Bazar

Mitrovitsa

SOFIA

Pristina

BULGARIA

Podgoritsa

Kustendil

MONTE-NEGRO

Prizren

Kachanik

SECOND BULGARIAN ARMY

Scutari

Kumanovo

San Giovanni di Medua

Skoplje

MACEDONIAN ARMY

ALBANIA

Gostivar

Velés

Vardar

ADRIATIC SEA

Durazzo

to Corfu

Crna

Monastir

5 October 1915, Allies land here in vain bid to assist Serbians.

Salonika

THE AUSTRO-GERMAN-BULGARIAN COMBINED ASSAULT UPON SERBIA OCTOBER 1915

GREECE

Arthur Banks 1973

0 — 50 Miles

THE CONFRONTATION OF THE BRITISH & GERMAN BATTLE FLEETS AT JUTLAND BANK ON 31 MAY 1916

❶ The Approach of the Rival Fleets

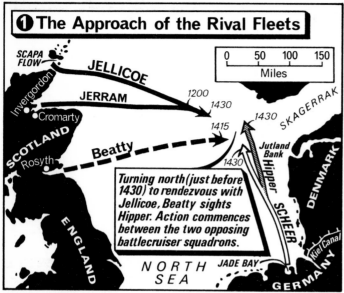

0 50 100 150
Miles

SCAPA FLOW
JELLICOE
JERRAM
Invergordon
Cromarty
SCOTLAND
Rosyth
Beatty
1200
1430
1415
1430
1430
1415
SKAGERRAK
Jutland Bank
Hipper
SCHEER
DENMARK
ENGLAND
NORTH SEA
JADE BAY
Kiel Canal
GERMANY

Turning north (just before 1430) to rendezvous with Jellicoe, Beatty sights Hipper. Action commences between the two opposing battlecruiser squadrons.

The Battle of Jutland ("Skagerrak" to Germans) was a direct confrontation between the British Grand Fleet and the German High Seas Fleet. Jellicoe possessed numerical and armament superiority and wished to fight in the northern North Sea, away from U-boats and minefields. Scheer wished to avoid a head-on clash and had perfected a "turn-away" manoeuvre for this event.

❸ Jellicoe versus Scheer

Note: mist prevalent. Maximum visibility 5 miles.

Jellicoe's deployment commences at 1815.

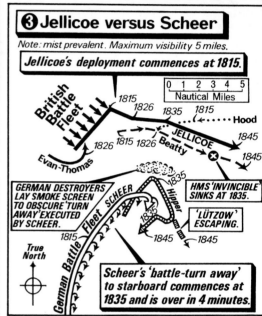

0 1 2 3 4 5
Nautical Miles

British Battle Fleet
1815
1826
1835
1815
Hood
1826
1815 1826
Beatty
JELLICOE
1845
1845
Evan-Thomas
SCHEER
German Battle Fleet
Hipper
1815
1835
1835
1845
1845

GERMAN DESTROYERS LAY SMOKE SCREEN TO OBSCURE 'TURN AWAY' EXECUTED BY SCHEER.

HMS 'INVINCIBLE' SINKS AT 1835.

'LÜTZOW' ESCAPING.

True North

Scheer's 'battle-turn away' to starboard commences at 1835 and is over in 4 minutes.

❷ Beatty versus Hipper

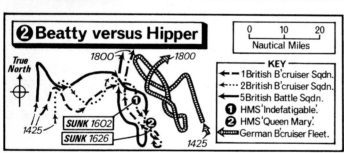

0 10 20
Nautical Miles

True North
1800
1800
1425
1425
SUNK 1602
SUNK 1626

KEY
←— 1 British B'cruiser Sqdn.
←·· 2 British B'cruiser Sqdn.
←·· 5 British Battle Sqdn.
❶ HMS 'Indefatigable'.
❷ HMS 'Queen Mary'.
◀■■ German B'cruiser Fleet.

HMS "IRON DUKE" — *JELLICOE'S FLAGSHIP*

Main armament:	Ten 13·5-in. guns.
Secondary arm.:	Twelve 6-in. guns.
Laid down:	1912.
Completed:	1914.
Length:	620 feet.
Displacement:	25,000 tons.
Maximum speed:	23 knots.

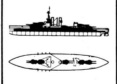

SMS "FRIEDRICH DER GROSSE" — *SCHEER'S FLAGSHIP*

Main armament:	Ten 12-inch guns.
Secondary arm.:	Fourteen 6-in. gs.
Laid down:	1909.
Completed:	1912.
Length:	564 feet.
Displacement:	24,700 tons.
Maximum speed:	23 knots.

HMS "LION" — *BEATTY'S FLAGSHIP*

Main armament:	Eight 13·5-in. guns.
Secondary arm.:	Sixteen 4-in. guns.
Laid down:	1909.
Completed:	1912.
Length:	675 feet.
Displacement:	26,350 tons.
Maximum speed:	29 knots.

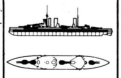

SMS "LÜTZOW" — *HIPPER'S FLAGSHIP (until disabled)*

Main armament:	Eight 12-in. guns.
Secondary arm.:	Twelve 6-in. guns.
Laid down:	1912.
Completed:	1915.
Length:	590 feet.
Displacement:	28,000 tons.
Maximum speed:	29 knots.

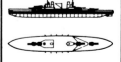

❹ The Second Clash of the Fleets

Steering west following his 'battle turn'(1835-1839), Scheer was moving away from his Jade base. Under cover of the mist, he turned for home only to meet Jellicoe for the second time, whereupon he executed a further 'turn away'. A running chase now commenced.

1922, British turn away to make torpedoes outrun their range. At the same time, British lengthen range of their own gunfire.

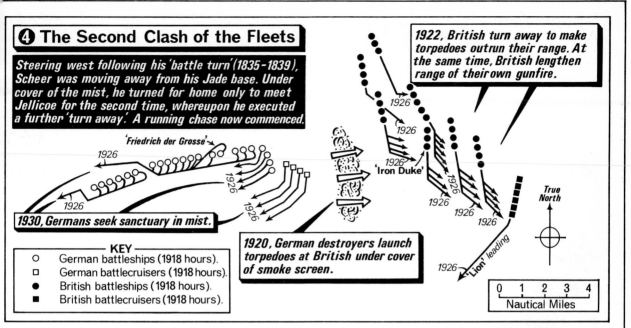

'Friedrich der Grosse'

1926

1926

1926

1930, Germans seek sanctuary in mist.

1926

1926

1926
'Iron Duke'

1926

1926

1926

True North

1926
'Lion' leading

1920, German destroyers launch torpedoes at British under cover of smoke screen.

KEY
○	German battleships (1918 hours).
□	German battlecruisers (1918 hours).
●	British battleships (1918 hours).
■	British battlecruisers (1918 hours).

Scale: 0 1 2 3 4 Nautical Miles

❺ The Night Chase: Scheer's Escape

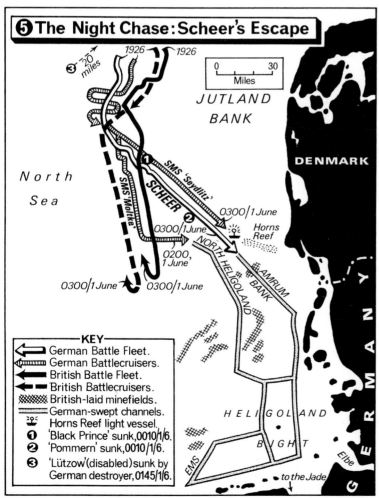

③ 20 miles

1926 — 1926

Scale: 0 30 Miles

JUTLAND BANK

DENMARK

North Sea

SMS 'Seydlitz'

① SCHEER

SMS 'Moltke'

② 0300/1 June

0300/1 June

Horns Reef

0200, 1 June

NORTH HELIGOLAND

0300/1 June

0300/1 June

AMRUM BANK

HELIGOLAND BIGHT

GERMANY

EMS

Elbe

to the Jade

KEY
⇦	German Battle Fleet.
⇐	German Battlecruisers.
←	British Battle Fleet.
◄--	British Battlecruisers.
▨▨▨	British-laid minefields.
≡≡≡	German-swept channels.
⚓	Horns Reef light vessel.
❶	'Black Prince' sunk,0010/1/6.
❷	'Pommern' sunk,0010/1/6.
❸	'Lützow'(disabled) sunk by German destroyer, 0145/1/6.

Despite British efforts to intercept the Germans on their homeward dash, the bulk of the High Seas Fleet made the Jade, battered but intact. Based upon ships lost and casualties, the encounter was a German success, but the North Sea strategical aspect remained as hitherto so far as the surface (not U-boat) war was concerned.

BRITISH DETAILS
Ships involved:	151
Sailors involved:	60,000
Battleships lost:	0
Battlecruisers lost:	3
Cruisers lost:	3
Destroyers lost:	8
Casualties:	6,097

GERMAN DETAILS
Ships involved:	99
Sailors involved:	36,000
Battleships lost:	1
Battlecruisers lost:	1
Cruisers lost:	4
Destroyers lost:	5
Casualties:	2,551

© Arthur Banks 1975

THE VERDUN BATTLE 1916

Geographical note: the River Meuse split the front into two sections, thus allowing Germans to launch two consecutive opening attacks.

Note: much of this lost territory was regained by French (October onwards).

GERMAN LINES

AREA OVERRUN BY GERMANS

Maucourt

Damloup

★ Ft.Tavannes

Ornes

★ Ft. Douaumont

Beaumont

★ Ft. Vaux

FRENCH INNER FORTRESSES STRENGTHEN DEFENCES.

★ Ft. Belrupt

Louvemont

★ Ft. Souville

★ Ft.St. Michel

Haumont

Bras

★ Ft. Thiaumont

★ Ft. Belleville

LINES

Brabant

MEUSE

Champneuville

Côtes de Meuse

Champ

Charny

★ Ft. Vacherauville

VERDUN

MEUSE

Consenvoye

Forges

Marre

★ Ft. Marre

Thierville

to Bar-le-Duc

★ Ft. Chaume

Drillancourt

★ Ft. Bois Bourrus

★ Ft. Choisel

★ Ft. Chana

★ Ft. Sartelles

Montfaucon

Bethincourt

Le Mort Homme

Chattancourt

FRENCH OUTER FORTRESS ZONE GUARDING VERDUN.

FRENCH

Esnes

Malancourt

Avocourt

This map shows the extent of the German advance between 21 February and 1 July (when the Allied attack on the Somme front commenced)

KEY

······ German lines on 21 March.
– – – German lines on 1 July.

0   1   2   3

Miles

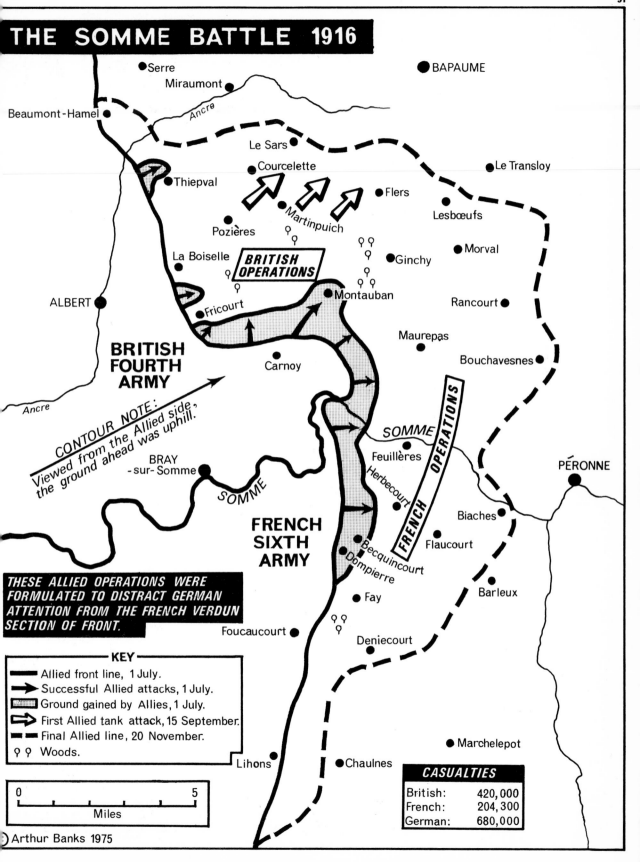

THE SOMME BATTLE 1916

BAPAUME

Serre

Miraumont

Ancre

Beaumont-Hamel

Le Sars

Courcelette

Le Transloy

Thiepval

Flers

Lesbœufs

Pozières

Martinpuich

BRITISH OPERATIONS

La Boiselle

Ginchy

Morval

Fricourt

Montauban

Rancourt

ALBERT

Maurepas

Carnoy

Bouchavesnes

BRITISH FOURTH ARMY

CONTOUR NOTE: Viewed from the Allied side, the ground ahead was uphill.

Ancre

SOMME

Feuillères

PÉRONNE

BRAY -sur- Somme

Herbecourt

FRENCH OPERATIONS

SOMME

FRENCH SIXTH ARMY

Biaches

Becquincourt

Flaucourt

Dompierre

THESE ALLIED OPERATIONS WERE FORMULATED TO DISTRACT GERMAN ATTENTION FROM THE FRENCH VERDUN SECTION OF FRONT.

Fay

Barleux

Foucaucourt

Deniecourt

KEY

— Allied front line, 1 July.
➤ Successful Allied attacks, 1 July.
▨ Ground gained by Allies, 1 July.
⇨ First Allied tank attack, 15 September.
--- Final Allied line, 20 November.
♀ ♀ Woods.

Marchelepot

Lihons

Chaulnes

0   5

Miles

CASUALTIES	
British:	420,000
French:	204,300
German:	680,000

© Arthur Banks 1975

THE BRUSILOV OFFENSIVE JUNE–OCTOBER 1916

ARMY GROUP LINSINGEN (4 JUNE)

ABORTIVE ATTACKS 100 MILES TO NORTH (IN JUNE AND JULY)

RUSSIAN THIRD ARMY (Lesh)

EVERT (Commander: Russian Centre Army Group)

Pripet

Stokhod

Goryn

Sluch

FOURTH AUSTRIAN ARMY (Archduke Josef Ferdinand)

Kovel

Lutsk

BRUSILOV'S PLANS
To spread heavy pressure over the whole front simultaneously rather than to concentrate at fixed points, thus preventing the enemy switching reserves from point to point at will.

Krilov

FIRST AUSTRIAN ARMY (Pulhallo von Brlog)

Rovno

Dubno

HQ, RUSSIAN EIGHTH ARMY

R U S S I A

SECOND AUSTRIAN ARMY (Böhm-Ermolli)

Styr

Brody

RUSSIAN EIGHTH ARMY (Kaledin) (11 INF. & 4 CAV. DIVISIONS)

BRUSILOV'S G.H.Q.

Lemberg

SOUTHERN 'GERMAN' ARMY (von Bothmer)

Brzezany

Tarnopol

Volochisk

RUSSIAN ELEVENTH ARMY (Sakharov) (8 INF. & 1 CAV. DIVISIONS)

BRUSILOV (Commander: Russian S.W. Army Group)

HQ RUSSIAN ELEVENTH ARMY

HQ, RUSSIAN SEVENTH ARMY

RUSSIAN SEVENTH ARMY (Shcherbachev) (7 INF. & 3½ CAV. DIVISIONS)

ACTING IN CONCERT

AUSTRIA-HUNGARY

Dniester

Stanislau

Gusyatin

HQ, RUSSIAN NINTH ARMY

RUSSIAN NINTH ARMY (Lechitsky) 10 INF. & 4 CAV. DIVISIONS

SEVENTH AUSTRIAN ARMY (Pflanzer-Baltin)

Kolomea

Kamenets-Podolski

NOTE: BRUSILOV'S DIVISIONS 4 JUNE.

TOTAL DIVISIONS 4 JUNE=38.

CARPATHIAN MTS.

Kuty

Czernowitz

Pruth

0   30
Miles

The Brusilov Offensive was the most competent Russian operation of the war. It weakened the offensives of the Central Powers at Verdun and in Italy, and without German assistance being forthcoming, Austria probably would have collapsed. It was a direct cause of the Habsburg Empire's disintegration. On both sides casualties were colossal, over two million men being involved. The offensive halted through sheer exhaustion on the Russian side, and discontent in the rear areas eventually led to the Russian Revolution.

Kimpolung

Sereth

— **KEY** —
━━━ Russian front line 4 June.
╍╍╍ Russian front line 10 October.
░░░ Ground gained by Russians.
◄━ Main Russian advances.
╂╂╂ Double track railways.
⚊ Pripet marshes.
⚑ Russian Army H.Q.
⊠ Russian Army Group G.H.Q.

RUMANIA

DIVISIONAL COMPARISONS. Most Russian divisions had 16 battalions, the remainder 12. Austrian divisions had 12 battalions: German had 9.

© Arthur Banks 1973

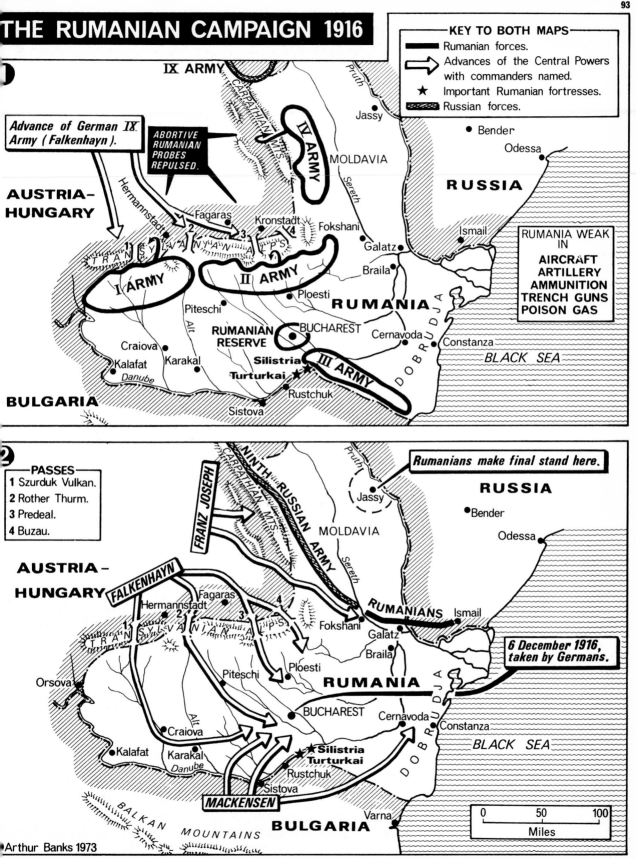

THE RUMANIAN CAMPAIGN 1916

KEY TO BOTH MAPS

Rumanian forces.
Advances of the Central Powers with commanders named.
★ Important Rumanian fortresses.
Russian forces.

Advance of German IX Army (Falkenhayn).

ABORTIVE RUMANIAN PROBES REPULSED.

IX ARMY

Pruth

Jassy

● Bender

Odessa ●

IV ARMY

MOLDAVIA

Sereth

RUSSIA

AUSTRIA-HUNGARY

Hermannstadt

Fagaras

2

3

Kronstadt

4

Fokshani

Ismail ●

RUMANIA WEAK IN

AIRCRAFT ARTILLERY AMMUNITION TRENCH GUNS POISON GAS

T R A N S Y L V A N I A N   A L P S

1

I ARMY

II ARMY

Galatz

Braila

Piteschi

Alt

Ploesti

RUMANIA

Craiova

Karakal

RUMANIAN RESERVE

BUCHAREST

Cernavoda

D O B R U D J A

Constanza

BLACK SEA

Kalafat

Danube

Silistria
Turturkai

★ III ARMY

Rustchuk

BULGARIA

Sistova

2

PASSES
1 Szurduk Vulkan.
2 Rother Thurm.
3 Predeal.
4 Buzau.

FRANZ JOSEPH

CARPATHIAN MTS

NINTH RUSSIAN ARMY

Pruth

Rumanians make final stand here.

Jassy

RUSSIA

MOLDAVIA

Sereth

● Bender

Odessa ●

AUSTRIA-HUNGARY

FALKENHAYN

Hermannstadt

Fagaras

2

3

4

1

T R A N S Y L V A N I A N   A L P S

Fokshani

RUMANIANS

Ismail ●

Galatz

Braila

6 December 1916, taken by Germans.

Orsova

Piteschi

Ploesti

RUMANIA

BUCHAREST

Cernavoda

Constanza

D O B R U D J A

BLACK SEA

Craiova

Alt

Kalafat

Karakal

Danube

★ **Silistria**
Turturkai

Rustchuk

MACKENSEN

Sistova

B A L K A N   MOUNTAINS

Varna ●

BULGARIA

0   50   100
Miles

Arthur Banks 1973

"THIRD YPRES"(PASSCHENDAELE):JULY – NOVEMBER 1917

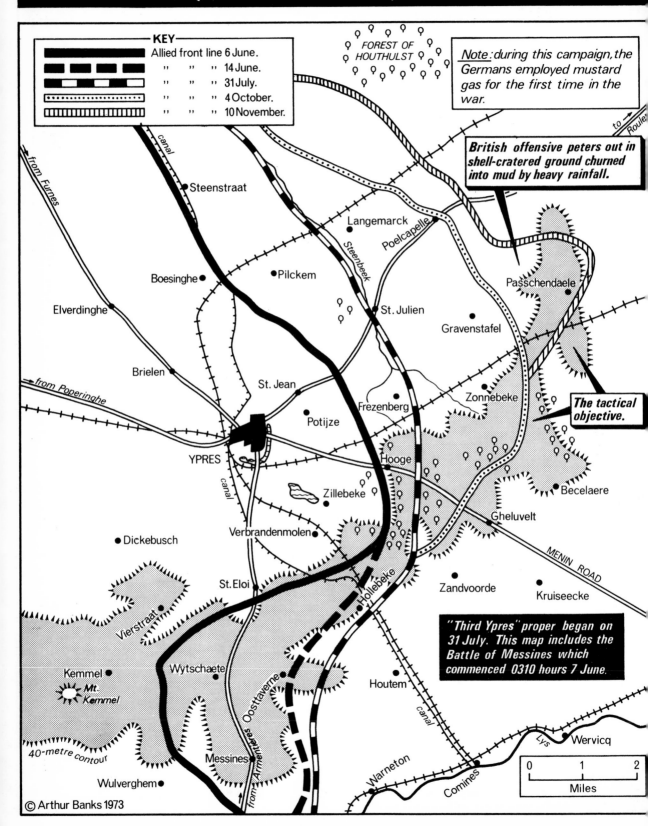

KEY

▬▬▬▬	Allied front line 6 June.
▬▪▬▪▬	,, ,, ,, 14 June.
▬▫▬▫▬	,, ,, ,, 31 July.
·······	,, ,, ,, 4 October.
▥▥▥▥	,, ,, ,, 10 November.

FOREST OF HOUTHULST

Note: during this campaign, the Germans employed mustard gas for the first time in the war.

to Roule[r]

British offensive peters out in shell-cratered ground churned into mud by heavy rainfall.

Steenstraat

Langemarck

Poelcapelle

Passchendaele

Boesinghe

Pilckem

Steenbeek

St. Julien

Gravenstafel

Elverdinghe

The tactical objective.

Brielen

St. Jean

Frezenberg

Zonnebeke

from Poperinghe

Potijze

Becelaere

YPRES

Hooge

Zillebeke

Gheluvelt

Dickebusch

Verbrandenmolen

MENIN ROAD

St. Eloi

Hollebeke

Zandvoorde

Kruiseecke

Vierstraat

Oosttaverne

"Third Ypres" proper began on 31 July. This map includes the Battle of Messines which commenced 0310 hours 7 June.

Kemmel

Wytschaete

Houtem

Mt. Kemmel

Messines

Warneton

Lys

Wervicq

40-metre contour

Wulverghem

Comines

0	1	2

Miles

from Furnes

canal

canal

from Armentières

canal

© Arthur Banks 1973

THE BRITISH TANK-SPEARHEADED OFFENSIVE AT CAMBRAI 1917

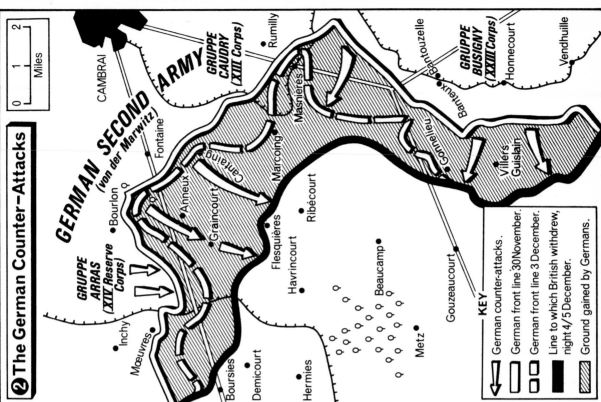

② The German Counter–Attacks

KEY

- German counter-attacks.
- German front line 30 November.
- German front line 3 December.
- Line to which British withdrew, night 4/5 December.
- Ground gained by Germans.

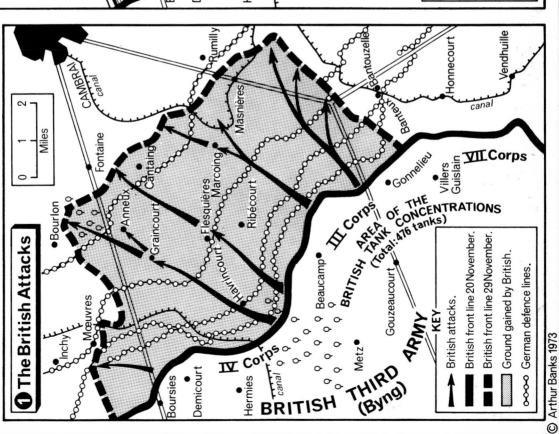

① The British Attacks

KEY

- British attacks.
- British front line 20 November.
- British front line 29 November.
- Ground gained by British.
- German defence lines.

AREA OF THE BRITISH TANK CONCENTRATIONS
(Total: 476 tanks)

© Arthur Banks 1973

THE GERMAN SOMME AND LYS OFFENSIVES 1918

The Lys 9-30 April

KEY

④ German Armies.

② British Armies.

EXTENT OF ADVANCE

MAXIMUM

START LINE

'GEORGETTE'

MENIN ROAD

Poelcapelle

Hooge

Ypres

Dickebusch

Poperinghe

Messines

Steenwerck

Armentières

Bailleul

Meteren

Éstaires

Merville

Hinges

Béthune

Fromelles

Aubers

Neuve Chapelle

La Bassée

La Bassée Canal

Cuinchy

Lille Canal

Loos

④ ② ⑥ ① Lys

German casualties totalled some 348,300.

British casualties totalled 260,000.

© Arthur Banks 1975

Ypres

Lys

Poperinghe

Lille

La Bassée

Loos

Lens

Douai

Cambrai

Miraumont

Albert

Péronne

St. Quentin

La Fère

Noyon

Somme

The Somme 21 March-5 April

KEY

⑥ German Armies.

③ British Armies.

Miles
0 ____ 10

MAXIMUM EXTENT OF ADVANCE

START LINE

'MICHAEL'

Lens

Gavrelle

Douai

Riencourt

Arras

Lys

Bapaume

Miraumont

Albert

Combles

Ytres

Péronne

Estrees

Chaulnes

Nesle

Moreuil

Montdidier

Lassigny

Noyon

Ham

St. Quentin

Barisis

Somme

Somme

① ⑥ ⑰ ② ⑱ ③ ⑤ ⑥

Miles
0 ___ 4

THE GERMAN AISNE AND MATZ OFFENSIVES 1918

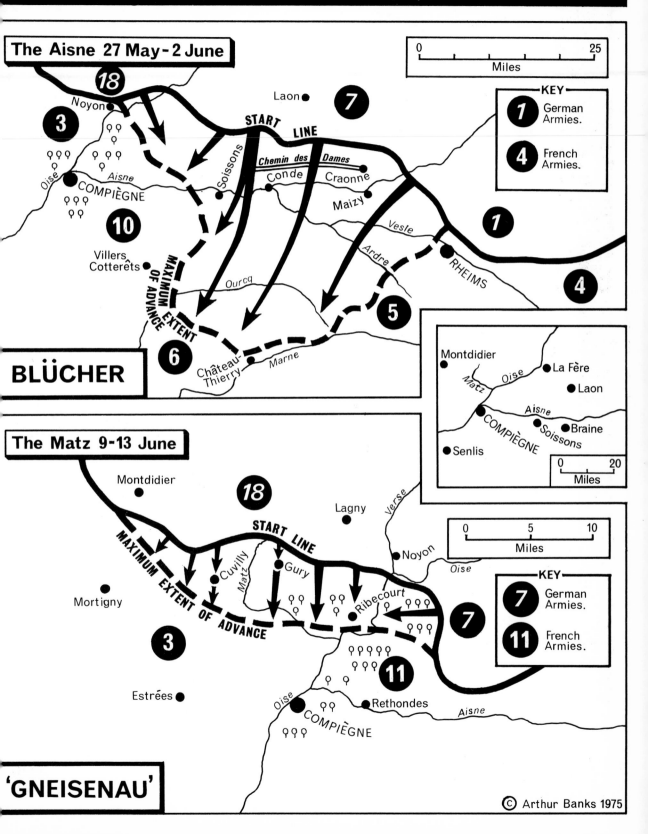

The Aisne 27 May - 2 June

0 — Miles — 25

KEY
- **1** German Armies.
- **4** French Armies.

Laon • 7

18 Noyon

3

Oise Aisne COMPIÈGNE

START LINE

Soissons Chemin des Dames Craonne
Condé

Maizy

10

Vesle

1

Villers Cotterêts

Ardre

RHEIMS

Ourcq

4

6 5

BLÜCHER

Château-Thierry Marne

Montdidier La Fère
Matz Oise Laon
COMPIÈGNE Aisne Braine
Soissons
Senlis

0 — Miles — 20

The Matz 9-13 June

Montdidier • 18 Lagny • Verse

START LINE

Mortigny • Cuvilly Matz Gury Ribecourt Noyon

Oise

3 7

0 — 5 — 10
Miles

KEY
- **7** German Armies.
- **11** French Armies.

Estrées • 11

Oise COMPIÈGNE Rethondes Aisne

'GNEISENAU'

© Arthur Banks 1975

THE ALLIED OFFENSIVES
18 JULY–11 NOVEMBER 1918

KEY

———	Allied line on 18 July.
— — —	Allied line on 25 August.
▨▨▨	Allied line on 15 October.
▦▦▦	Allied line on 6 November.
▨▨▨	Allied line on 11 November.
·······	Allied army boundaries.
▲▲▲	German defence lines.

NORTH SEA

HOLLAND

GERMANY

BELGIUM

LUXEMBOURG

FRANCE

Zeebrugge
Ostend
Calais
Boulogne
Dunkirk
KING ALBERT'S H.Q.
Nieuport
Bruges
Thielt
Ghent
Malines
ANTWERP
Louvain
BRUSSELS
Ypres
Hondschoote
Cassel
Hazebrouck
St. Omer
Aire
Armentières
LILLE
Courtrai
Audenarde
Tournai
Ath
Mons
Maubeuge
La Cateau
Avesnes
GERMAN O.H.L.
Liége
Namur
Charleroi
Dinant
Spa
GERMAN O.H.L.
Malmédy
Trier
Saarbrücken
Dieuze
Diedenhofen
Metz
Nancy
Toul
St. Mihiel
12 Sept.
AMERICANS
Verdun
Bar-le-Duc
St. Dizier
Vitry-le-François
Châlons-sur-Marne
Fère Champenoise
Épernay
Rheims
Dormans
Montmirail
La Ferté
Coulommiers
PARIS
Meaux
Senlis
Chantilly
Creil
Pontoise
Beauvais
Clermont
Compiègne
Aumale
Abbeville
Montreuil
HAIG'S G.H.Q.
St. Pol
Doullens
Béthune
La Bassée
Lens
Douai
Cambrai
Bapaume
Albert
Péronne
Chaulnes
Nesle
Roye
Noyon
Montdidier
Ham
Chauny
Soissons
Château Thierry
Laon
Vervins
Guise
Marle
Hirson
Charleville-Mézières
Rethel
Montmédy
Longwy
Arlon
LUXEMBOURG
Bastogne
Neufchâteau

ARDENNES
EIFEL

Moselle
Meuse
Sambre
Scheldt
Yser
Lys
Scarpe
Somme
Aisne
Marne
Seine

FLANDERN
WOTAN
HERMANN
SIEGFRIED
HUNDING
BRUNHILD
KRIEMHILD
CHEMIN DES DAMES

BELGIANS
BRITISH
FRENCH

FOCH'S H.Q.
PETAIN'S G.Q.G.

MOVED 5 SEPTEMBER

12 Sept.
26 Sept.
28 Sept.
27 Sept.
8 Aug.
18 July

Miles
0   50

© Arthur Banks 1973

THE ALLIED ADVANCE INTO GERMANY 1918

© Arthur Banks 1975

GERMANY

Gie

Frankfurt

Mannheim

FRENCH

Mainz

Neutral zone

AMERICAN
Rhine

Coblenz

Worms

Speier

Line 8 Dec.

BRITISH

Line 12 Dec.

Cologne

Düren

ZONE 2
(American)

ZONE 1
(French)

Line 1 Dec.

Strassburg

EIFEL

Line 18 Nov.

HOLLAND

Liége

LUX.

Luxembourg

Metz

Nancy

Arnhem

Hasselt

ZONE 4
(Belgian)

ZONE 3 (British)

Namur

BELGIUM

ARDENNES

Verdun

BRUSSELS

Mons

ARMISTICE LINE 11 November

Rheims

Bruges

Ghent

Lille

Cambrai

F R A N C E

A L S A C E

Dunkirk

PARIS

50

0

Miles

MILITARY CASUALTIES OF THE 1914–1918 WAR

KEY

Deaths.
Wounded.

300

0 Miles

JAPAN →
300
950

RUSSIA
1,700,000
5,000,000

TURKEY
326,000
400,000

RUMANIA
335,800
150,000

BULGARIA
77,000
153,000

6,000
25,000

AUSTRIA–HUNGARY
922,500
3,630,000

GREECE
133,500
48,000

SERBIA
48,000

ALBANIA

MONTENEGRO
3,000
10,000

GERMANY
1,809,000
4,260,000

MAIN CASUALTIES OF THE WAR ARE SUFFERED BY THESE FOUR NATIONS.

ITALY
954,000

463,000

SWITZ.

HOLLAND

BELG.
13,700
45,000

FRANCE
1,358,000
4,350,000

BRITAIN & EMPIRE
908,400
2,090,250

U.S.A.
50,600
205,700

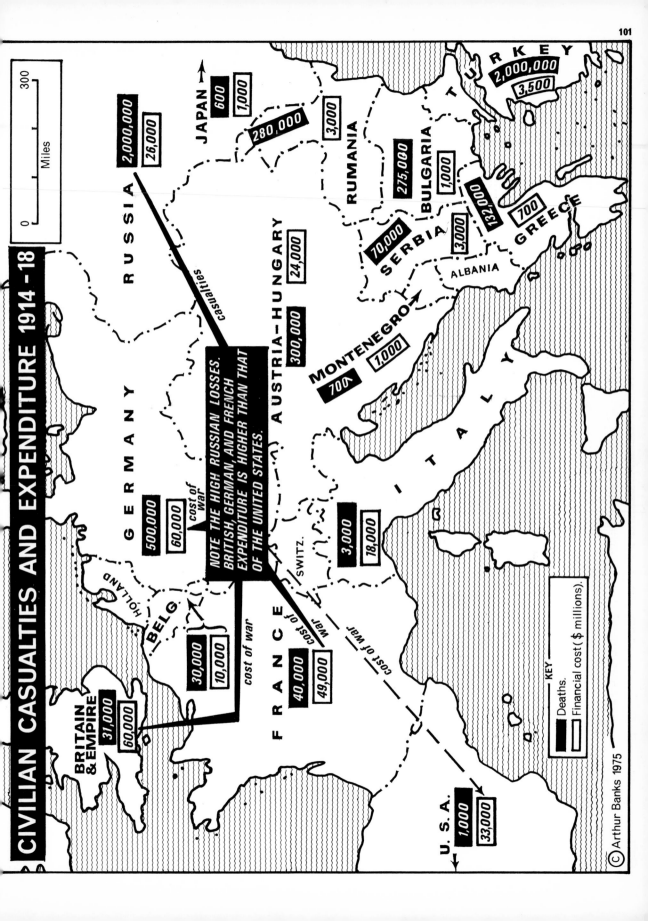

CIVILIAN CASUALTIES AND EXPENDITURE 1914-18

300

Miles

0

KEY

Deaths.

Financial cost ($ millions).

NOTE THE HIGH RUSSIAN LOSSES. BRITISH, GERMAN, AND FRENCH EXPENDITURE IS HIGHER THAN THAT OF THE UNITED STATES.

cost of war

casualties

JAPAN
600
1,000

TURKEY
2,000,000
3,500

RUSSIA
2,000,000
26,000

RUMANIA
280,000
3,000

BULGARIA
275,000
1,000

132,000

GREECE
700

SERBIA
70,000
3,000

ALBANIA

AUSTRIA-HUNGARY
300,000
24,000

MONTENEGRO
700
1,000

GERMANY
500,000
60,000

cost of war

HOLLAND

BELG.
30,000
10,000

SWITZ.

3,000
18,000

ITALY

FRANCE
40,000
49,000

cost of war

cost of war

BRITAIN & EMPIRE
31,000
60,000

U.S.A.
1,000
33,000

© Arthur Banks 1975

V
THE INTER-WAR YEARS

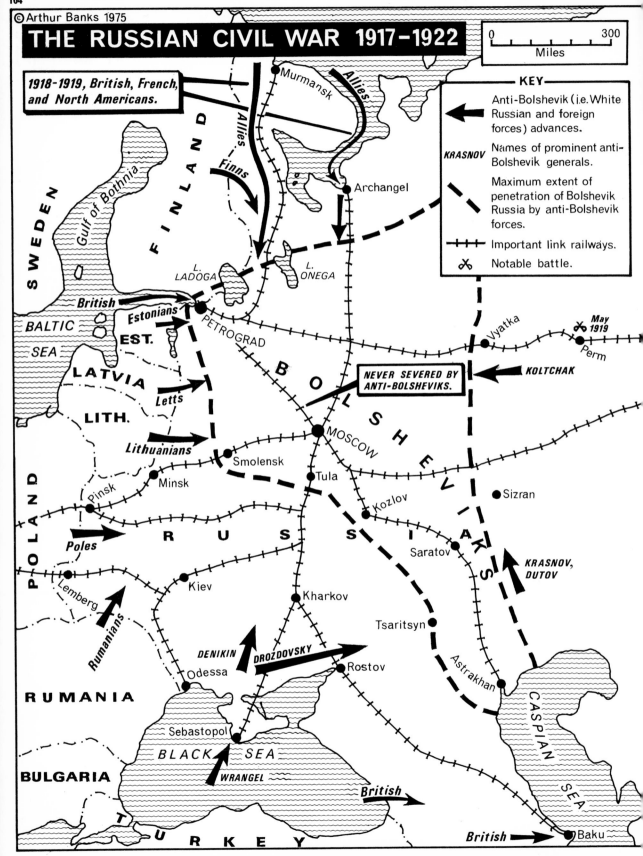

© Arthur Banks 1975

THE RUSSIAN CIVIL WAR 1917-1922

0 — 300
Miles

1918-1919, British, French, and North Americans.

— KEY —

Anti-Bolshevik (i.e. White Russian and foreign forces) advances.

KRASNOV — Names of prominent anti-Bolshevik generals.

Maximum extent of penetration of Bolshevik Russia by anti-Bolshevik forces.

┼┼┼ Important link railways.

✂ Notable battle.

Murmansk

Allies

Allies

Finns

Archangel

SWEDEN

FINLAND

Gulf of Bothnia

L. LADOGA

L. ONEGA

British

BALTIC SEA

Estonians

EST.

PETROGRAD

May 1919

Vyatka

Perm

LATVIA

Letts

LITH.

NEVER SEVERED BY ANTI-BOLSHEVIKS.

← *KOLTCHAK*

Lithuanians

Smolensk

B O L S H E V I K S

Minsk

MOSCOW

Pinsk

Tula

Sizran

POLAND

Poles →

R U S S I A

Kozlov

Saratov

Lemberg

Kiev

Kharkov

KRASNOV, DUTOV

Rumanians

DENIKIN

DROZDOVSKY →

Tsaritsyn

Odessa

Rostov

Astrakhan

RUMANIA

Sebastopol

CASPIAN SEA

BLACK SEA

BULGARIA

WRANGEL

British →

Baku

T U R K E Y

British →

THE GRAECO–TURKISH WAR 1919–1922

BLACK SEA

Adrianople

CONSTANTINOPLE

Thrace

1919

Sinope

RUSSIA

Black Sea

Kars

ARMENIANS 1919

TURKEY

Nationalists

April 1920, new government established under Mustapha Kemal.

ANGORA

Anatolia

TURKEY

Izmid

1922

1922

Sakkaria

Eski-shehr

Inönü

Brusa

1921

1921

Konia

Ushak

1919

1922

Smyrna

Aldin

Mughla

1919

Adalia

Adana

MEDITERRANEAN SEA

KEY

Turks.	
Greeks.	
Italians.	
✗	Battles.

0 100 200
Miles

© Arthur Banks 1975

THE RUSSO–POLISH WAR 1920

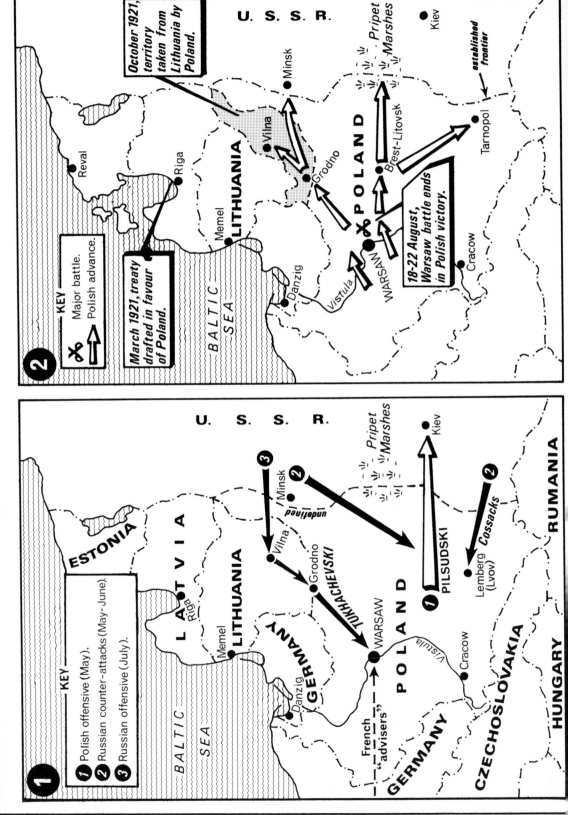

THE WEIMAR REPUBLIC

BALTIC SEA

Memel

East Prussia

Danzig

POLISH "CORRIDOR"

P o s e n

Katowice

Kolberg

Oder

Breslau

NORTH SEA

BERLIN

Elbe

Leipzig

Dresden

WEIMAR

Erfurt

G E R M A N Y

Nuremberg

Munich

Hamburg

Hanover

Bremen

Weser

Münster

Cassel

Frankfurt

Stuttgart

NORTH SCHLESWIG

Rhine

Cologne

Coblenz

Mainz

SAAR

1919, new Republican Constitution formed: Chancellor (rather than President) is main figure.

1920, Hitler forms National Socialist Party. 1923, "putsch" ends in failure: 1924, Hitler is imprisoned: he writes "MEIN KAMPF."

1923, American occupation force returns home.

This map shows Germany in 1919, following the Treaty of Versailles.

© Arthur Banks 1975

KEY
Germany's losses.

0   100
Miles

IRELAND

❶ Before the Treaty of 1921

Miles
0 ————— 100

1912, Carson's Ulster Volunteers drill openly in defiance of British government.

April 1914, rifles smuggled in from Germany.

Larne

BELFAST

ULSTER

Easter 1916, rising is put down by British: ringleaders executed.

Howth

Curragh Camp

DUBLIN

LEINSTER

March 1914, British officers resign commissions upon orders to stand ready for possible Ulster revolt.

CONNAUGHT

"Black and Tans" in conflict with Sinn Feiners

MUNSTER

NOTE: "SINN FEIN" MEANS 'OURSELVES ALONE'.

July 1914, Irish volunteers smuggle in arms.

Good Friday 1916, Sir Roger Casement lands here from a German submarine. He is arrested and his cargo-ship laden with arms for revolutionaries is confiscated.

Houses and property set ablaze

Tralee Bay

THE 'BLACK AND TANS' WERE A SPECIAL FORCE OF ARMED POLICE SENT TO IRELAND BY THE BRITISH GOVERNMENT.

© Arthur Paul 1975

❷ Following the Treaty of 1921

NORTHERN IRELAND
"The Six Counties"

British naval base (until 1938).

ANTRIM
BELFAST
DOWN
LONDON-DERRY
ARMAGH
TYRONE
FERMANAGH
DONEGAL

Almost isolated from the rest of the Irish Free State.

1925, boundary problem is resolved.

Kingstown gets new name.

Dun Laoghaire

DUBLIN

IRISH FREE STATE

OFFALY
LEIX

Kings County gets new name.

Queens County gets new name.

1922–1923, civil war between government and extremists

Cork (Cobh)

Seat of Senate and Dáil.

British naval bases (until 1938).

The Irish Free State became Eire in 1937. During the Second World War it adopted neutral status, but did not become an independent republic until 1948.

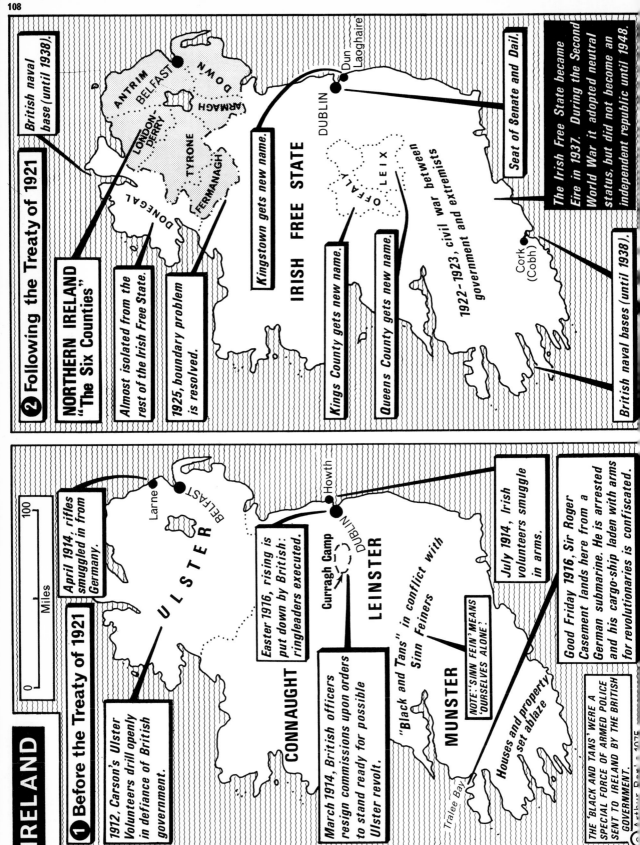

ITALIAN EXPANSION 1889-1939

1939, annexed to Italy.

1919, ceded to Italy by Austria.

1919-1924, disputed with Yugoslavia.

1919-1921, occupied by 'volunteer patriots': 1924, Italian.

Black Sea

ITALY

Fiume

Zara

ALBANIA

Sardinia

1912, occupied by Italy.

Sicily

Mediterranean Sea

Dodecanese Islands

Abortive attempt to establish control of Smyrna-Adalia region in 1919.

L I B Y A

1912-1925, ceded to Italy by Britain.

Red Sea

1911-1912, conquered by Italy from Ottoman Empire.

1890, declared an Italian province.

1919, ceded to Italy by France.

Italian from 1889.

1912, conquered by Italy (but not completely pacified until 1931).

ERITREA

1935-1936, conquered by Italy.

A B Y S S I N I A

ITALIAN SOMALILAND

1925, ceded to Italy by Britain.

0   500

Miles

INDIAN OCEAN

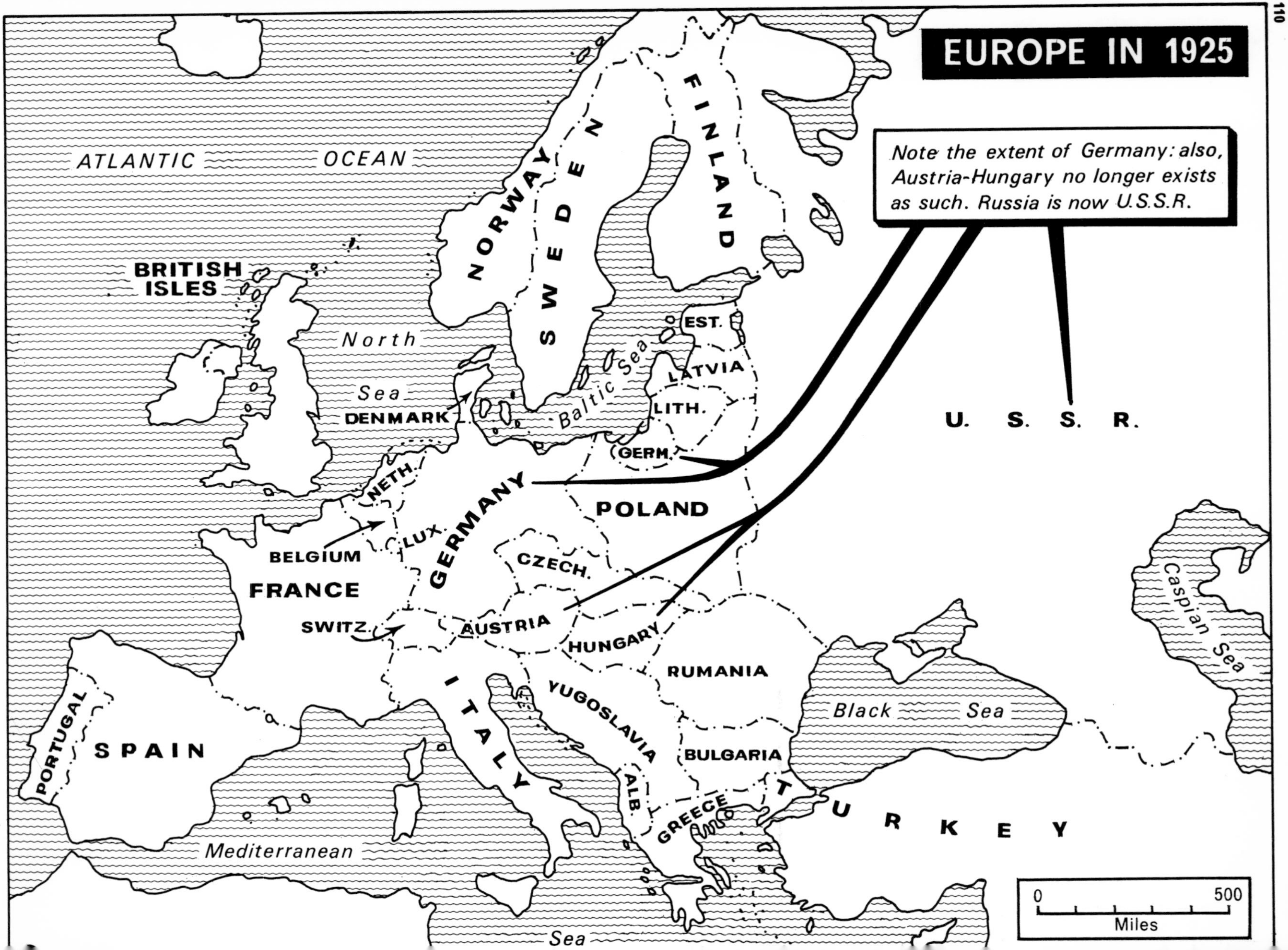

EUROPE IN 1925

Note the extent of Germany: also, Austria-Hungary no longer exists as such. Russia is now U.S.S.R.

500

Miles

0

U. S. S. R.

Caspian Sea

Black Sea

TURKEY

RUMANIA

BULGARIA

GREECE

HUNGARY

YUGOSLAVIA

ALB.

AUSTRIA

ITALY

CZECH.

POLAND

GERMANY

GERM.

LITH.

LATVIA

EST.

FINLAND

NORWAY

SWEDEN

Baltic Sea

DENMARK

NETH.

LUX.

BELGIUM

SWITZ.

FRANCE

North Sea

BRITISH ISLES

ATLANTIC OCEAN

SPAIN

PORTUGAL

Mediterranean Sea

EUROPE BETWEEN THE WORLD WARS

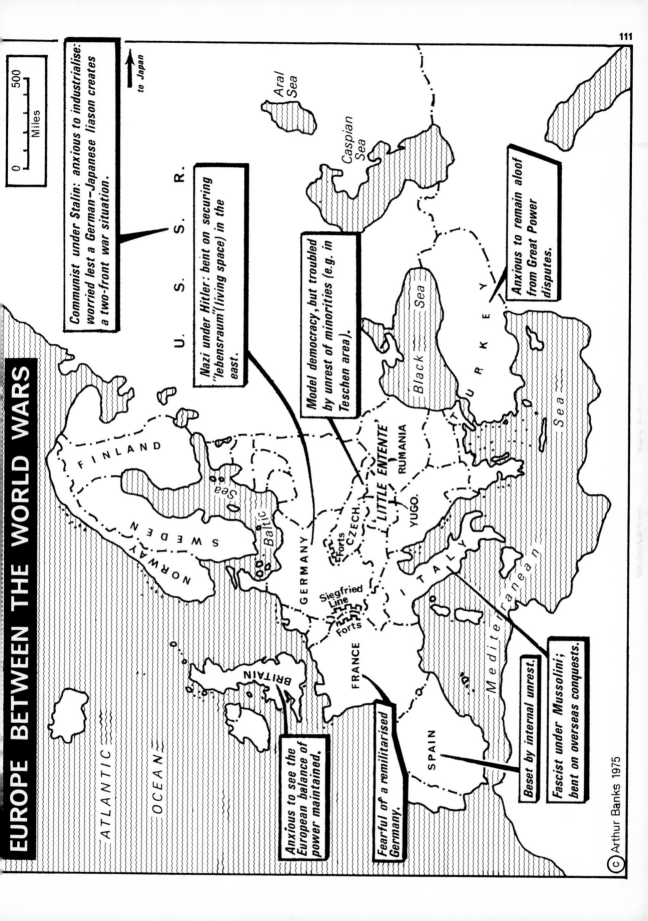

0 — 500 Miles

to Japan

Communist under Stalin: anxious to industrialise; worried lest a German–Japanese liason creates a two-front war situation.

Nazi under Hitler: bent on securing "lebensraum" (living space) in the east.

Model democracy, but troubled by unrest of minorities (e.g. in Teschen area).

Anxious to remain aloof from Great Power disputes.

Anxious to see the European balance of power maintained.

Fearful of a remilitarised Germany.

Beset by internal unrest.

Fascist under Mussolini; bent on overseas conquests.

Aral Sea

Caspian Sea

Black Sea

T U R K E Y

U. S. S. R.

FINLAND

NORWAY

SWEDEN

Baltic Sea

GERMANY

Forts

CZECH.

LITTLE ENTENTE

RUMANIA

YUGO.

Siegfried Line

Forts

FRANCE

BRITAIN

SPAIN

ITALY

Mediterranean Sea

ATLANTIC OCEAN

© Arthur Banks 1975

CHINA 1926-1933

PEKING

1928, captured by the Nationalists. Name is changed to Peiping (Northern Peace).

1928

S H A N T U N G

YELLOW SEA

0   200
Miles

Tsinan

1927

1928-1929, occupied by Japanese.

Hwang Ho

Hwang Ho

Suchow

1927

1932

Nanking

1927

Shanghai

EAST CHINA SEA

1926

Yangtse

Yangtse

Hankow

Wuchang

Hangchow

C H I N A

Nanchang

CHANGSHA ✂

1930, Nationalists defeat Communists who flee west.

1927, Communist uprising suppressed by Nationalists.

1932, occupied by Japanese forces.

1926

Foochow

1927, Communist uprising suppressed by Nationalists.

Formosa

Canton

The period was marked by rivalry between Nationalists and Communists to achieve supremacy, and by Japanese infiltration.

SOUTH CHINA SEA

── KEY ──

⬅   Nationalist advances, 1926-1928.

◯   Nationalist campaigning areas, 1927.

◗   Nationalist campaign against Communists.

© Arthur Banks 19

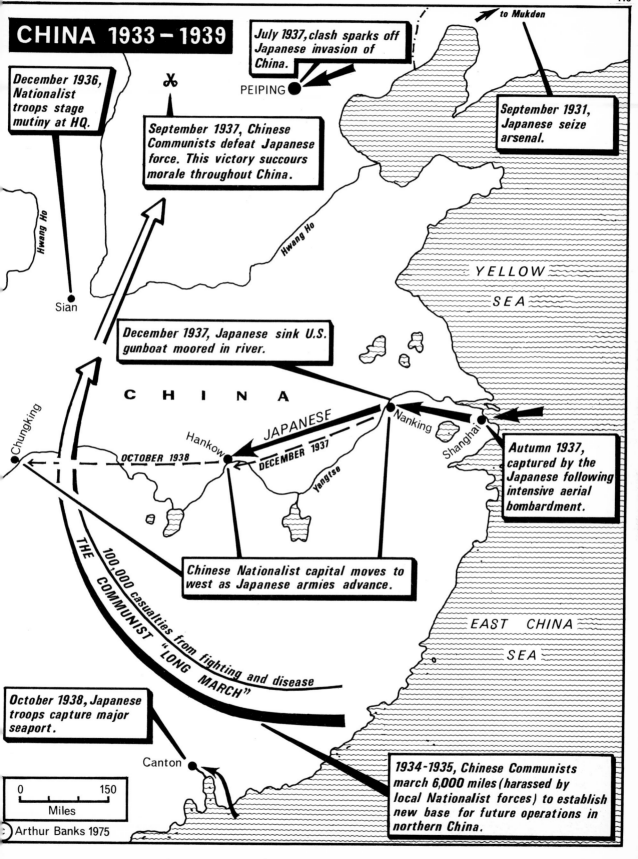

114

STRIFE IN INDIA PRE-1939

500 Miles

1919-1920, British operations against tribesmen and guerrillas.

1920's and 1930's, Gandhi leads campaign of civil disobedience against British.

1919, riot occurs here during which Europeans are killed. British troops fire on unarmed mob causing 1,600 casualties. Public indignation aroused in Britain.

Pathans in skirmishes with British during 1920's.

1919, peace treaty between Afghans and British.

CHINA

TIBET

NEPAL

BURMA

SIAM

GULF OF SIAM

BAY OF BENGAL

CEYLON

Calcutta

Madras

RIOTS AND UNREST

INDIA

RIOTS AND UNREST

Kashmir

Punjab

UNREST

Amritsar

DELHI

KHYBER PASS

NORTH-WEST FRONTIER

UNREST

Kabul

AFGHANISTAN

ARABIAN SEA

Bombay

KHYBER PASS

Kabul

Peshawar

Rawalpindi

SPAIN: THE AXIS "TRAINING GROUND" 1936–1939

The Spanish Civil War between the Nationalists and Republicans attracted foreign contingents and volunteers to both sides. The Nationalists were the victors. Total casualties: at least 750,000.

KEY

- **R** Military revolts, 1936.
- Spanish Nationalist advances.
- Spanish government moves from Madrid to east coast.
- Spanish Nationalist naval blockade (from Nov. 1937).
- Important battles.
- Heavily bombed by Germans.

September 1937, nine-power conference held at Nyon in Switzerland; anti-submarine naval patrol zones established.

Mid-1937, submarines of "unknown" origin attack British, French, Soviet, and Spanish Government shipping.

Non-interventionist policy.

April 1937, devastated by German aircraft.

Nationalist HQ.

December 1937–February 1938, bitter fighting here.

26 January 1939, falls to Nationalists.

March 1937, Italian reverses.

Besieged at intervals, 1936–1939.

28 March 1939, both cities surrender to Nationalists; civil war ends.

May 1937, shelled by German pocket-battleship: bombed by German Air Force.

July 1936, Franco arrives here to command Spanish Nationalist forces.

1928, dictatorship established.

MEDITERRANEAN SEA

Balearic Islands

FRANCE

Andorra

Barcelona

Vinaroz

Valencia

Oct. 1937

1939

1938

1939

Ebro

Teruel

Brihuega
Guadalajara

Nov. 1936

1937–1938

Guernica

Bilbao

1937

BURGOS R

OVIEDO R

Duero

MADRID R

TOLEDO

S P A I N

1936

Tagus

Badajoz

1936

R SEVILLE

Guadalquivir

Malaga

Almeria

Melilla

1936

CADIZ R

Tangier

1936

SPANISH MOROCCO

P O R T U G A L

LISBON

0   100
Miles

© Arthur Banks 1975

VI
THE SECOND
WORLD WAR

HITLER'S ROAD TO WAR 1936-1939

U. S. S. R.

LATVIA

LITHUANIA

Memel

EAST PRUSSIA (GERMANY)

Danzig

P O L A N D

SWEDEN

BALTIC SEA

DENMARK

Berlin

Sudetenland

CZECHO-SLOVAKIA

AUSTRIA

HUNGARY

RUMANIA

BULGARIA

YUGOSLAVIA

ALB.

Rhineland

Rhine

SWITZ.

I T A L Y

ROME

NETH.

BELGIUM

LUX.

F R A N C E

BRITAIN

S P A I N

500

Miles

0

MUSSOLINI
Hitler's "ally and friend"

KEY

- Hitler's "Third Reich".
- - - - Training ground for Luftwaffe (in Spain).
- (1) Hitler's first "exploratory" move (1936).
- (2) Austria annexed (1938).
- (3) Sudetenland annexed (later, western Czechoslovakia, 1939).
- (4) Memel annexed (1939).
- ▨ Territories gained by Hitler (1936-1939).
- (5) Danzig attacked (September 1939).

THE INVASION OF POLAND BY GERMANY (1 SEPTEMBER) & U.S.S.R. (17 SEPTEMBER) 1939

...aneously with their land attack, the Germans bombed the Poles from the air.

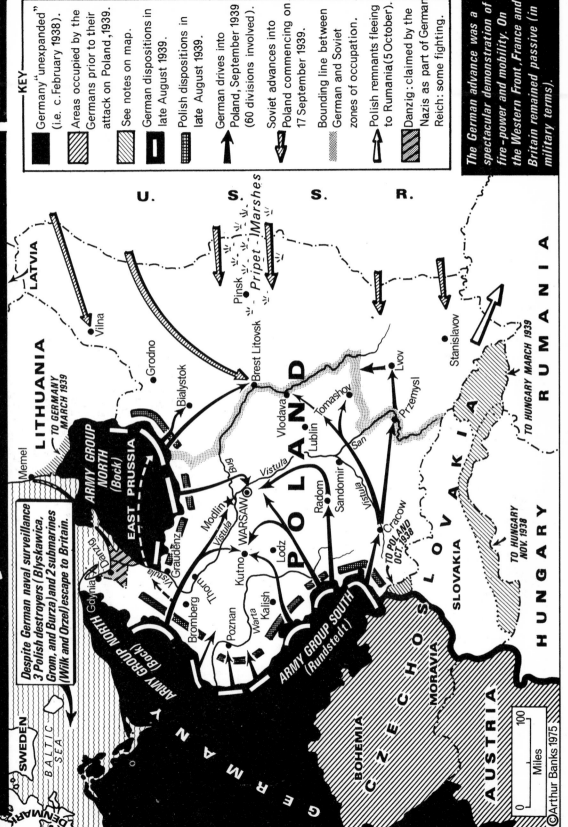

KEY

- Germany "unexpanded" (i.e. c.February 1938).
- Areas occupied by the Germans prior to their attack on Poland, 1939.
- See notes on map.
- German dispositions in late August 1939.
- Polish dispositions in late August 1939.
- German drives into Poland, September 1939 (60 divisions involved).
- Soviet advances into Poland commencing on 17 September 1939.
- Bounding line between German and Soviet zones of occupation.
- Polish remnants fleeing to Rumania (5 October).
- Danzig: claimed by the Nazis as part of German Reich: some fighting.

The German advance was a spectacular demonstration of fire-power and mobility. On the Western Front, France and Britain remained passive (in military terms).

Despite German naval surveillance 3 Polish destroyers (Blyskawica, Grom, and Burza) and 2 submarines (Wilk and Orzel) escape to Britain.

U. S. S. R.

SWEDEN

BALTIC SEA

DENMARK

GERMANY

LATVIA

LITHUANIA

Memel

TO GERMANY MARCH 1939

Vilna

Grodno

Bialystok

Pinsk

Pripet - Marshes

Brest Litovsk

Vlodava

Lvov

Stanislavov

Przemysl

ARMY GROUP NORTH (Bock)

EAST PRUSSIA

Gdynia

Danzig

Graudenz

Modlin

WARSAW

Vistula

Bug

Vistula

Tomashov

San

Lublin

Radom

Sandomir

Vistula

Thorn

Bromberg

Kutno

Lodz

Poznan

Warta

Kalish

ARMY GROUP NORTH (Bock)

ARMY GROUP SOUTH (Rundstedt)

Cracow

TO POLAND OCT.1938

TO HUNGARY NOV.1938

POLAND

CZECHO SLOVAKIA

SLOVAKIA

BOHEMIA

MORAVIA

AUSTRIA

HUNGARY

RUMANIA

TO HUNGARY MARCH 1939

0   100   Miles

©Arthur Banks 1975

THE CRUISE OF 'ADMIRAL GRAF SPEE' 21 AUGUST-13 DECEMBER 1939

KEY
Track of German pocket-battleship 'Admiral Graf Spee', with dates.

❶ The Quarry–'Admiral Graf Spee'

Note: in an attempt to confuse the British Admiralty, 'Graf Spee' frequently displayed false name-plates of the other two German pocket-battleships, the 'Admiral Scheer' and 'Deutschland'.

During 'Graf Spee's' voyage, her supplies were replenished by the tanker 'Altmark'.

Total tonnage of merchant shipping sunk by 'Graf Spee' during her 115-day cruise a commerce raider amounted to 50,089 gross tons.

Note: Allied naval groups hunting the 'Graf Spee' are shown by their official force designations, thus **F G H** *etc.*

NORTH AMERICA

ATLANTIC OCEAN

SOUTH AMERICA

EUROPE

Wilhelmshaven
GERMANY

AFRICA

INDIAN

21 Aug.
23 Aug.
25 Aug.
27 Aug.
29 Aug.
31 Aug.
2 Sept.
4 Sept.
6 Sept.
8 Sept.
30 Sept. ❶
29 Sept.
10 Sept.
3 Oct.
10 Oct. ❹
8 Oct.
❷
5 Oct.
13 Oct.
23 Oct.
❸ 7 Oct.
❺ 22 Oct.
2 Dec. ❼
2 Dec.
❽ 3 Dec.
4 Dec.
27 Sept.
17 Sept.
7 Dec. ❾
13 Dec.
7 Dec.
28 Oct.
24 Nov.
1 Nov.
20 Nov.
❻ 15 Nov.
14 Nov.
8

13 December 1939, the Battle of the River Plate.

Plate ✂

VICTIMS OF THE 'GRAF SPEE'
❶ SS 'Clement' ❷ SS 'Newton Beech' ❸ SS 'Ashlea' ❹ SS 'Huntsman'
❺ SS 'Trevanion' ❻ SS 'Africa Shell' ❼ SS 'Doric Star' ❽ SS 'Tairoa' ❾ SS 'Streonshalh'

© Arthur Banks 1975

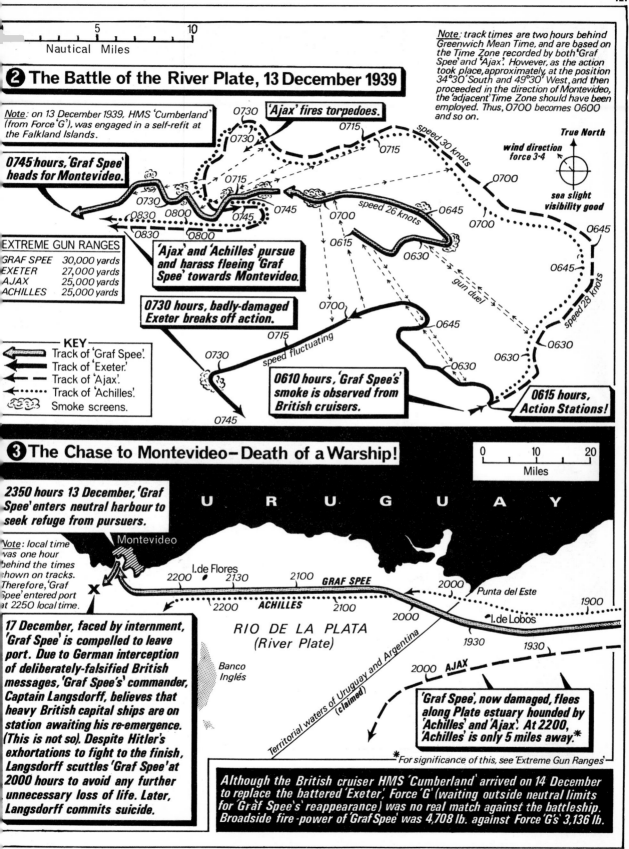

THE SOVIET–FINNISH WAR 30 NOVEMBER 1939 – 12 MARCH 1940

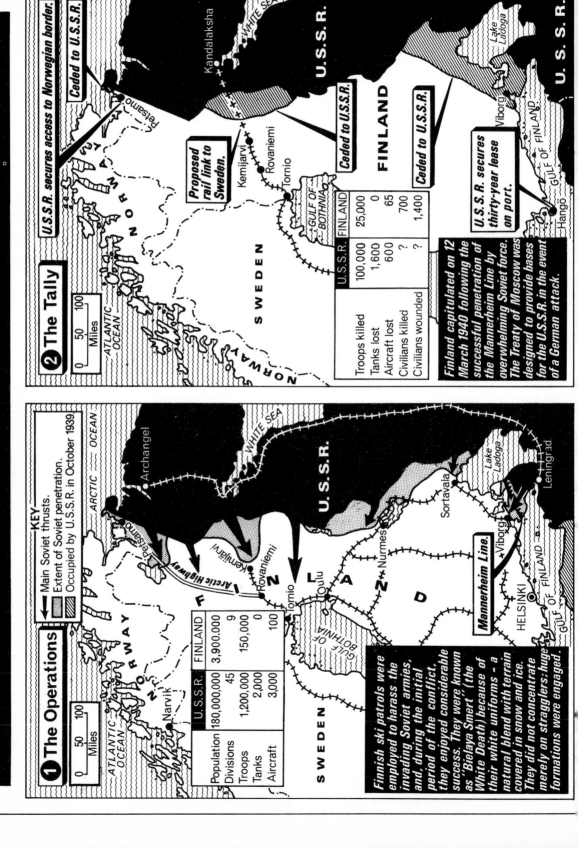

② The Tally

U.S.S.R. secures access to Norwegian border.

Ceded to U.S.S.R.

Proposed rail link to Sweden.

Ceded to U.S.S.R.

Ceded to U.S.S.R.

U.S.S.R. secures thirty-year lease on port.

	U.S.S.R.	FINLAND
Troops killed	100,000	25,000
Tanks lost	1,600	0
Aircraft lost	600	65
Civilians killed	?	700
Civilians wounded	?	1,400

Finland capitulated on 12 March 1940 following the successful penetration of the Mannerheim Line by overwhelming Soviet force. The Treaty of Moscow was designed to provide bases for the U.S.S.R. in the event of a German attack.

① The Operations

KEY
- ➤ Main Soviet thrusts.
- Extent of Soviet penetration.
- Occupied by U.S.S.R. in October 1939.

	U.S.S.R.	FINLAND
Population	180,000,000	3,900,000
Divisions	45	9
Troops	1,200,000	150,000
Tanks	2,000	0
Aircraft	3,000	100

Mannerheim Line.

Finnish ski patrols were employed to harass the invading Soviet armies, and, during the initial period of the conflict, they enjoyed considerable success. They were known as "Bielaya Smert" (the White Death) because of their white uniforms – a natural blend with terrain covered in snow and ice. They did not concentrate merely on stragglers: huge formations were engaged.

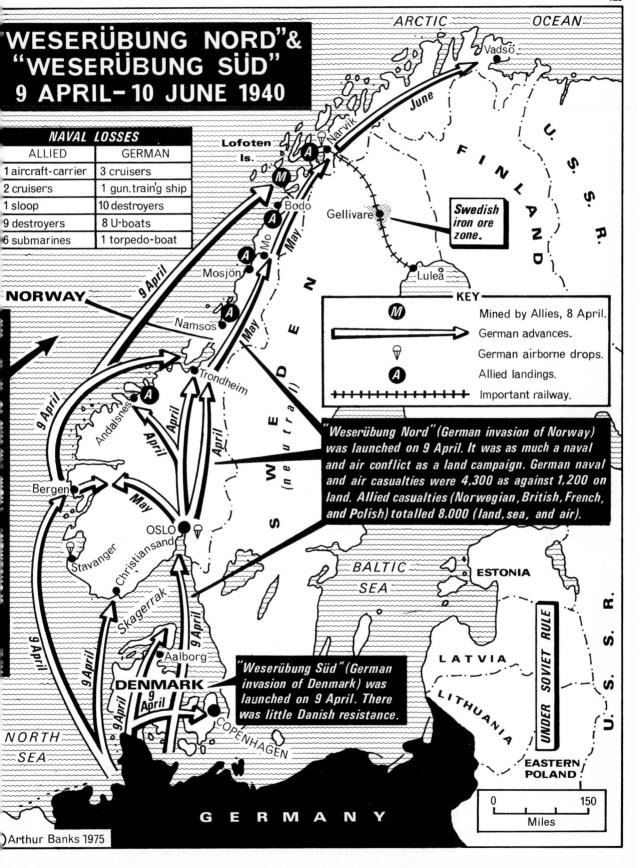

"WESERÜBUNG NORD"& "WESERÜBUNG SÜD" 9 APRIL– 10 JUNE 1940

ARCTIC OCEAN

Vadsö

June

Narvik

Lofoten Is.

FINLAND

U.S.S.R.

NAVAL LOSSES	
ALLIED	GERMAN
1 aircraft-carrier	3 cruisers
2 cruisers	1 gun.train'g ship
1 sloop	10 destroyers
9 destroyers	8 U·boats
6 submarines	1 torpedo-boat

Bodo

Gellivare

Swedish iron ore zone.

Mo

May

Luleå

Mosjön

NORWAY

9 April

Namsos

May

S W E D E N (neutral)

KEY

M — Mined by Allies, 8 April.
→ German advances.
✈ German airborne drops.
A — Allied landings.
+++++ Important railway.

Trondheim

April

April

April

9 April

Andalsnes

A

"Weserübung Nord" (German invasion of Norway) was launched on 9 April. It was as much a naval and air conflict as a land campaign. German naval and air casualties were 4,300 as against 1,200 on land. Allied casualties (Norwegian, British, French, and Polish) totalled 8,000 (land, sea, and air).

Bergen

May

BALTIC SEA

ESTONIA

OSLO

Stavanger

Christiansand

Skagerrak

9 April

LATVIA

UNDER SOVIET RULE

U.S.S.R.

9 April

9 April

Aalborg

9 April

LITHUANIA

"Weserübung Süd" (German invasion of Denmark) was launched on 9 April. There was little Danish resistance.

DENMARK 9 April

9 April

COPENHAGEN

EASTERN POLAND

NORTH SEA

GERMANY

0	150
Miles	

Arthur Banks 1975

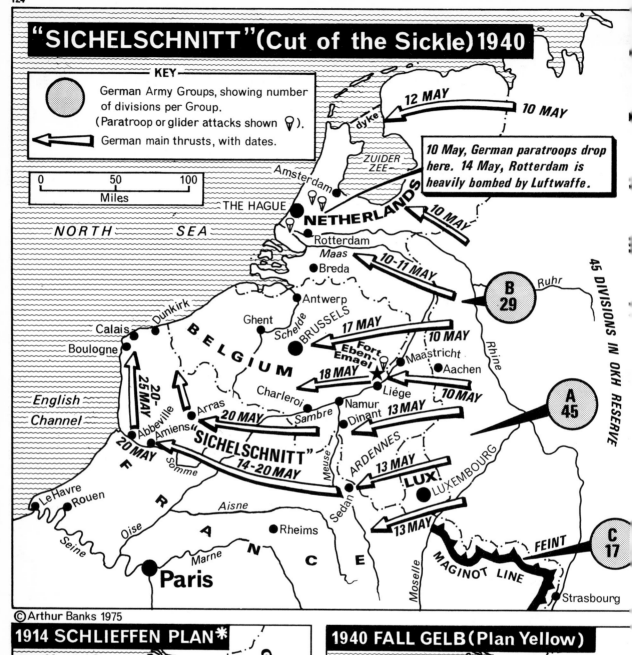

"SICHELSCHNITT" (Cut of the Sickle) 1940

KEY

German Army Groups, showing number of divisions per Group.
(Paratroop or glider attacks shown ▽).

German main thrusts, with dates.

0   50   100
Miles

12 MAY

10 MAY

dyke

ZUIDER ZEE

Amsterdam

THE HAGUE

NETHERLANDS

10 MAY, German paratroops drop here. 14 May, Rotterdam is heavily bombed by Luftwaffe.

NORTH   SEA

Rotterdam

Maas

10 MAY

10-11 MAY

Breda

Antwerp

B 29

Ruhr

Dunkirk

Calais

Ghent

Schelde

BRUSSELS

17 MAY

Fort Eben-Emael

10 MAY

Rhine

Boulogne

BELGIUM

18 MAY

Liége

10 MAY

Maastricht

Aachen

English Channel

20-25 MAY

Charleroi

Namur

Dinant

13 MAY

A 45

Arras

20 MAY

Sambre

ARDENNES

Abbeville

Amiens

"SICHELSCHNITT"
14-20 MAY

Meuse

13 MAY

LUXEMBOURG

LUX

20 MAY

F R A N C E

Somme

Sedan

13 MAY

45 DIVISIONS IN OKH RESERVE

Le Havre

Rouen

Aisne

Rheims

13 MAY

FEINT

C 17

Seine

Oise

Marne

Moselle

MAGINOT LINE

Paris

Strasbourg

© Arthur Banks 1975

1914 SCHLIEFFEN PLAN ✱

North Sea

HOLLAND

G E R M A N Y

BELGIUM

Antwerp

Maubeuge

Namur

Liége

ENGLISH CHANNEL

LUX.

UNSUCCESSFUL

F R A N C E

PARIS

✱ Moltke's 1914 version of original 1905 Plan.

1940 FALL GELB (Plan Yellow)

NETH.

Capitulates on 15 May.

Dunkirk

Calais

BELGIUM

Boulogne

Capitulates on 28 May.

G E R M A N Y

SUCCESSFUL

ARDENNES

LUX.

later

PARIS

Inspired by Manstein.

Maginot Line

F R A N C E

OPERATIONS IN THE VICINITY OF DUNKIRK IN 1940

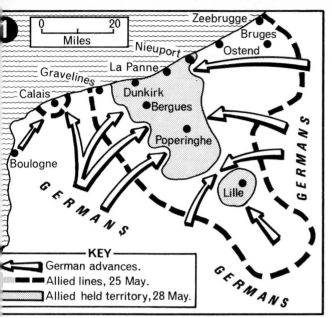

1

Miles 0 — 20

Zeebrugge
Bruges
Ostend
Nieuport
La Panne
Gravelines
Calais
Dunkirk
Bergues
Poperinghe
Boulogne
Lille

GERMANS
GERMANS
GERMANS
GERMANS

KEY
- German advances.
- Allied lines, 25 May.
- Allied held territory, 28 May.

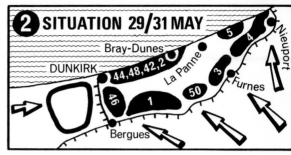

2 SITUATION 29/31 MAY

DUNKIRK
Bray-Dunes
La Panne
Nieuport
Furnes
Bergues
44, 48, 42, 2
46
1
50
3
5
4

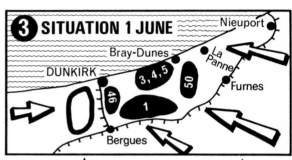

3 SITUATION 1 JUNE

DUNKIRK
Bray-Dunes
La Panne
Nieuport
Furnes
Bergues
46
1
3, 4, 5
50

KEY
- British divisions.
- French troops.
- German advances.
- Canals.

THE FALL OF FRANCE JUNE 1940

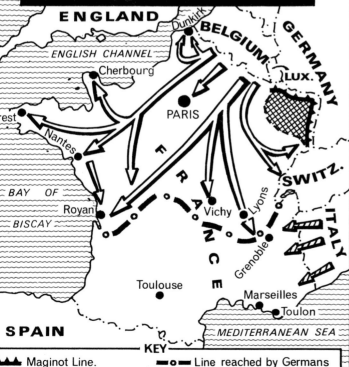

ENGLAND
ENGLISH CHANNEL
Dunkirk
BELGIUM
GERMANY
LUX.
Cherbourg
PARIS
FRANCE
SWITZ.
Brest
Nantes
BAY OF BISCAY
Royan
Vichy
Lyons
ITALY
Grenoble
Toulouse
Marseilles
Toulon
MEDITERRANEAN SEA
SPAIN

KEY
- Maginot Line.
- German advances.
- Italian attacks (20 June).
- Line reached by Germans at the armistice (22 June).
- Trapped French troops.

Operation "DYNAMO"

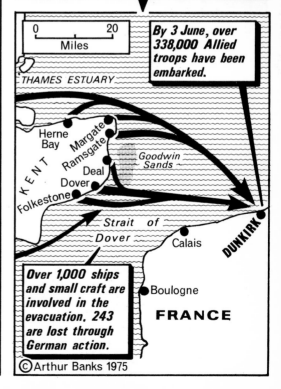

Miles 0 — 20

By 3 June, over 338,000 Allied troops have been embarked.

THAMES ESTUARY
Herne Bay
Margate
Ramsgate
Deal
Dover
Goodwin Sands
KENT
Folkestone
Strait of Dover
Calais
DUNKIRK
Boulogne
FRANCE

Over 1,000 ships and small craft are involved in the evacuation. 243 are lost through German action.

© Arthur Banks 1975

THE BATTLE OF BRITAIN 1940

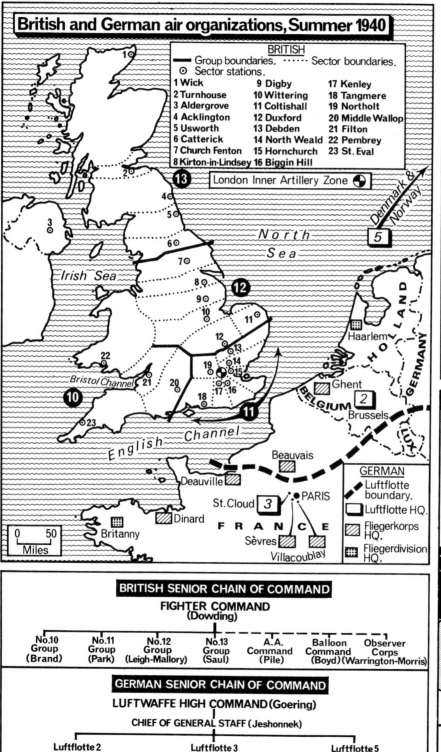

British and German air organizations, Summer 1940

BRITISH
— Group boundaries.   ···· Sector boundaries.
⊙ Sector stations.

1 Wick	9 Digby	17 Kenley
2 Turnhouse	10 Wittering	18 Tangmere
3 Aldergrove	11 Coltishall	19 Northolt
4 Acklington	12 Duxford	20 Middle Wallop
5 Usworth	13 Debden	21 Filton
6 Catterick	14 North Weald	22 Pembrey
7 Church Fenton	15 Hornchurch	23 St. Eval
8 Kirton-in-Lindsey	16 Biggin Hill	

London Inner Artillery Zone ⊕

North Sea

Irish Sea

Bristol Channel

English Channel

Haarlem

HOLLAND

GERMANY

Ghent   2

BELGIUM

Brussels

LUX.

Beauvais

Deauville

St.Cloud   3   ● PARIS

F R A N C E

Sèvres

Villacoublay

Dinard

Britanny

Denmark & Norway

5

GERMAN
▬ ▬ Luftflotte boundary.
▫ Luftflotte HQ.
▨ Fliegerkorps HQ.
▦ Fliegerdivision HQ.

0   50
Miles

BRITISH SENIOR CHAIN OF COMMAND
FIGHTER COMMAND
(Dowding)

No.10 Group (Brand)	No.11 Group (Park)	No.12 Group (Leigh-Mallory)	No.13 Group (Saul)	A.A. Command (Pile)	Balloon Command (Boyd)	Observer Corps (Warrington-Morris)

GERMAN SENIOR CHAIN OF COMMAND
LUFTWAFFE HIGH COMMAND (Goering)
CHIEF OF GENERAL STAFF (Jeshonnek)

Luftflotte 2 (Kesselring)	Luftflotte 3 (Sperrle)	Luftflotte 5 (Stumpff)

© Arthur Banks 1975

GERMAN OFFENSIVE PLAN

1. RECONNAISSAN[CE]
Initial phase for Luftwaffe t[o] probe R.A.F. defences, and [gain] general knowledge of the unfamiliar airspace.

2. BATTLE WITH R.[A.F.]
This phase to be a "direct [air] fight to eliminate Fighter Command and its airfields.

3. DESTRUCTION O[F] BRITAIN'S WAR ECONOMY
An offensive against urban centres in general and Lond[on] in particular.

BRITISH DEFENSIVE PLAN

1. R.A.F. Fighter Command to concentrate on the destruct[ion] of enemy bombers; "fighter [v. fighter] clashes to be avoided.
2. Protection of airfields and [the] important radiolocation sit[es.]

BRITISH RADIOLOCATION

0   200
Miles

NORWA[Y]

BRITAIN

FRANCE

BEL[GIUM]

KEY

▦ High altitude co[ver]
▨ Low altitude cov[er]

FROM NORWAY

LUFTFLOTTE 5
15 August

FROM DENMARK

NORTH SEA

, R.A.F. FIGHTER COMMAND

, No.11 GROUP

B R I T A I N

Stanmore

Uxbridge

Ventnor

LUFTFLOTTE 2

Ostend

Dunkirk

Calais

Boulogne

Etaples

ENGLISH CHANNEL

Dieppe

Cherbourg

LUFTFLOTTE 3

F R A N C E

AIRCRAFT LOSSES

Luftwaffe:	1,733
R.A.F. :	915

━ KEY ━

German embarkation ports (invasion-craft attacked by British bombers, August–September).

British radiolocation stations attacked by Luftwaffe, 12 August (Ventnor put out of action).

R.A.F. sector stations and airfields attacked by Luftwaffe (18 August–6 September).

London: main German target (7 September onwards).

Main air-battle area.

Direction of German attacks.

thur Banks 1975

DAILY AIRCRAFT LOSSES

The main period of the battle was from 13 August (Adler Tag or 'Eagle Day') until 15 September (the day when the Germans made their heaviest attack).

━ KEY ━

German losses shown thus: ■

British losses shown thus: □

Note:— On some days flying was restricted, or aircraft grounded because of bad weather. These days are shown thus: ▨

Date	German	British
13 AUGUST	45	13
14 August	▨	
15 August	75	34
16 August	45	21
17 August	▨	
18 August	71	27
19 August	▨	
20 August	▨	
21 August	▨	
22 August	▨	
23 August	▨	
24 August	38	22
25 August	20	16
26 August	41	31
27 August	3	0
28 August	30	20
29 August	17	9
30 August	36	26
31 August	41	39
1 September	14	15
2 September	35	31
3 September	16	16
4 September	25	17
5 September	23	20
6 September	35	23
7 September	41	28
8 September	15	2
9 September	28	19
10 September	3	0
11 September	29	25
12 September	4	0
13 September	4	1
14 September	14	14
15 SEPTEMBER	60	26
Totals	**808**	**495**

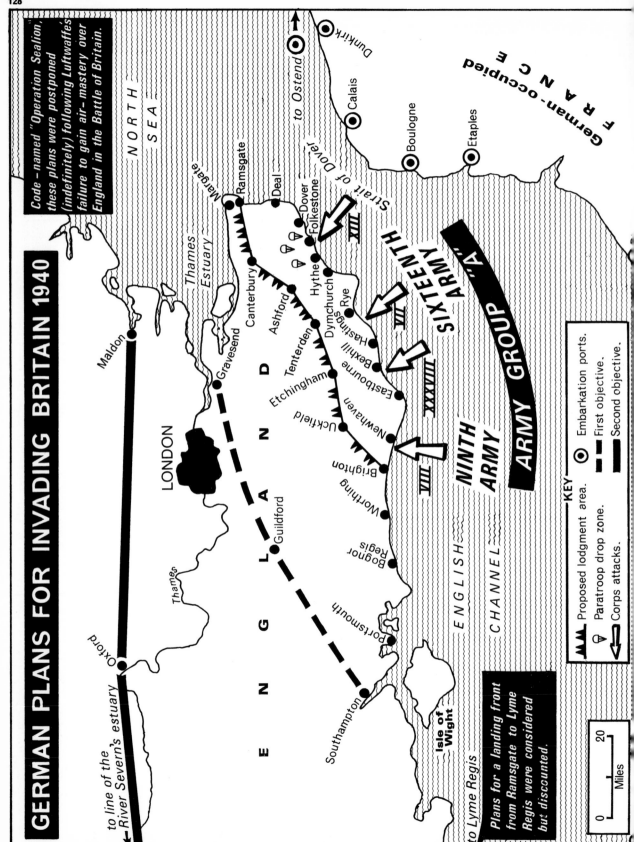

GERMAN PLANS FOR INVADING BRITAIN 1940

Code-named "Operation Sealion", these plans were postponed (indefinitely) following Luftwaffe's failure to gain air-mastery over England in the Battle of Britain.

to line of the River Severn's estuary

Oxford

LONDON

Maldon

Thames Estuary

Gravesend

Guildford

ENGLAND

Canterbury

Ashford

Tenterden

Etchingham

Uckfield

Margate

Ramsgate

Deal

Dover

Folkestone

Hythe

Dymchurch

Rye

Hastings

Bexhill

Eastbourne

Newhaven

Brighton

Worthing

Bognor Regis

Portsmouth

Southampton

Isle of Wight

Thames

NORTH SEA

Strait of Dover

XIII

SIXTEENTH ARMY

VII

XXXVIII

NINTH ARMY

VIII

ARMY GROUP "A"

ENGLISH CHANNEL

to Ostend

Dunkirk

Calais

Boulogne

Etaples

German-occupied FRANCE

to Lyme Regis

Plans for a landing front from Ramsgate to Lyme Regis were considered but discounted.

KEY

⊚	Embarkation ports.
---	First objective.
▬	Second objective.
▲▲▲	Proposed lodgment area.
⊕	Paratroop drop zone.
⇨	Corps attacks.

0   20
Miles

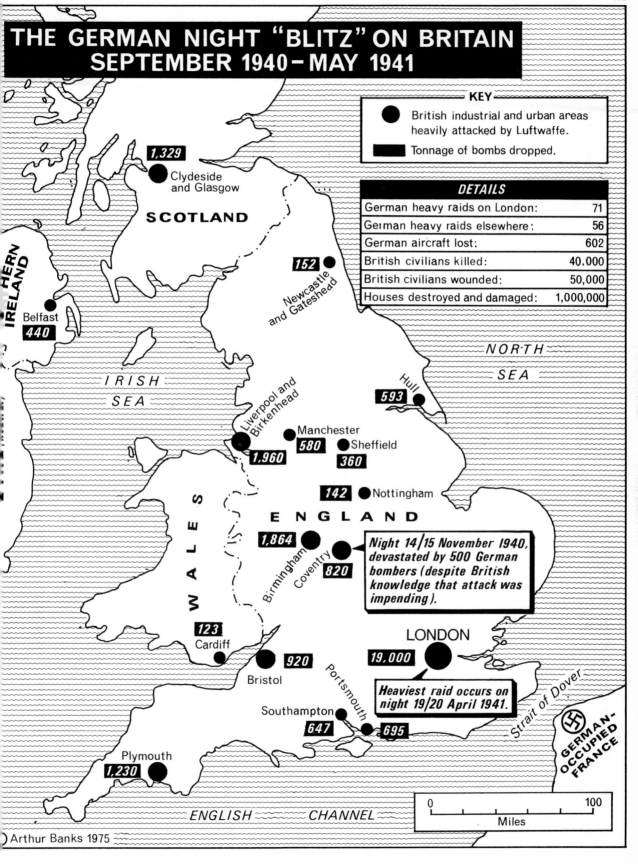

THE GERMAN NIGHT "BLITZ" ON BRITAIN
SEPTEMBER 1940 – MAY 1941

KEY

⬤ British industrial and urban areas heavily attacked by Luftwaffe.

▬ Tonnage of bombs dropped.

DETAILS	
German heavy raids on London:	71
German heavy raids elsewhere:	56
German aircraft lost:	602
British civilians killed:	40,000
British civilians wounded:	50,000
Houses destroyed and damaged:	1,000,000

1,329 Clydeside and Glasgow

SCOTLAND

152 Newcastle and Gateshead

NORTHERN IRELAND

Belfast **440**

IRISH SEA

NORTH SEA

Hull **593**

Liverpool and Birkenhead **1,960**

Manchester **580**

Sheffield **360**

142 Nottingham

WALES

ENGLAND

Birmingham **1,864**

Coventry **820**

Night 14/15 November 1940, devastated by 500 German bombers (despite British knowledge that attack was impending).

123 Cardiff

920 Bristol

LONDON **19,000**

Heaviest raid occurs on night 19/20 April 1941.

Portsmouth

Southampton **647**

695

Strait of Dover

GERMAN-OCCUPIED FRANCE

Plymouth **1,230**

ENGLISH CHANNEL

0 — 100
Miles

© Arthur Banks 1975

SECOND BATTLE OF THE ATLANTIC

1 Phase One: July 1940 – April 1941

GREENLAND

ICELAND

BRITISH ISLES

NORTH AMERICA

NEWFOUNDLAND

Lorient

EUROPE

Azores

Bermuda

Madeira

Gulf of Mexico

Canary Is.

Bahamas

ATLANTIC OCEAN

AFRICA

West Indies

Caribbean Sea

PACIFIC OCEAN

Cape Verde Is.

SOUTH AMERICA

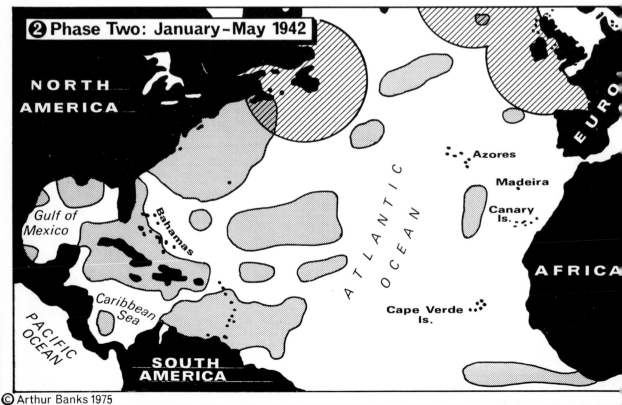

2 Phase Two: January – May 1942

NORTH AMERICA

EUROPE

Azores

Madeira

Gulf of Mexico

Canary Is.

Bahamas

ATLANTIC OCEAN

AFRICA

Caribbean Sea

PACIFIC OCEAN

Cape Verde Is.

SOUTH AMERICA

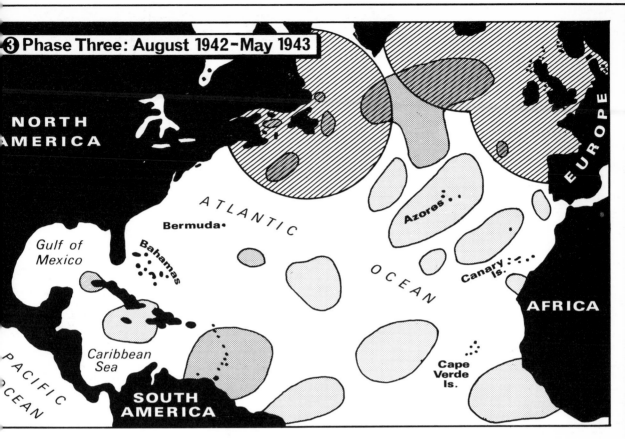

③ Phase Three: August 1942 – May 1943

NORTH AMERICA

ATLANTIC

Bermuda·

Gulf of Mexico

Bahamas

OCEAN

Azores

Canary Is.

AFRICA

EUROPE

Caribbean Sea

Cape Verde Is.

PACIFIC OCEAN

SOUTH AMERICA

── KEY ──

Areas where German U-boats sank large numbers of Allied and neutral ships.

Ranges of Allied land-based air cover.

Lorient. First German U-boat base on Atlantic coast (operational from July 1940).

Allied convoy routes.

Allied bases.

ese map sections illustrate phases the naval fight in the vital north antic theatre. The German assault ainst Allied merchant shipping was ee-pronged: via U-boats, surface ders, and long-range aircraft. 1,163 boats were involved (often in 'pack' mations) of which 784 were sunk. lied (plus neutral) losses totalled 326 ships (a tonnage of 14,680,000).

ALLIED CONVOY ROUTES AND BASES

TO U.S.S.R.

NORTH AMERICA

Reykjavik

Liverpool

EUROPE

St.John's

Sydney

Halifax

Azores

Gibraltar

Bermuda

ATLANTIC OCEAN

AFRICA

Freetown

Georgetown

SOUTH AMERICA

© Arthur Banks 1975

THE MEDITERRANEAN AND NORTH AFRICA 1940–1941

KEY
- Italian-held territory.
- British advances.
- Important naval clash.
- Important tank clash.

February 1941, bombarded by British Force "H" (from Gibraltar).

November 1940, British carrier-borne aircraft inflict heavy damage on Italian naval units.

February 1941, British 'U'-class submarines commence operations against Axis shipping plying between Italy and Libya.

March 1941, battle off Cape Matapan: British sink three Italian cruisers and two Italian destroyers, but battleship "Vittorio Veneto" escapes.

September 1940, British fleet attacks targets and repels Italian E-boat sortie.

December 1941, Italian-manned slow-speed torpedoes ("pigs") incapacitate two British battleships in harbour.

March 1941, German aircraft drop accoustic and magnetic mines in Suez Canal, closing it for three weeks.

March 1941, British troops to Greece

Following hesitant Italian advance into Egypt in September 1940, British launch counter-offensive in December. This develops into full-scale advance and victory: British take 130,000 prisoners.

February 1941, Rommel arrives here to command German Afrika Korps in Libya.

BLACK SEA, Aegean Sea, Adriatic Sea, MEDITERRANEAN SEA, ALBANIA, ITALY, Corsica, Sardinia, Sicily, TUNISIA, EGYPT, LIBYA

Genoa, Taranto, Malta, Tripoli, Castel Benito Airfield, Rhodes, Scarpanto, Crete, Alexandria, Sidi Barrani, Bardia, Tobruk, Derna, Msus, Beda Fomm, Benghazi, El Agheila

0 200 Miles

BRITISH NAVAL LOSSES OFF GREECE AND CRETE 1941

0 — 200
Miles

GREECE
TURKEY
Rhodes
Scarpanto
CRETE
MEDITERRANEAN SEA
NORTH AFRICA

— KEY —
✸ British warships sunk or badly damaged.
✱ British transports „ „ „ „ .

26 May, H.M.S. "Formidable" (sole British aircraft-carrier in area dominated by 500 Axis aircraft) is dive-bombed and put out of action.

THE TOLL

Warships sunk:	**9**
Warships seriously damaged:	**7**
Warships damaged:	**6**

© Arthur Banks 1975

ROMMEL IN NORTH AFRICA 1941–1942

1 His advance.
2 His retreat.
3 His second advance.

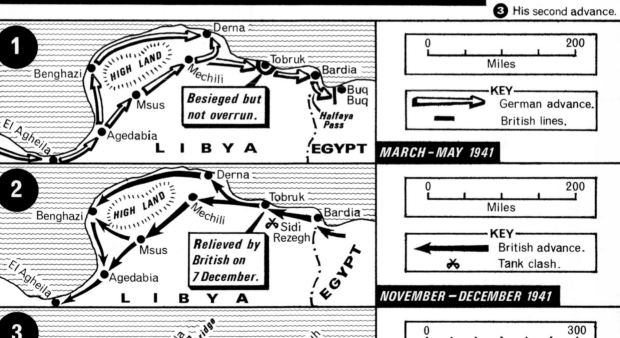

1
Derna
Benghazi
HIGH LAND
Mechili
Tobruk
Bardia
Buq Buq
Msus
Besieged but not overrun.
Halfaya Pass
El Agheila
Agedabia
L I B Y A
EGYPT

0 — 200 Miles
KEY
→ German advance.
▬ British lines.
MARCH – MAY 1941

2
Derna
Benghazi
HIGH LAND
Mechili
Tobruk
Bardia
✂ Sidi Rezegh
Msus
Relieved by British on 7 December.
El Agheila
Agedabia
L I B Y A
EGYPT

0 — 200 Miles
KEY
← British advance.
✂ Tank clash.
NOVEMBER – DECEMBER 1941

3
Benghazi
Gazala
Cauldron
Knightsbridge
Mersa Matruh
El Alamein
February–June: stalemate situation.
ALAM HALFA
El Agheila
Qattara Depression

0 — 300 Miles
KEY
→ German advance.
✂ ✱ Battle / positions.
JANUARY – JULY 1942

SECURING THE BALKAN FLANK SPRING 1941

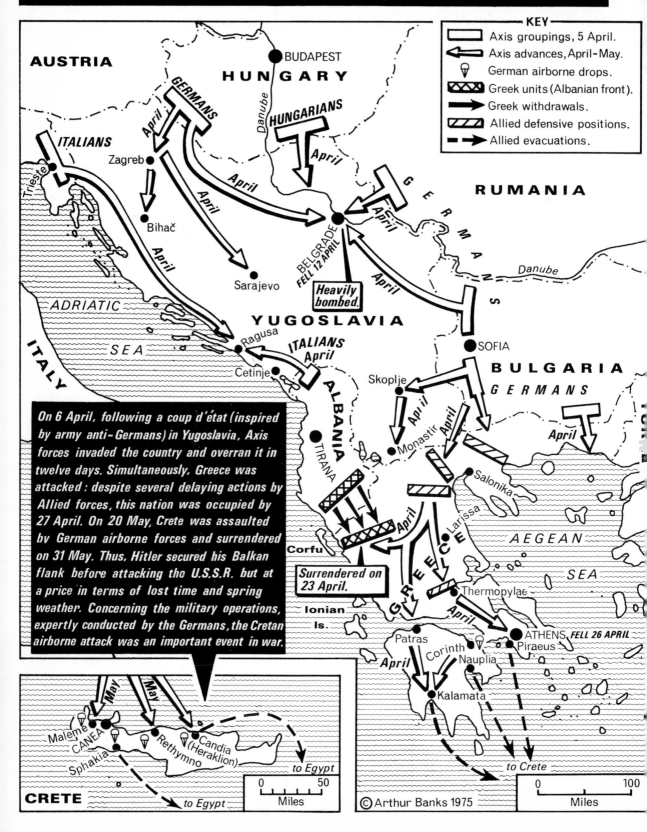

KEY

- Axis groupings, 5 April.
- Axis advances, April–May.
- German airborne drops.
- Greek units (Albanian front).
- Greek withdrawals.
- Allied defensive positions.
- Allied evacuations.

AUSTRIA

HUNGARY

BUDAPEST

GERMANS

April

ITALIANS

Trieste

Danube

HUNGARIANS

April

April

Zagreb

April

April

Bihač

RUMANIA

GERMANS

April

BELGRADE FELL 12 APRIL

Heavily bombed.

April

Danube

ADRIATIC

SEA

Sarajevo

YUGOSLAVIA

ITALY

April

Ragusa

ITALIANS April

Cetinje

ALBANIA

SOFIA

Skoplje

BULGARIA

GERMANS

April

April

On 6 April, following a coup d'état (inspired by army anti-Germans) in Yugoslavia, Axis forces invaded the country and overran it in twelve days. Simultaneously, Greece was attacked: despite several delaying actions by Allied forces, this nation was occupied by 27 April. On 20 May, Crete was assaulted by German airborne forces and surrendered on 31 May. Thus, Hitler secured his Balkan flank before attacking the U.S.S.R. but at a price in terms of lost time and spring weather. Concerning the military operations, expertly conducted by the Germans, the Cretan airborne attack was an important event in war.

TIRANA

Monastir

Salonika

April

Corfu

April

Larissa

AEGEAN

SEA

Surrendered on 23 April.

Ionian Is.

G R E E C E

April

Thermopylae

April

Patras

Corinth

Nauplia

ATHENS *FELL 26 APRIL*

Piraeus

April

Kalamata

to Crete

May

May

Maleme

CANEA

Rethymno

Candia (Heraklion)

Sphakia

to Egypt

CRETE

0   50
Miles

to Egypt

0   100
Miles

© Arthur Banks 1975

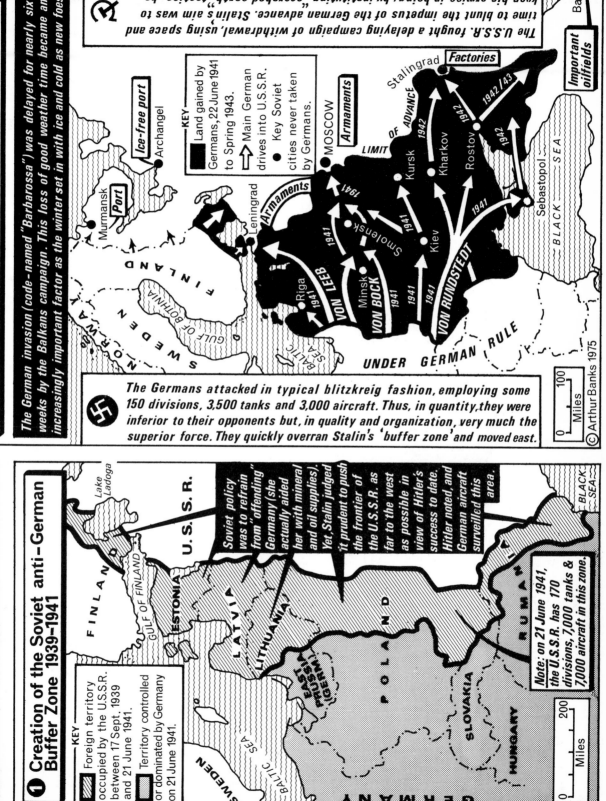

OPERATION BARBAROSSA

② The German Assault on the U.S.S.R. (22 June 1941)

The German invasion (code-named "Barbarossa") was delayed for nearly six weeks by the Balkans campaign. This loss of good weather time became an increasingly important factor as the winter set in with ice and cold as new foes.

The U.S.S.R. fought a delaying campaign of withdrawal, using space and time to blunt the impetus of the German advance. Stalin's aim was to keep his armies in being : by instituting "scorched earth" tactics, he denied Soviet crops and resources to the invaders.

KEY
- Land gained by Germans, 22 June 1941 to Spring 1943.
- Main German drives into U.S.S.R.
- Key Soviet cities never taken by Germans.

Ice-free port — Archangel
Port — Murmansk
Leningrad
MOSCOW — *Armaments*
Riga
Minsk
Smolensk
Kiev
Kursk
Kharkov
Rostov
Sebastopol
Stalingrad — *Factories*
Baku — *Important oilfields*

Armaments
LIMIT OF ADVANCE
VON LEEB
VON BOCK
VON RUNDSTEDT
UNDER GERMAN RULE
1941
1942
1942/43

BALTIC SEA
BLACK SEA
GULF OF BOTHNIA
NORWAY
SWEDEN
FINLAND

0 — 100 Miles
© Arthur Banks 1975

The Germans attacked in typical blitzkreig fashion, employing some 150 divisions, 3,500 tanks and 3,000 aircraft. Thus, in quantity, they were inferior to their opponents but, in quality and organization, very much the superior force. They quickly overran Stalin's 'buffer zone' and moved east.

① Creation of the Soviet anti-German Buffer Zone 1939–1941

KEY
- Foreign territory occupied by the U.S.S.R. between 17 Sept. 1939 and 21 June 1941.
- Territory controlled or dominated by Germany on 21 June 1941.

Soviet policy was to refrain from "offending" Germany (she actually aided her with mineral and oil supplies). Yet, Stalin judged it prudent to push the frontier of the U.S.S.R. as far to the west as possible in view of Hitler's success to date. Hitler noted, and German aircraft surveilled this area.

Note: on 21 June 1941, the U.S.S.R. has 170 divisions, 7,000 tanks & 7,000 aircraft in this zone.

Lake Ladoga
U.S.S.R.
FINLAND
GULF OF FINLAND
ESTONIA
LATVIA
LITHUANIA
EAST PRUSSIA (GERM.)
POLAND
SLOVAKIA
HUNGARY
RUMANIA
GERMANY
SWEDEN
BALTIC SEA
BLACK SEA

0 — 200 Miles

THE JAPANESE ASSAULT ON PEARL HARBOR 1941

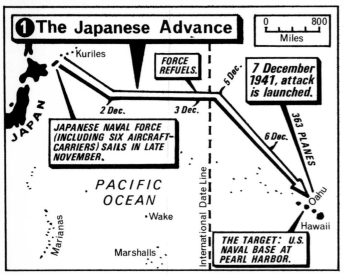

❶ The Japanese Advance

0 — 800
Miles

Kuriles

FORCE REFUELS.

5 Dec.

7 December 1941, attack is launched.

JAPAN

2 Dec.   3 Dec.

JAPANESE NAVAL FORCE (INCLUDING SIX AIRCRAFT-CARRIERS) SAILS IN LATE NOVEMBER.

6 Dec.

363 PLANES

PACIFIC OCEAN

Oahu

•Wake

Hawaii

Marianas

Marshalls

International Date Line

THE TARGET: U.S. NAVAL BASE AT PEARL HARBOR.

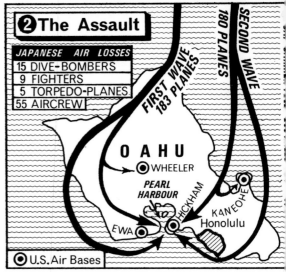

❷ The Assault

JAPANESE AIR LOSSES	
15	DIVE-BOMBERS
9	FIGHTERS
5	TORPEDO-PLANES
55	AIRCREW

FIRST WAVE 183 PLANES

180 PLANES

SECOND WAVE

O A H U

WHEELER

PEARL HARBOUR

HICKHAM

KANEOHE

EWA

Honolulu

⊙ U.S. Air Bases

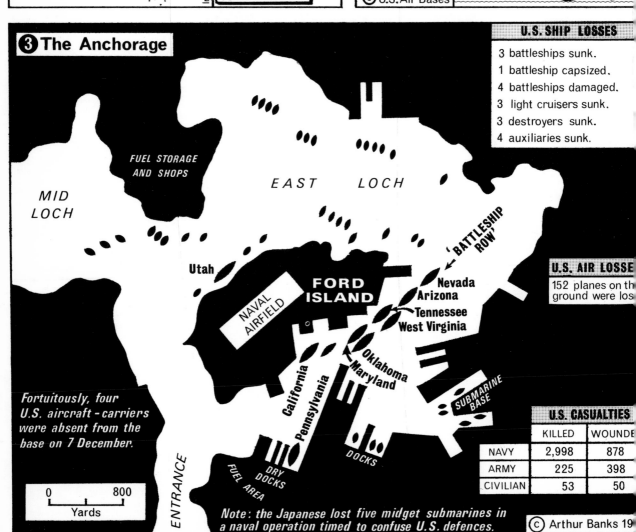

❸ The Anchorage

U.S. SHIP LOSSES

3 battleships sunk.
1 battleship capsized.
4 battleships damaged.
3 light cruisers sunk.
3 destroyers sunk.
4 auxiliaries sunk.

FUEL STORAGE AND SHOPS

EAST LOCH

MID LOCH

U.S. AIR LOSSE
152 planes on th
ground were los

Utah

FORD ISLAND

'BATTLESHIP ROW'

NAVAL AIRFIELD

Nevada
Arizona
Tennessee
West Virginia

California
Pennsylvania

Oklahoma
Maryland

SUBMARINE BASE

DOCKS

Fortuitously, four U.S. aircraft-carriers were absent from the base on 7 December.

ENTRANCE

FUEL AREA

DRY DOCKS

0 — 800
Yards

U.S. CASUALTIES

	KILLED	WOUNDE
NAVY	2,998	878
ARMY	225	398
CIVILIAN	53	50

Note: the Japanese lost five midget submarines in a naval operation timed to confuse U.S. defences.

© Arthur Banks 19

JAPANESE CONQUESTS 1941–1942

KEY

The Japanese Empire on the eve of its attack on Pearl Harbor in December 1941.

Japanese strikes, Dec. 1941.

Greatest extent of Japanese conquests (January 1943).

Important naval/air clashes.

1000

Miles

0

Dutch Harbor

Aleutian Is.

Attu Kiska

U.S.S.R.

SAKHALIN

Kurile Is.

HOKKAIDO

J A P A N

HONSHU

Tokyo

SHIKOKU

KYUSHU

Iwojima

Ryukyu Is.

Formosa

Midway I.

June 1942

P A C I F I C   O C E A N

Hawaiian Is.

Pearl Harbor

Wake I.

Marshall Is.

Guam

Caroline Is.

NEW GUINEA

Coral Sea

May 1942

AUSTRALIA

U.S.S.R.

MONGOLIA

Manchuria

C H I N A

Chungking

BURMA ROAD

BURMA

TIBET

INDIA

FR. INDO-CHINA

THAI-LAND

Dec. 1941

MALAYA

Singapore

Sumatra

DUTCH EAST INDIES

Java

Feb. 1942

Borneo

Jan. 1942

Celebes

Hainan

Manila

PHILIPPINE IS.

© Arthur Banks 1975

THE JAPANESE ASSAULT ON BURMA 1942

KEY

Japanese advances, with dates.

Important railways.

Clashes.

CASUALTIES	
JAPANESE:	**7,000**
BRITISH:	**13,000**
BURMESE:	**5,000**
CHINESE (estimate):	**15,000**

This area, peopled by Chins and Kashins, is not conquered by Japanese.

INDIA

INDIA

CHINA

Chindwin

Waza

Linhpa

Myitkyina

Maungkan

Indaw

Bhamo

Mawlaik
Kalewa

Irrawaddy

Shwebo

Lashio

Burma Road

MAY

MAY

MAY

MANDALAY

APRIL

Taunglau

Paletwa

Lai-kha

Kengtung

B   U   R   M   A

FRENCH
INDO-
CHINA

Magwe

Loikaw

Salween

APRIL

APRIL

Akyab

APRIL

Toungoo

APRIL

MARCH

THAILAND
(SIAM)

BAY   OF

Sittang

Prome

Irrawaddy

MARCH

Moulmein

JAN.

BENGAL

FEB.

RANGOON

OPENING ATTACKS

JAN.

0   100

Miles

JAN.
from
Kra Isthmus

© Arthur Banks 1975

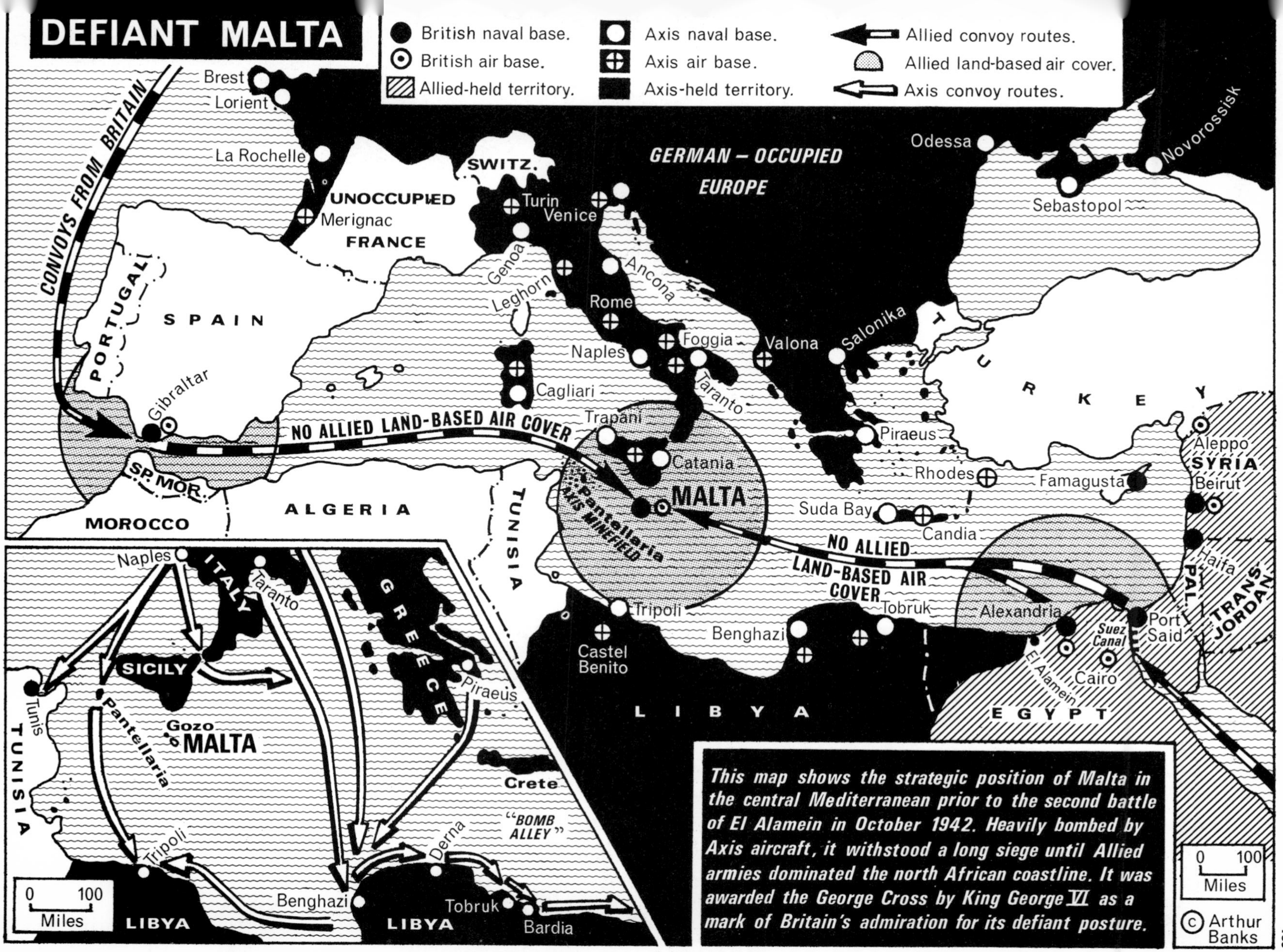
DEFIANT MALTA
British naval base.
British air base.
Allied-held territory.
Axis naval base.
Axis air base.
Axis-held territory.
Allied convoy routes.
Allied land-based air cover.
Axis convoy routes.
CONVOYS FROM BRITAIN
Brest
Lorient
La Rochelle
Merignac
UNOCCUPIED
FRANCE
SWITZ.
GERMAN – OCCUPIED EUROPE
PORTUGAL
SPAIN
Gibraltar
SP. MOR.
MOROCCO
ALGERIA
TUNISIA
NO ALLIED LAND-BASED AIR COVER
Turin
Venice
Genoa
Leghorn
Ancona
Rome
Naples
Foggia
Taranto
Cagliari
Trapani
Catania
MALTA
Pantellaria
AXIS MINEFIELD
Tripoli
Castel Benito
Valona
Salonika
Odessa
Sebastopol
Novorossisk
TURKEY
Piraeus
Rhodes
Famagusta
Aleppo
SYRIA
Beirut
Haifa
PAL.
TRANS JORDAN
Suda Bay
Candia
NO ALLIED LAND-BASED AIR COVER
Tobruk
Benghazi
LIBYA
Alexandria
El Alamein
Suez Canal
Port Said
Cairo
EGYPT
0 100 Miles
Arthur Banks
Naples
ITALY
Taranto
SICILY
Gozo
MALTA
Pantellaria
Tunis
TUNISIA
Tripoli
Benghazi
Derna
Tobruk
Bardia
LIBYA
GREECE
Piraeus
Crete
"BOMB ALLEY"
0 100 Miles

This map shows the strategic position of Malta in the central Mediterranean prior to the second battle of El Alamein in October 1942. Heavily bombed by Axis aircraft, it withstood a long siege until Allied armies dominated the north African coastline. It was awarded the George Cross by King George VI as a mark of Britain's admiration for its defiant posture.

ALLIED AID TO THE U.S.S.R.

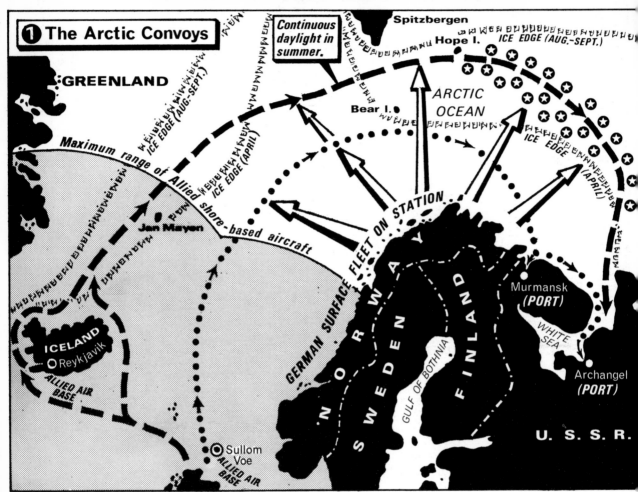

① The Arctic Convoys

GREENLAND

Continuous daylight in summer.

Spitzbergen

Hope I.

ICE EDGE (AUG.-SEPT.)

ARCTIC OCEAN

Bear I.

ICE EDGE (AUG.-SEPT.)

ICE EDGE (APRIL)

Maximum range of Allied shore-based aircraft

Jan Mayen

ICE EDGE (APRIL)

GERMAN SURFACE FLEET ON STATION

N O R W A Y

S W E D E N

FINLAND

GULF OF BOTHNIA

Murmansk (PORT)

WHITE SEA

Archangel (PORT)

ICELAND

Reykjavik

ALLIED AIR BASE

Sullom Voe

ALLIED AIR BASE

U. S. S. R.

② The Caspian Route

| 0 | 300 |
Miles

GERMAN LAND THREAT

Astrakhan

Black Sea

U.S.S.R.

U.S.S.R. CASPIAN SEA

Baku

Tehran

ALLIED AID

PERSIA (IRAN)

I R A Q

Basra

Persian Gulf

© Arthur Banks 1975

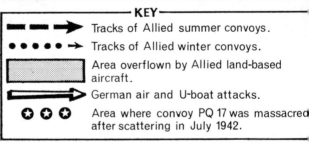

--- KEY ---

Tracks of Allied summer convoys.

Tracks of Allied winter convoys.

Area overflown by Allied land-based aircraft.

German air and U-boat attacks.

Area where convoy PQ 17 was massacred after scattering in July 1942.

Anglo – American aid to the U.S.S.R. equalled about 5% of Soviet internal production. It included over 20,000 aircraft, 13,000 tanks, food, clothing, medical supplies, petroleum, and electronic equipment. It went via two main routes (see maps). 40 Allied convoys made the northern journey despite German interference in transit (815 merchant ships sailed: 98 were sunk). The Caspian route, although safer, was indirect from the west

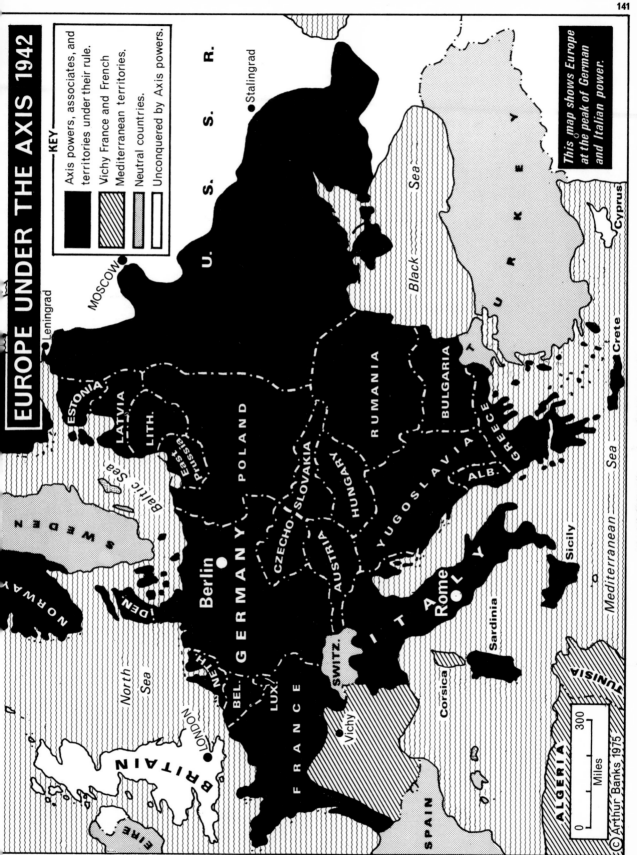

EUROPE UNDER THE AXIS 1942

KEY

- Axis powers, associates, and territories under their rule.
- Vichy France and French Mediterranean territories.
- Neutral countries.
- Unconquered by Axis powers.

This map shows Europe at the peak of German and Italian power.

Leningrad

MOSCOW

Stalingrad

U. S. S. R.

SWEDEN

NORWAY

ESTONIA

LATVIA

LITH.

East Prussia

Baltic Sea

POLAND

Berlin

GERMANY

DEN.

CZECHO-SLOVAKIA

AUSTRIA

HUNGARY

RUMANIA

Black Sea

BULGARIA

YUGOSLAVIA

ALB.

GREECE

TURKEY

Crete

Cyprus

NETH.

BEL.

LUX.

SWITZ.

FRANCE

Vichy

ITALY

Rome

Sardinia

Corsica

Sicily

Mediterranean Sea

ALGERIA

TUNISIA

SPAIN

North Sea

LONDON

BRITAIN

EIRE

300

Miles

0

© Arthur Banks 1975

STRATEGY: VIEWPOINTS AND INTENTIONS AUTUMN 1942

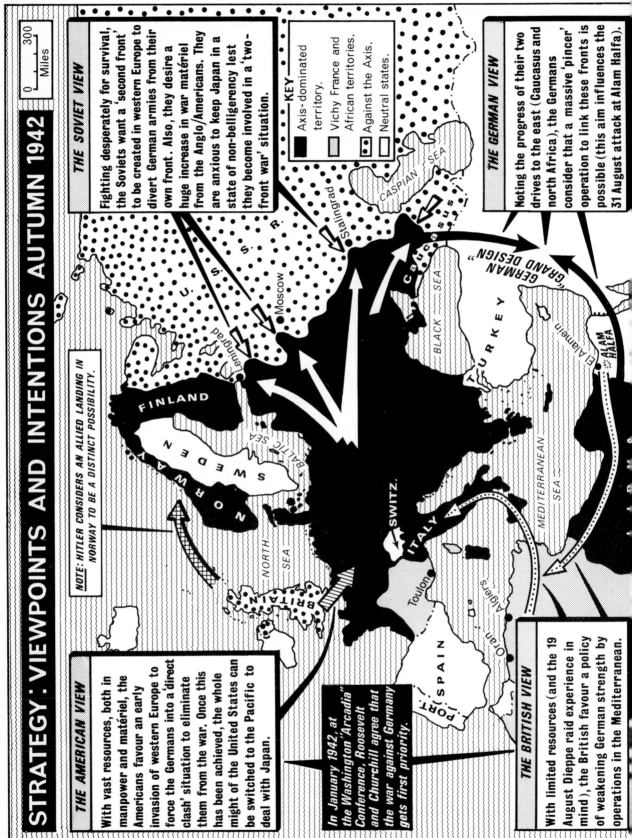

0   300
Miles

THE SOVIET VIEW

Fighting desperately for survival, the Soviets want a 'second front' to be created in western Europe to divert German armies from their own front. Also, they desire a huge increase in war matériel from the Anglo/Americans. They are anxious to keep Japan in a state of non-belligerency lest they become involved in a 'two-front war' situation.

KEY

■ Axis-dominated territory.

▨ Vichy France and African territories.

⚬•⚬ Against the Axis.

☐ Neutral states.

THE GERMAN VIEW

Noting the progress of their two drives to the east (Caucasus and north Africa), the Germans consider that a massive 'pincer' operation to link these fronts is possible (this aim influences the 31 August attack at Alam Halfa).

NOTE: HITLER CONSIDERS AN ALLIED LANDING IN NORWAY TO BE A DISTINCT POSSIBILITY.

GERMAN "GRAND DESIGN"

FINLAND

NORWAY

SWEDEN

BALTIC SEA

U.S.S.R.

Leningrad

Moscow

Stalingrad

CASPIAN SEA

Caucasus

BLACK SEA

TURKEY

El Alamein

ALAM HALFA

NORTH SEA

BRITAIN

SWITZ.

ITALY

MEDITERRANEAN SEA

Toulon

SPAIN

PORT.

Algiers

Oran

THE AMERICAN VIEW

With vast resources, both in manpower and matériel, the Americans favour an early invasion of western Europe to force the Germans into a 'direct clash' situation to eliminate them from the war. Once this has been achieved, the whole might of the United States can be switched to the Pacific to deal with Japan.

In January 1942, at the Washington "Arcadia" Conference, Roosevelt and Churchill agree that the war against Germany gets first priority.

THE BRITISH VIEW

With limited resources (and the 19 August Dieppe raid experience in mind), the British favour a policy of weakening German strength by operations in the Mediterranean.

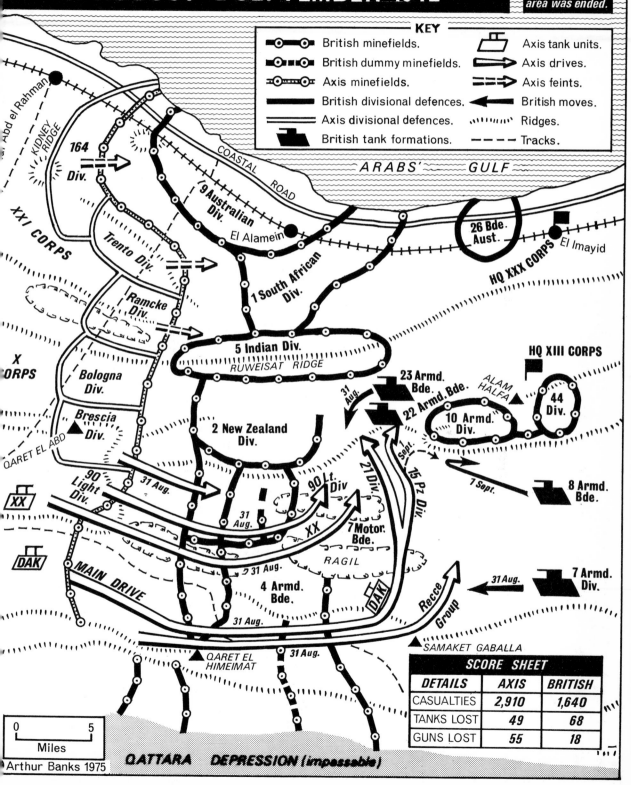

THE GERMAN REBUFF AT ALAM HALFA 31 AUGUST - 2 SEPTEMBER 1942

This battle was decisive: German expansion in the area was ended.

KEY

- British minefields.
- British dummy minefields.
- Axis minefields.
- British divisional defences.
- Axis divisional defences.
- British tank formations.
- Axis tank units.
- Axis drives.
- Axis feints.
- British moves.
- Ridges.
- Tracks.

Jebel Abd el Rahman

KIDNEY RIDGE

164 Div.

XXI CORPS

Trento Div.

Ramcke Div.

X CORPS

Bologna Div.

Brescia Div.

QARET EL ABD

90 Light Div.

DAK

MAIN DRIVE

COASTAL ROAD

ARABS' GULF

9 Australian Div.

El Alamein

1 South African Div.

5 Indian Div.

RUWEISAT RIDGE

2 New Zealand Div.

90 Lt. Div.

31 Aug.

31 Aug.

XX

7 Motor. Bde.

RAGIL

4 Armd. Bde.

31 Aug.

31 Aug.

21 Div.

DAK

QARET EL HIMEIMAT

31 Aug.

26 Bde. Aust.

El Imayid

HQ XXX CORPS

23 Armd. Bde.

22 Armd. Bde.

10 Armd. Div.

1 Sept.

15 Pz. Div.

7 Sept.

ALAM HALFA

HQ XIII CORPS

44 Div.

8 Armd. Bde.

Recce Group

7 Armd. Div.

31 Aug.

SAMAKET GABALLA

SCORE SHEET		
DETAILS	**AXIS**	**BRITISH**
CASUALTIES	2,910	1,640
TANKS LOST	49	68
GUNS LOST	55	18

0 ___ 5
Miles

Arthur Banks 1975

QATTARA DEPRESSION (impassable)

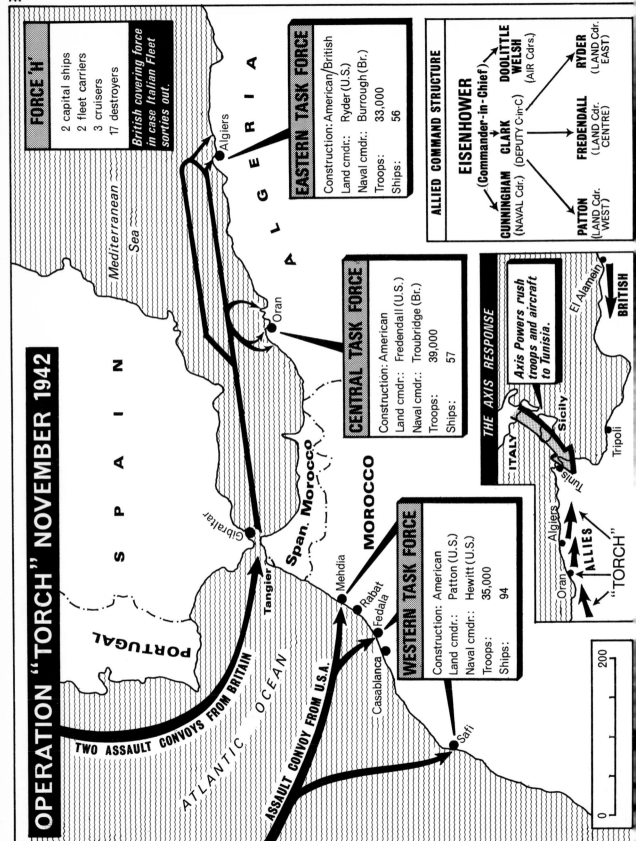

OPERATION "TORCH" NOVEMBER 1942

FORCE 'H'

- 2 capital ships
- 2 fleet carriers
- 3 cruisers
- 17 destroyers

British covering force in case Italian Fleet sorties out.

EASTERN TASK FORCE

Construction:	American/British
Land cmdr.:	Ryder (U.S.)
Naval cmdr.:	Burrough (Br.)
Troops:	33,000
Ships:	56

CENTRAL TASK FORCE

Construction:	American
Land cmdr.:	Fredendall (U.S.)
Naval cmdr.:	Troubridge (Br.)
Troops:	39,000
Ships:	57

WESTERN TASK FORCE

Construction:	American
Land cmdr.:	Patton (U.S.)
Naval cmdr.:	Hewitt (U.S.)
Troops:	35,000
Ships:	94

ALLIED COMMAND STRUCTURE

EISENHOWER
(Commander-in-Chief)

CLARK
(DEPUTY C-in-C)

DOOLITTLE WELSH
(AIR Cdrs.)

CUNNINGHAM
(NAVAL Cdr.)

RYDER
(LAND Cdr. EAST)

FREDENDALL
(LAND Cdr. CENTRE)

PATTON
(LAND Cdr. WEST)

THE AXIS RESPONSE

Axis Powers rush troops and aircraft to Tunisia.

BRITISH

ALLIES

"TORCH"

Mediterranean Sea

ALGERIA

Algiers

Oran

SPAIN

Gibraltar

Tangier

Span. Morocco

PORTUGAL

MOROCCO

Mehdia

Rabat

Fedala

Casablanca

Safi

ATLANTIC OCEAN

TWO ASSAULT CONVOYS FROM BRITAIN

ASSAULT CONVOY FROM U.S.A.

ITALY

Sicily

Tunis

Tripoli

Algiers

Oran

El Alamein

0   200

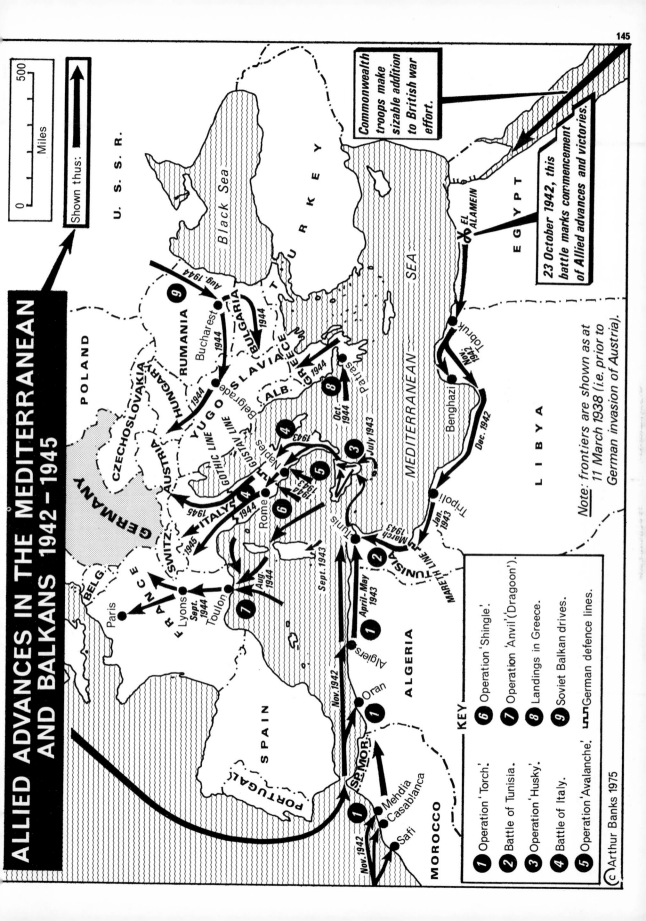

ALLIED ADVANCES IN THE MEDITERRANEAN AND BALKANS 1942–1945

500

0

Miles

Shown thus:

Commonwealth troops make sizable addition to British war effort.

23 October 1942, this battle marks commencement of Allied advances and victories.

Note: frontiers are shown as at 11 March 1938 (i.e. prior to German invasion of Austria).

U. S. S. R.

Black Sea

T U R K E Y

POLAND

CZECHOSLOVAKIA

GERMANY

AUSTRIA

HUNGARY

RUMANIA

Bucharest 1944

Aug. 1944

BULGARIA

1944

YUGOSLAVIA

Belgrade 1944

GOTHIC LINE

GUSTAV LINE

ALB.

GR 1944

GREECE

Piraeus

Oct. 1944

SWITZ.

BELG.

FRANCE

Paris

Lyons Sept. 1944

Toulon Sept. 1944

Aug. 1944

ITALY

Rome 1944

Naples 1943

1945

1945

July 1943

MEDITERRANEAN SEA

EGYPT

EL ALAMEIN

Tobruk Nov. 1942

Benghazi Dec. 1942

Tripoli Jan. 1943

L I B Y A

Tunis

March 1943

MARETH LINE

TUNISIA

April-May 1943

Sept. 1943

Nov. 1942

Algiers

ALGERIA

Oran

SP.MOR.

Mehdia Casablanca

Safi

Nov. 1942

MOROCCO

SPAIN

PORTUGAL

KEY

① Operation 'Torch'.
② Battle of Tunisia.
③ Operation 'Husky'.
④ Battle of Italy.
⑤ Operation 'Avalanche'.
⑥ Operation 'Shingle'.
⑦ Operation 'Anvil' ('Dragoon').
⑧ Landings in Greece.
⑨ Soviet Balkan drives.
⊔⊔ German defence lines.

© Arthur Banks 1975

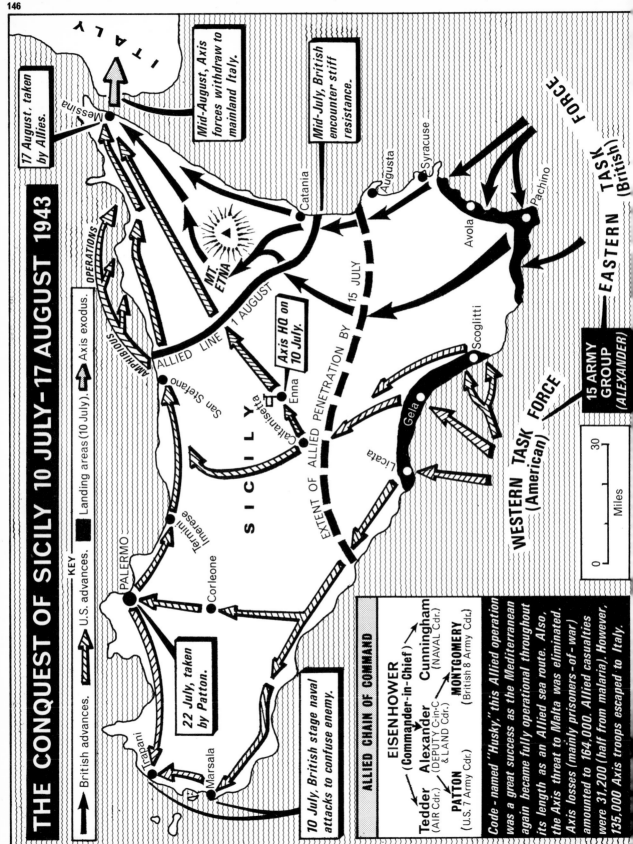

THE CONQUEST OF SICILY 10 JULY–17 AUGUST 1943

KEY
- British advances.
- U.S. advances.
- Landing areas (10 July).
- Axis exodus.

17 August, taken by Allies.

Mid-August, Axis forces withdraw to mainland Italy.

Mid-July, British encounter stiff resistance.

ITALY

Messina

Catania

Augusta

Syracuse

Pachino

Avola

MT. ETNA

AMPHIBIOUS OPERATIONS

ALLIED LINE 1 AUGUST

Axis HQ on 10 July.

Enna

Caltanissetta

San Stefano

EXTENT OF ALLIED PENETRATION BY 15 JULY

SICILY

Scoglitti

Gela

Licata

EASTERN TASK FORCE (British)

15 ARMY GROUP (ALEXANDER)

WESTERN TASK FORCE (American)

0   30
Miles

Termini Imerese

PALERMO

Corleone

22 July, taken by Patton.

Trapani

Marsala

10 July, British stage naval attacks to confuse enemy.

ALLIED CHAIN OF COMMAND

EISENHOWER (Commander-in-Chief)

Tedder (AIR Cdr.)

Alexander (DEPUTY C-in-C & LAND Cdr.)

Cunningham (NAVAL Cdr.)

PATTON (U.S. 7 Army Cdr.)

MONTGOMERY (British 8 Army Cdr.)

Code-named "Husky," this Allied operation was a great success as the Mediterranean again became fully operational throughout its length as an Allied sea route. Also, the Axis threat to Malta was eliminated. Axis losses (mainly prisoners-of-war) amounted to 164,000. Allied casualties were 31,200 (half from malaria). However, 135,000 Axis troops escaped to Italy.

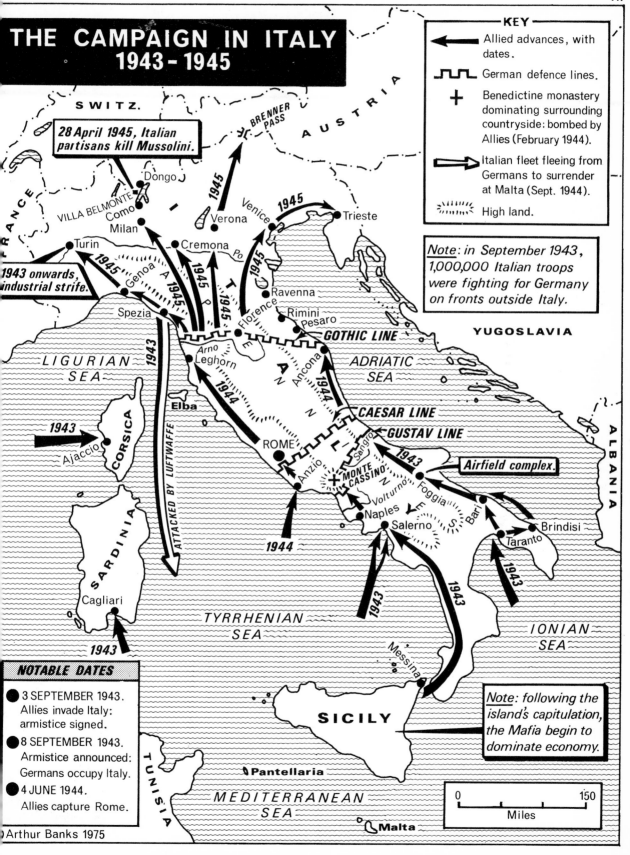

147

THE CAMPAIGN IN ITALY 1943-1945

KEY
← Allied advances, with dates.
⊓⊔ German defence lines.
✛ Benedictine monastery dominating surrounding countryside: bombed by Allies (February 1944).
⇨ Italian fleet fleeing from Germans to surrender at Malta (Sept. 1944).
High land.

Note: in September 1943, 1,000,000 Italian troops were fighting for Germany on fronts outside Italy.

SWITZ.

28 April 1945, Italian partisans kill Mussolini.

BRENNER PASS

AUSTRIA

Dongo

1945

VILLA BELMONTE Como
Milan
Verona
Venice
1945
Trieste

Turin
Cremona
Po
1945

1943 onwards, industrial strife.

Genoa
A 1945
1945
T 1945

Ravenna

Spezia

Florence
Rimini
Pesaro
GOTHIC LINE

YUGOSLAVIA

LIGURIAN SEA

Arno
Leghorn

Ancona

ADRIATIC SEA

1944

1944

CAESAR LINE

1943

CORSICA

Ajaccio

Elba

ATTACKED BY LUFTWAFFE

1944

ROME

Anzio
MONTE CASSINO
GUSTAV LINE

Sangro
1943

Airfield complex.

ALBANIA

SARDINIA

Cagliari

1943

Volturno
Naples
Salerno

Foggia
Bari
Taranto
Brindisi

1944

1943

1943

1943

TYRRHENIAN SEA

Messina

IONIAN SEA

NOTABLE DATES
● 3 SEPTEMBER 1943. Allies invade Italy: armistice signed.
● 8 SEPTEMBER 1943. Armistice announced: Germans occupy Italy.
● 4 JUNE 1944. Allies capture Rome.

SICILY

Pantellaria

TUNISIA

Note: following the island's capitulation, the Mafia begin to dominate economy.

MEDITERRANEAN SEA

Malta

0 ——————— 150
Miles

© Arthur Banks 1975

THE CARRIER CLASH IN MID-PACIFIC IN JUNE 1943

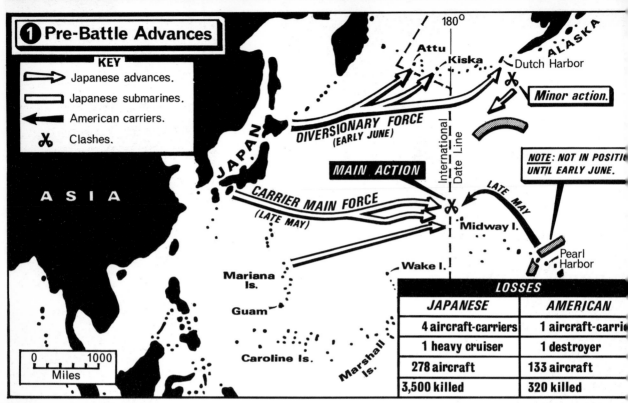

① Pre-Battle Advances

KEY
- ▭⟩ Japanese advances.
- ▭ Japanese submarines.
- ◄━ American carriers.
- ✂ Clashes.

180°

Attu
Kiska
ALASKA
Dutch Harbor

DIVERSIONARY FORCE (EARLY JUNE)

Minor action.

International Date Line

**NOTE: NOT IN POSITI[ON]
UNTIL EARLY JUNE.**

MAIN ACTION

CARRIER MAIN FORCE (LATE MAY)

LATE MAY

Midway I.

A S I A

Pearl Harbor

Wake I.

Mariana Is.

Guam

Caroline Is.

Marshall Is.

0   1000
Miles

LOSSES	
JAPANESE	**AMERICAN**
4 aircraft-carriers	1 aircraft-carri[er]
1 heavy cruiser	1 destroyer
278 aircraft	133 aircraft
3,500 killed	320 killed

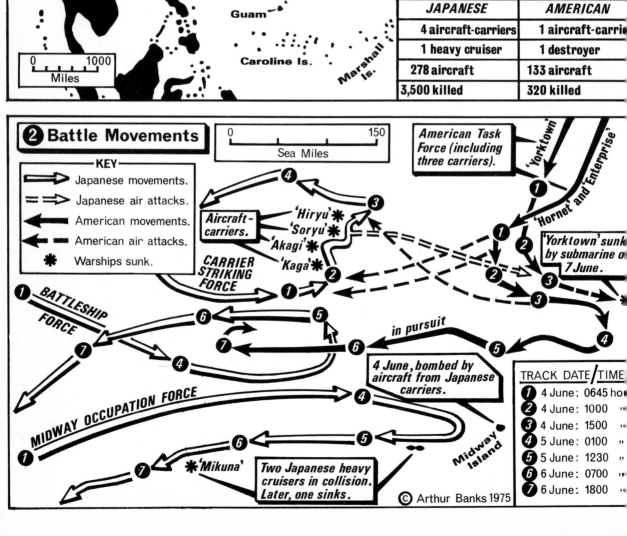

② Battle Movements

0   150
Sea Miles

American Task Force (including three carriers).

'Yorktown'

'Hornet and Enterprise'

KEY
- ▭⟩ Japanese movements.
- ≡⟩ Japanese air attacks.
- ◄━ American movements.
- ◄- - American air attacks.
- ✳ Warships sunk.

Aircraft-carriers.
'Hiryu' ✳
'Soryu' ✳
'Akagi' ✳
'Kaga' ✳

CARRIER STRIKING FORCE

'Yorktown' sunk by submarine o[n] 7 June.

BATTLESHIP FORCE

in pursuit

4 June, bombed by aircraft from Japanese carriers.

MIDWAY OCCUPATION FORCE

Midway Island

✳ 'Mikuna'

Two Japanese heavy cruisers in collision. Later, one sinks.

© Arthur Banks 1975

TRACK	DATE / TIME
❶	4 June: 0645 ho[urs]
❷	4 June: 1000 ,,
❸	4 June: 1500 ,,
❹	5 June: 0100 ,,
❺	5 June: 1230 ,,
❻	6 June: 0700 ,,
❼	6 June: 1800 ,,

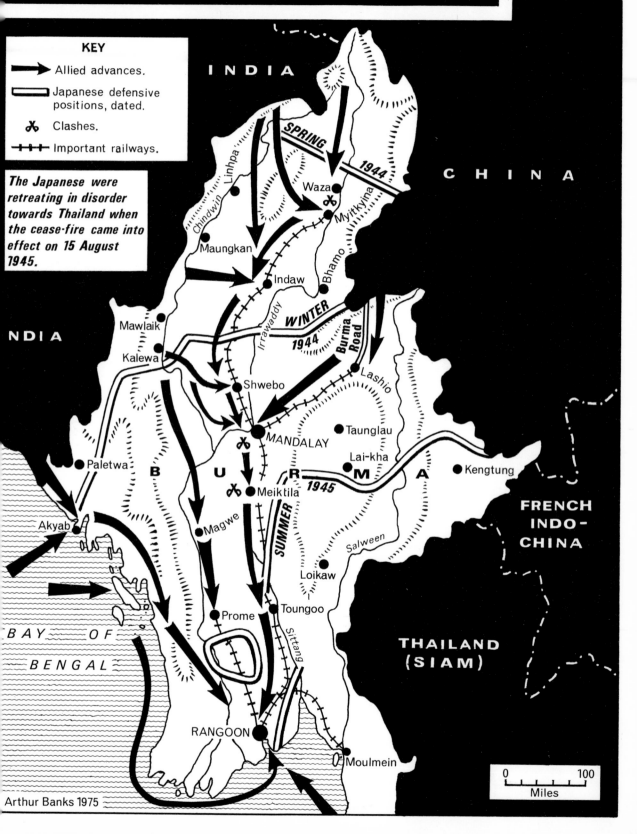

ALLIED ADVANCES IN BURMA 1944-1945

KEY

➤ Allied advances.

▭ Japanese defensive positions, dated.

✂ Clashes.

+++ Important railways.

The Japanese were retreating in disorder towards Thailand when the cease-fire came into effect on 15 August 1945.

INDIA

CHINA

SPRING 1944

Waza ✂

Myitkyina

Bhamo

Burma Road

Maungkan

Chindwin

Linhpa

Indaw

Mawlaik

Kalewa

WINTER 1944

Irrawaddy

Shwebo

Lashio

Taunglau

✂ MANDALAY

Lai-kha

Paletwa

B U R M A 1945

Kengtung

✂ Meiktila

Magwe

SUMMER 1945

Salween

Akyab

Loikaw

FRENCH INDO-CHINA

Prome

Toungoo

BAY OF

BENGAL

Sittang

THAILAND (SIAM)

RANGOON

Moulmein

0   100
Miles

Arthur Banks 1975

THE LIBERATION OF WESTERN EUROPE 1944

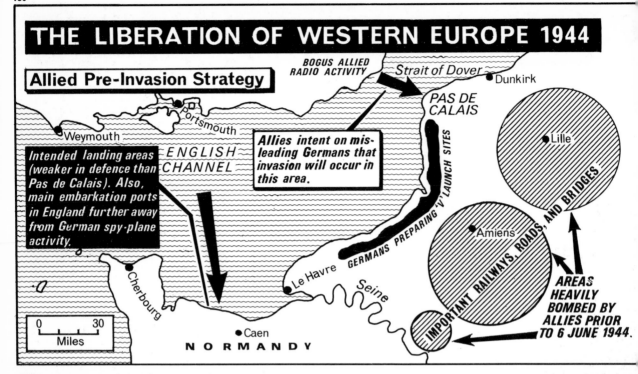

Allied Pre-Invasion Strategy

BOGUS ALLIED RADIO ACTIVITY

Strait of Dover

Dunkirk

PAS DE CALAIS

Portsmouth

Weymouth

ENGLISH CHANNEL

Allies intent on misleading Germans that invasion will occur in this area.

Lille

GERMANS PREPARING 'V' LAUNCH SITES

Intended landing areas (weaker in defence than Pas de Calais). Also, main embarkation ports in England further away from German spy-plane activity.

Amiens

IMPORTANT RAILWAYS, ROADS, AND BRIDGES

Cherbourg

Le Havre

Seine

AREAS HEAVILY BOMBED BY ALLIES PRIOR TO 6 JUNE 1944.

0   30
Miles

Caen

N O R M A N D Y

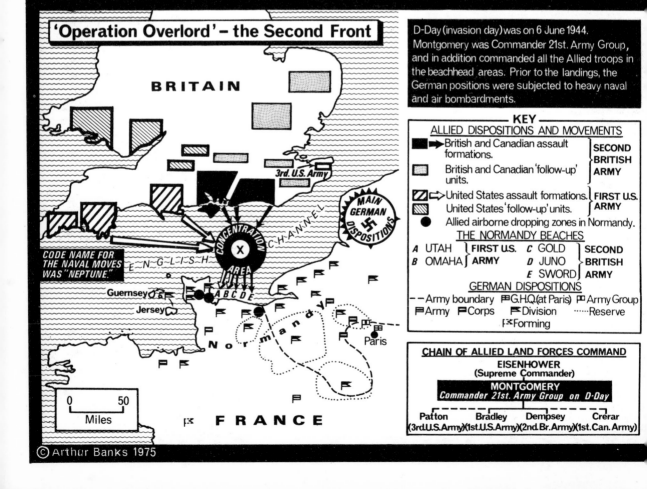

'Operation Overlord' – the Second Front

BRITAIN

3rd. U.S. Army

CODE NAME FOR THE NAVAL MOVES WAS "NEPTUNE."

E-N-G-L-I-S-H CHANNEL

MAIN GERMAN DISPOSITIONS

CONCENTRATION AREA

Guernsey

Jersey

A B C D E

N o r m a n d y

Paris

F R A N C E

0   50
Miles

© Arthur Banks 1975

D-Day (invasion day) was on 6 June 1944. Montgomery was Commander 21st. Army Group, and in addition commanded all the Allied troops in the beachhead areas. Prior to the landings, the German positions were subjected to heavy naval and air bombardments.

KEY

ALLIED DISPOSITIONS AND MOVEMENTS

- British and Canadian assault formations.
- British and Canadian 'follow-up' units.

SECOND BRITISH ARMY

- United States assault formations.
- United States 'follow-up' units.

FIRST U.S. ARMY

- Allied airborne dropping zones in Normandy.

THE NORMANDY BEACHES

A	UTAH	**FIRST U.S.**	C	GOLD
B	OMAHA	**ARMY**	D	JUNO
			E	SWORD

SECOND BRITISH ARMY

GERMAN DISPOSITIONS

- – – Army boundary
- G.H.Q. (at Paris)
- Army Group
- Army
- Corps
- Division
- ...... Reserve
- Forming

CHAIN OF ALLIED LAND FORCES COMMAND

EISENHOWER
(Supreme Commander)

MONTGOMERY
Commander 21st. Army Group on D-Day

Patton	Bradley	Dempsey	Crerar
(3rd.U.S.Army)	(1st.U.S.Army)	(2nd.Br.Army)	(1st.Can.Army)

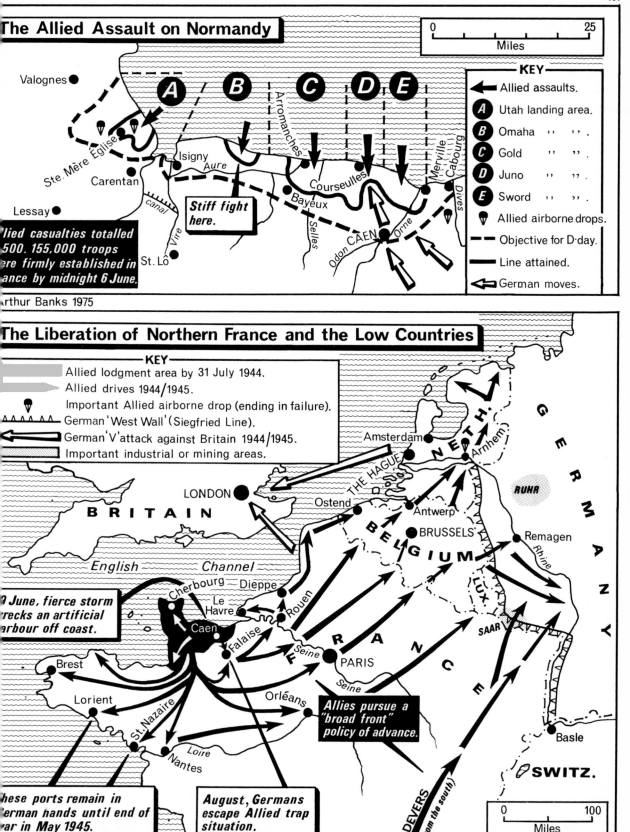

The Allied Assault on Normandy

0   25
Miles

KEY
- ⬅ Allied assaults.
- **A** Utah landing area.
- **B** Omaha ,, ,, .
- **C** Gold ,, ,, .
- **D** Juno ,, ,, .
- **E** Sword ,, ,, .
- Allied airborne drops.
- --- Objective for D-day.
- ▬ Line attained.
- ⬅ German moves.

Valognes

A **B** **C** **D** **E**

Ste. Mère Eglise

Isigny
Carentan
Aure
Arromanches
Courseulles
Merville
Cabourg
Dives
Bayeux
Selles
Odon CAEN
Orne

Lessay
canal
Vire
St. Lô

Stiff fight here.

Allied casualties totalled 8,500. 155,000 troops were firmly established in France by midnight 6 June.

Arthur Banks 1975

The Liberation of Northern France and the Low Countries

KEY
- Allied lodgment area by 31 July 1944.
- Allied drives 1944/1945.
- Important Allied airborne drop (ending in failure).
- ᴧᴧᴧᴧ German 'West Wall' (Siegfried Line).
- ⬅ German 'V' attack against Britain 1944/1945.
- Important industrial or mining areas.

BRITAIN

LONDON

English   Channel

Amsterdam
THE HAGUE
NETH.
Arnhem
GERMANY
RUHR
Ostend
Antwerp
BELGIUM
BRUSSELS
Remagen
Rhine
LUX.
SAAR

Cherbourg — Dieppe
Le Havre
Rouen
Caen
Falaise
Seine
F R A N C E
PARIS
Seine
Brest
Orléans
Lorient
St. Nazaire
Loire
Nantes
DEVERS (from the south)
Basle
SWITZ.

19 June, fierce storm wrecks an artificial harbour off coast.

Allies pursue a "broad front" policy of advance.

These ports remain in German hands until end of war in May 1945.

August, Germans escape Allied trap situation.

0   100
Miles

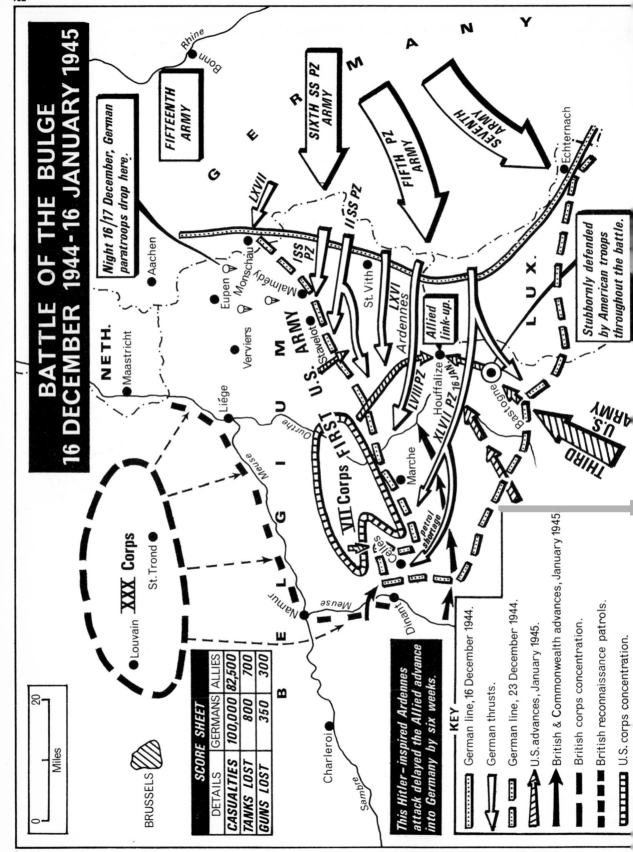

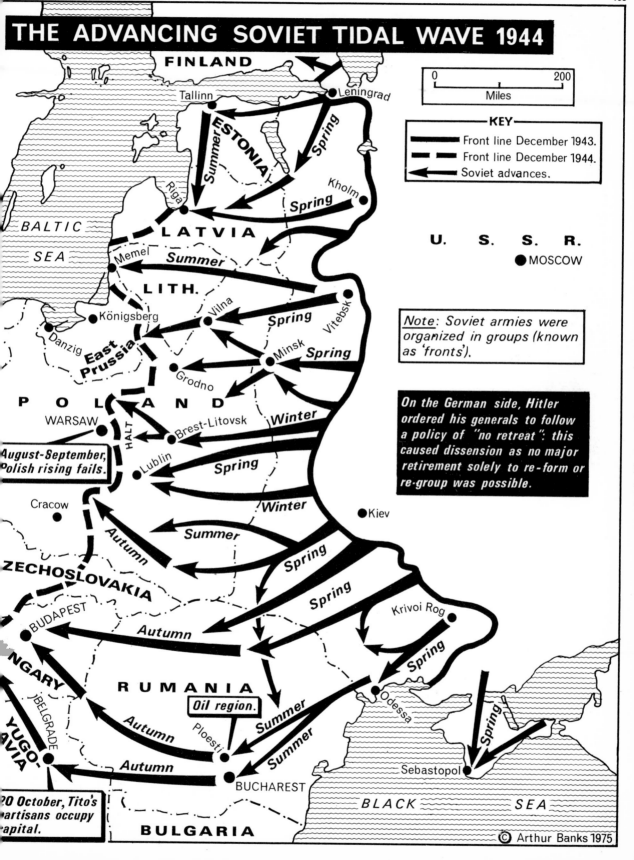

THE ADVANCING SOVIET TIDAL WAVE 1944

FINLAND

Tallinn · Leningrad

ESTONIA

Summer

Spring

Spring

Riga · Kholm

BALTIC

SEA

LATVIA

Memel

Summer

LITH.

Königsberg · Vilna

Danzig

East Prussia

Spring · Vitebsk

Grodno · Minsk · Spring

P O L A N D

WARSAW

Brest-Litovsk · Winter

HALT

August-September,
Polish rising fails.

Lublin · Spring

Cracow

Winter

ZECHOSLOVAKIA

Summer

Autumn

Kiev

Spring

BUDAPEST

Spring

Autumn

Krivoi Rog

NGARY

R U M A N I A

Autumn

Oil region.

BELGRADE

YUGO-
AVIA

Autumn · Ploesti · Summer

Spring

Summer

Odessa

20 October, Tito's
artisans occupy
capital.

Autumn · BUCHAREST

Sebastopol · Spring

BLACK   SEA

BULGARIA

© Arthur Banks 1975

KEY

0 ———— 200
Miles

——— Front line December 1943.
- - - Front line December 1944.
←— Soviet advances.

U. S. S. R.

● MOSCOW

Note: Soviet armies were
organized in groups (known
as 'fronts').

On the German side, Hitler
ordered his generals to follow
a policy of "no retreat": this
caused dissension as no major
retirement solely to re-form or
re-group was possible.

© Arthur Banks 1975

GERMANY AT BAY
JANUARY-MAY 1945

Note: frontiers shown as they were in early 1938 (prior to the German annexation of Austria and the Sudetenland).

DENMARK

SWEDEN

Memel

NORTH SEA

BALTIC SEA

Flensburg

Königsberg

CHERNYAKHOVS

Kiel Canal

Kiel

Danzig

East Prussia

RENDULIC

ROKOSSOVSKY

Lübeck

Rostock

Kolberg

Allenstein

Hamburg

Lüneburg

Stettin

HIMMLER

Elbe

Oder

ZHUKOV

NETHERLANDS

Bremen

Hanover

BLASKOWITZ

Brunswick

Berlin

Posen

Arnhem

Frankfurt

Oder

Warsaw

MONTGOMERY

Magdeburg

ZHUKOV

Lodz

BRADLEY

Kassel

POLAND

Cologne

Leipzig

Neisse

Breslau

BRADLEY

Erfurt

Dresden

KONIEV

Cracow

GERMANY

Elbe

Vistula

Frankfurt

Prague

Main

MODEL

Mainz

CZECHOS

SCHÖRNER

DEVERS

Nuremberg

L O V A K I A

PETROV

FRANCE

Danube

Brünn

BELG LUX

Stuttgart

Danube

Vienna

MALINOVSKY

HAUSSER

Augsburg

WÖHLER

Budapest

Berchtesgaden

Salzburg

Basle

Innsbruck

A U S T R I A

TOLBUKHIN

H U N G A R Y

Berne

Brenner Pass

Szeged

SWITZERLAND

Y

U

Zagreb

G

O

S

KESSELRING

L

WEICHS

Como

Milan

Trieste

A

V

I

A

Danube

Turin

Venice

Pola

Belgrade

Po

CLARK

ADRIATIC

Genoa

SEA

FRANCE

GULF OF GENOA

Florence

I T A L Y

0	50	100

Miles

KEY

Allied-held territory, 27 January 1945

Allied gains, 27 January–8 May 1945

The battlefronts on 27 January 1945

The battlefronts on 8 May 1945.

Main Allied advances.

DEVERS Allied commanders.

MODEL German commanders.

Neutral states throughout the war.

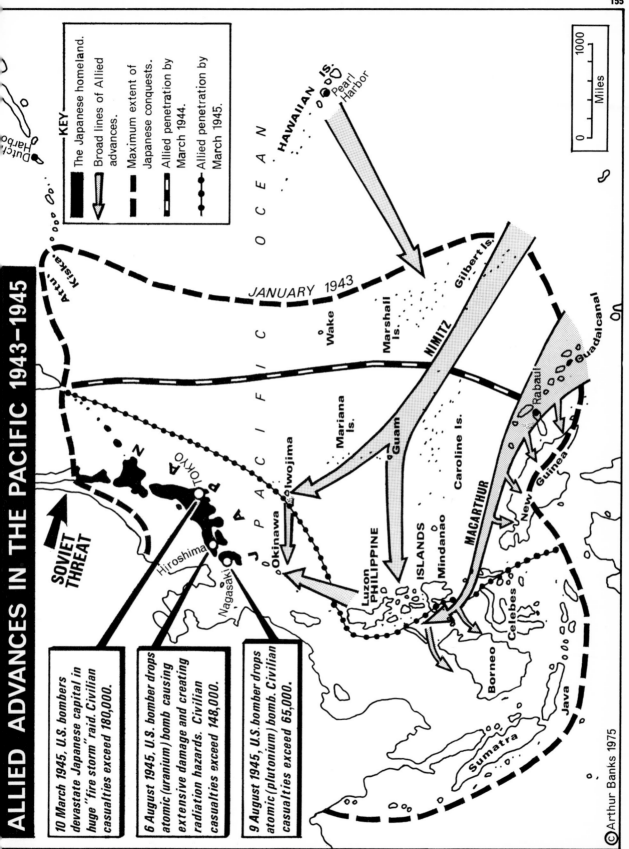

ALLIED ADVANCES IN THE PACIFIC 1943–1945

KEY

- The Japanese homeland.
- Broad lines of Allied advances.
- Maximum extent of Japanese conquests.
- Allied penetration by March 1944.
- Allied penetration by March 1945.

1000

Miles

0

PACIFIC OCEAN

HAWAIIAN IS.

Pearl Harbor

Dutch Harbor

Kiska

Attu

JANUARY 1943

Wake

Gilbert Is.

Marshall Is.

NIMITZ

Guadalcanal

Rabaul

Mariana Is.

Guam

Caroline Is.

MACARTHUR

New Guinea

JAPAN

TOKYO

Hiroshima

Nagasaki

SOVIET THREAT

Iwojima

Okinawa

Luzon

PHILIPPINE ISLANDS

Mindanao

Borneo

Celebes

Java

Sumatra

10 March 1945, U.S. bombers devastate Japanese capital in huge "fire storm" raid. Civilian casualties exceed 180,000.

6 August 1945, U.S. bomber drops atomic (uranium) bomb causing extensive damage and creating radiation hazards. Civilian casualties exceed 148,000.

9 August 1945, U.S. bomber drops atomic (plutonium) bomb. Civilian casualties exceed 65,000.

© Arthur Banks 1975

THE RECONQUEST OF THE PHILIPPINES 1944-1945

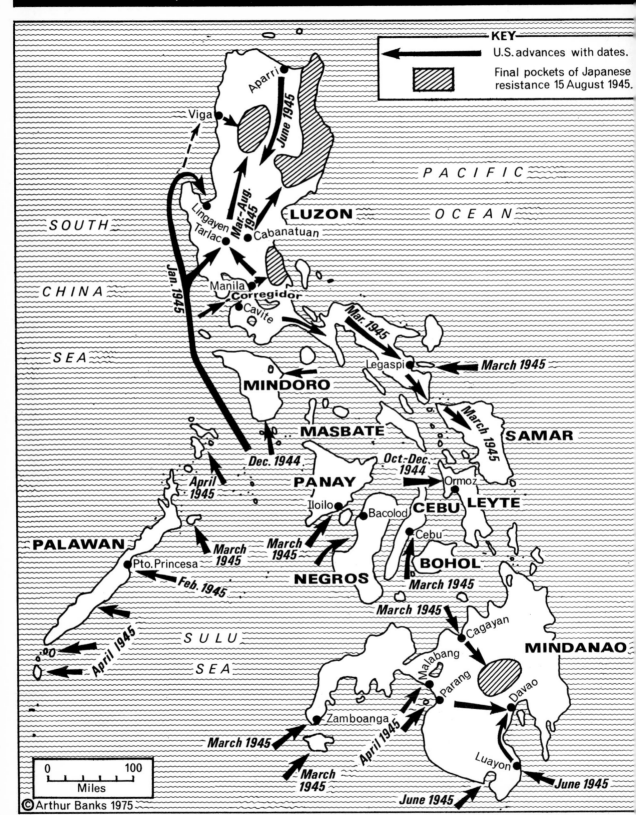

KEY

U.S. advances with dates.

Final pockets of Japanese resistance 15 August 1945.

Aparri

Viga

June 1945

PACIFIC

OCEAN

SOUTH

Lingayen

Tarlac

Mar.-Aug. 1945

LUZON

Cabanatuan

CHINA

Jan. 1945

Manila

Corregidor

Cavite

SEA

Mar. 1945

Legaspi

March 1945

MINDORO

March 1945

MASBATE

SAMAR

Dec. 1944

April 1945

PANAY

Oct.-Dec. 1944

Ormoz

CEBU **LEYTE**

Iloilo

Bacolod

Cebu

PALAWAN

March 1945

BOHOL

Pto. Princesa

Feb. 1945

March 1945

NEGROS

March 1945

March 1945

Cagayan

SULU

MINDANAO

April 1945

Malabang

Parang

SEA

Davao

Zamboanga

March 1945

April 1945

Luayon

March 1945

June 1945

June 1945

0   100

Miles

© Arthur Banks 1975

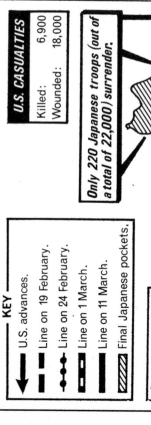

THE OKINAWA CAMPAIGN 1 APRIL–22 JUNE 1945

KEY
- U.S. advances.
- ⊕ Japanese airfields.
- ⊣⊢ Japanese defence lines.
- ▨ Final Japanese pocket.

Note: the British Royal Navy aided the U.S. Fifth Fleet during the naval operations.

OKINAWA

PACIFIC OCEAN

East China Sea

Aha

Tako

Ie-Shima

Bise

Nago

Iheya

Izena

Hagushi

Shuri

Naha

April
May
June

Tsugen

U.S. feint attacks (1 April)

Kerama

U.S. III MARINE AMPHIBIOUS CORPS (Geiger)

1 April

U.S. XXIV CORPS (Hodge)

0   10
Miles

CASUALTIES

Japanese troops:	125,000
Japanese sailors:	3,700
Japanese airmen:	7,800
U.S. troops:	40,000
U.S. sailors:	9,600
U.S. airmen:	1,200

HISTORICAL NOTE

IN 1281, KUBLAI KHAN'S MONGOL FLEET INVADING JAPAN WAS DISPERSED BY A 'DIVINE WIND' (KAMI KAZE): see Vol 1, page 152.

Both campaigns were marked by a large number of attacks on Allied warships by enemy kamikaze suicidal pilots.

THE IWOJIMA CAMPAIGN 19 FEBRUARY–16 MARCH 1945

KEY
- U.S. advances.
- Line on 19 February.
- Line on 24 February.
- •─•─• Line on 1 March.
- Line on 11 March.
- ▨ Final Japanese pockets.

0   1
Mile

U.S. CASUALTIES

Killed:	6,900
Wounded:	18,000

Only 220 Japanese troops (out of a total of 22,000) surrender.

Nishi

AIRFIELD

AIRFIELD

AIRFIELD

PACIFIC OCEAN

PACIFIC OCEAN

MT. SURIBACHI

5 Marine Div.

19 February

3 Marine Div.

4 Marine Div.

19 February

U.S. FIFTH AMPHIBIOUS CORPS (Schmidt)

© Arthur Banks 1975

MILITARY CASUALTIES OF THE 1939–1945 WAR

KEY
Deaths.
Wounded.

NOTE THESE HUGE CASUALTIES

CHINA
650,000
1,800,000

JAPAN
1,510,000
500,000

U.S.S.R.
7,500,000
14,000,000

GREATEST NUMBER OF CASUALTIES OCCUR IN THIS AREA

GERMANY
2,850,000
7,300,000

ITALY
78,000
120,000

BRITAIN
398,000
480,000

FRANCE
211,000
400,000

ALL OTHER PARTICIPANTS
1,500,000
4,000,000

U.S.A.
293,000
590,000

400
0
Miles

CIVILIAN CASUALTIES AND EXPENDITURE 1939–1945

KEY
Deaths.
Cost ($ millions).

JAPAN →
300,000
100,000

CHINA →
1,000,000
no figs. available

U.S.S.R.
15,000,000
200,000

NOTE THESE HIGH CIVILIAN CASUALTIES

Approximately 6,000,000 Jews in Germany and 4,500,000 Poles were killed (1939–1945).

POLAND

GERMANY
500,000
300,000

ITALY
80,000
50,000

BRITAIN
70,000
150,000

FRANCE
110,000
100,000

ALL OTHER PARTICIPANTS
15,000,000 ?
350,000

U.S.A.
1,000 ?
350,000

NOTE THESE HIGH EXPENDITURES

0   400
Miles

© Arthur Banks 1975

THE WORLD'S SUPERPOWERS 1945

UNITED STATES OF AMERICA

Sole possessor of the atomic bomb makes her the world's leading military power: she possesses the largest air force and navy in the world. Furthermore, she is the world's leading industrial and manufacturing nation. Her homeland has remained inviolate throughout the war.

UNION OF SOVIET SOCIALIST REPUBLICS

Possessor of the largest army in the world and virtually self-sufficient in raw materials. However, due to German occupation, much of her industry is in ruins. She does not possess the over-riding weapon of all, the atomic bomb.

Britain, France, and Germany, the three European powers which had dominated the world scene prior to September 1939, emerged from the war much reduced in international status. From henceforth, the world's military spectrum was to be dominated by the U.S.A. and the U.S.S.R., the two new superpowers.

PACIFIC OCEAN

AUSTRALIA

ANTARCTICA

INDIAN OCEAN

ASIA

AFRICA

EUROPE

ATLANTIC OCEAN

NORTH AMERICA

SOUTH AMERICA

PACIFIC OCEAN

© Arthur Banks 1975

Index of Place Names

Aachen, 70, 124, 151
Aalborg, 123
Abbeville, 40, 98, 124
Abruzzi 38
Abyssinia, 45, 60; conquered by
    Italy, 1935-36, 109
Achi Baba, 86
Achilles, HMS, role in Battle of
    River Plate, 120-21
Acklington, RAF station, 126
Aconcagua, Mt, 5
Adalia, 105
Adana, 105
Aden, 55, 59-60
Adobe Walls, Battle of, 31
Adowa, Battle of, 34
Adrianople, 41, 56-57, 105
Afghanistan, 59-60, 114
Africa
    horn of, 34; physical features of,
    5; 79, 120-1, 130-1; in 1945,
    160
Africa, East, 34
Africa, North, 133; Rommel in,
    133
Africa Shell, SS, victim of *Graf
    Spee*, 120-1
Africa, South, 34-5, 43, 45, 55
Africa, West, 34
Agadir, 35, 54
Agedabia, 133
Aha, 157
Ahaggar, 6
Aire, 98
Aisne, R, 66, 68, 70, 72; German
    offensives, 1918, 97; 98, 124
Ajaccio, 147
Ajax, HMS, role in Battle of River
    Plate, 120-1
Akagi, Japanese ship, 148
Akyab, 138, 149
Alabama, 10, 13, 15-17
Ala Dagh, Battle of, 41
Alam Halfa, 133; German rebuff
    at, 142; 143
Alaska, 43, 61, 148
Albania, 42, 57, 64, 69, 80-82, 87,
    109-110, 118, 134, 141, 145,
    147

Alberga, R, 7
Albert, 66, 91, 96, 98
Aldergrove, RAF station, 126
Aldin, 105
Aleppo, 60; British air base, 139
Aleutian Islands, 61, 137
Alexandria, (Africa), 34, 46;
    Italian-manned slow-speed
    torpedoes, 'pigs', incapacitate 2
    British battleships in harbour,
    1941, 132; British naval base,
    139
Alexandria, (USA), 12, 16-17, 19
Algeçıras, 54
Algeria, 43, 45, 53, 64, 139, 141;
    'Operation Torch', 144; 145
Algiers, 142 'Operation Torch',
    144, 145
Aliakmon, R, 56-7
Alland, R, 71
Allatoona, 29
Allegehenny, Mts, 12-13
Allenstein, 74, 154
Almeria, shelled by German
    pocket battleship; bombed by
    German airforce, 115
Alsace, 39-40
Alt, R, 93
Altmark, German tanker used to
    replenish supplies of *Graf Spee*,
    120-1
Amazon, R, 5
Amelia Court House, 12, 30
Amiens, 66, 70, 72, 124, 150
Amritsar, Riot of 1919, 114
Amrun Bank, 89
Amsterdam, 124, 151
Anatolia, 105
Ancona, Axis naval base, 139, 147
Ancre, 66
Ancre, R, 91
Andalsnes, 123
Andaman Islands, 43, 55
Andes, Mts, 5
Andorra, 115
Angerburg, 74
Anglo-Egyptian Sudan, 59-60
Angola, 35, 43, 45
Angora, 59, 105

Anhalt, 39
Anna, North, R, 12
Anna, South, R, 12
Annapolis, 12
Anneux, 94
Anping, Battle of, 50
Antartica, 160
Antietam, Battle of, 15, 20-21, 24
Antietam, Creek, 24
Antrim, 108
Antwerp, 66, 68, 70, 72, 76, 98,
    124, 151
Anzac Cove, 86
Anzio, 147
Aôut, Mt, 71
Apaches, 31
Aparri, 156
Apennines, Mts, 2
Appalachian, Mts, 4
Appomattox Courthouse, 12; Lee
    surrenders to Grant, 17;
    campaign, 18; 20, 30
Apulia, 38
Aquia Creek, 12
Arabian Sea, 3
Araguaia, R, 5
Aral Sea, 3, 50
Aras, R, 58
Archangel, 58, 104, 122; ice-free
    port, never taken by Germans,
    135; 140
Arctic Ocean, 3
Ardennes, 'Battle of the Bulge ,
    152
Argentina, 36, 43
Argonne, R, 70
Ari Burnu, 86
Arizona, US battleship, 136
Arkansas, 10, 13, 15-17
Arkansas Post, 13; confederate
    surrender at, 16; 19
Arkansas, R, 4, 13, 15-16, 18-19,
    31
Arlon, 98
Armagh, 108
Armentières, 72, 96, 98
Arnhem, 99, 151, 154
Arno, 147
Arras, 66, 72, 76, 96, 124

Asan, 48
Ascension Islands, 43, 55
Ashburton, R, 7
Ashford, 128
Ashlea, SS, victim of *Graf Spee*, 120-1
Asia, physical features of, 3 ; 78, 148, 160
Aspromonte, Battle of, 38
Assir, 60
Astrakhan, 58, 104, 140
Atbara, Battle of, 34
Ath, 98
Athabaska, Lake, 4
Athens, 56, 57 ; fell to Axis powers, 1941, 134
Atlanta, 13, 17 ; campaign, 19, 29
Atlantic, second battle of the, phases 1 and 2, 130 ; phase 3, 131, allied convoy routes and bases during, 131
Atlas, Mts, 6
Atrek, R, 58
Attu, 136, 148, 155
Aubers, 96
Aubertin, R, 71
Auckland Is, 55
Audenarde, 98
Augsburg, 154
Augusta, 13, 146
Aumale, 98
Aure, R, 151
Austral Is, 55
Australasia, physical features of, 7
Australia, 43, 55, 77, 137, 160
Austria, 39, 110 ; annexed by Germans, 118 : 119, 134, 147
Austria-Hungary, 41, 54, 56-7, 64-5, 67-69, 80-82, 87, 92-3 ; military casualties 1914-18, 100 ; civilian casualties and expenditure, 1914-18, 101 ; 141, 145, 154
Austria, lower, 42
Austria, upper, 42
Avecapelle, 73
Averasboro, Battle of, 17
Avesnes, 98
Avocourt, 90
Avola, 146
Azores, 43, 79, 130 ; allied base during second battle of the Atlantic, 131
Azov, 58

Back, R, 4
Bacolod, 156
Badajoz, 115
Baden, 39
Baghdad, 59
Bagirmi, 35
Bahama Is, 43, 79, 130-1

Baikal, Lake, 3
Bailleul, 96
Baker Island, 61
Baku, 58, 104 ; important oilfields, never taken by Germans, 135 ; 140
Balearic Is, 115
Balkan, Mts, 2
Balkans, allies engaged in clashes with Bulgarian forces, 82 ; securing the Balkan flank, 1941, 134
Balkash, Lake, 3
Ball's Ford, 22
Baltic Fleet, (Russian), 51
Baltimore, 12
Baltimore Pike, 28
Baluchistan, 60
Banco Inglés, 120-1
Banks, (Union Offensive), 16-7
Banks Ford, 27
Banteux, 95
Bantouzelle, 95
Bapaume, Battle of, 40, 91, 96, 98
Barcelona, fell to nationalists, 115
Bardia, 132-3 ; Axis naval base, 139
Bari, 147
Barisis, 96
Bar-Le-Duc, 98
Barleux, 91
Basle, 40, 151, 154
Basra, 140
Bastogne, 98, 152
Basutoland, 49
Bath, 21
Baton Rouge, 13, 26 ; Battle of, 15-6
Batum, 58, 60
Bavaria, 39
Bavarian Palatinate, 39
Bayeux, 151
Bayeux Vidal, 26
Bear I, 140
Bearpaw, Battle of, 31
Beauchamp, 95
Beaufort Sea, 3
Beaumont, 90
Beaumont-Hamel, 91
Beau-Regard, (Confederate Offensive), 17
Beauvais, 40, 98, 126
Becelaere, 75, 94
Bechuanaland, 45
Becquincourt, 91
Beda Fomm, 132
Beirut, Axis naval and air base, 139
Belfast, 108 ; during Blitz, 129
Belfort, 69-70, 76
Belgium 39-40, 64-6, 68-9, 72, 76, 80-1, 98-9 ; military casualties 1914-18, 100 ;

civilian casualties and expenditure 1914-18, 101, 110, 118 ; capitulates, 124, 125-6, 141, 145, 151-2, 154
Belgrade 56-7, 67 ; fell to Germans, 87 ; heavily bombed, fell to Axis powers, 134 ; 145 ; occupied by Tito, 152 ; 154
Belmont, (S. Africa), Battle of, 49
Belmont, (USA), 13 ; failure of Grant's attack, 18
Bender, 93
Benevento, 38
Bengal, Bay of, 3
Benghazi, 53, 132-3 ; Axis air and naval base, 139 ; 145
Bentonville, Battle of, 17
Berchtesgaden, 154
Bergen, 123
Bergues, 125
Bering Sea, 59
Berlin, (Germany), 39, 107, 118, 141, 154
Berlin, (USA), 16
Bermuda, 43, 55, 130 ; allied base during second battle of Atlantic, 131
Berne, 154
Besançon, 70
Bessarabia, 58, 67
Bethincourt, 90
Béthune, 72, 96, 98
Bexhill, 128
Bhamo, 138, 149
Biaches, 91
Bialystok, 119
Big Black, R, 26
Biggin Hill RAF station, 126
Big Hole, Battle of, 31
Bihac, 134
Bilbao, 115
Bingen, 40
Birkenhead, during Blitz, 129
Birmingham, (UK), during Blitz, 129
Birmingham, (USA), 13
Biscay, Bay of, 2
Bise, 157
Bismarck Archipelago, 55
Bixschoote, 73
Bizerta, 34
Black Prince, HMS, sunk, 89
Black, R, 44
Black Sea, 2-3, 6, 41, 53-4, 56-9, 64
Blackburn's Ford, 22
Bloemfontein, 49
Blue Ridge, 12-13
Blunt, (Union Offensive), 15
Blyskawica, Polish destroyer, escapes to Britain despite German naval surveillance, 119
Bodo, 123

Boers, 35
Boesinghe, 73, 75, 94
Boghali, 86
Bognor Regis, 128
Bohemia, 39, 42, 119
Bohol, 156
Bolton, 26
Bombay, 60, 114
Bombon, (Foch's HQ), 98
Bonn, 76, 152
Boonville, 15
Borneo, 55, 137, 155
Bosnia, 41-2, 54, 56, 87
Bouchavesnes, 91
Boulogne, 66, 98, 124-5 ;
    German embarkation port, 127-8
Bounty I, 55
Bourlon, 95
Boursies, 95
Bouvet, French battleship, mined
    in Dardanelles, 84
Bowling Green, 13
Boxer Rebellion 1900, 50
Brabant, 90
Bragg, (Confederate Offensive),
    15-16
Braila, 93
Braine, 97
Branco, R, 5
Brandenburg, 16
Brandy Station, 12
Bras, 90
Brashear City, 16
Brasso, 42
Bray Dunes, 125
Bray-sur-Somme, 91
Brazil, 36, 43
Breda, 124
Bremen, 39, 107, 154
Brenner Pass, 147, 154
Breslau, 107, 154
Brest, 120-1, 125 ; Axis naval
    base, 139, 151
Brest-Litovsk, 67, 77, 106, 119 ;
    soviet advance through Europe,
    152
Bridgeport, 26
Brielen, 75, 94
Brighton, 128
Brihuega, Battle of, 115
Brindisi, 147
Bristol, during Blitz, 129
Britain
    43, 54-5, 64-5, 68, 79-82 ;
    military casualties 1914-18,
    100 ; civilian casualties and
    expenditure 1914-18, 101 ; in
    1925, 110 ; anxious to see
    European balance of power
    maintained, 111, 118 ; Battle of
    1940, 126 ; British and German
    air organisations, summer 1940,
    126 ; British defensive and

German offensive plans, 126 ;
    British and German senior
    chains of command, 126 ;
    British radio-location net, 126 ;
    daily aircraft losses, 127 ;
    invasion of, German plans for,
    128 ; 130, 141-2, 150-1 ;
    military casualties 1939-45,
    158 ; civilian casualties and
    expenditure 1939-45, 159 ;
    1945, 160
British East Africa, 45, 55
British Honduras, 37
Brittany, 126
Brody, 67, 92
Bromberg, 119
Broodseinde, 75
Brown's Gap, 21
Bruges, 66, 72, 76, 98-9, 125
Bruinsburg, 26
Brünn, 42, 154
Brunswick, 39, 154
Brusa, 105
Brussels, 66, 70, 72, 76, 98-9,
    124, 126, 151-2
Brzezany, 92
Bucharest, 41, 56-7, 67 ; taken by
    Germans, 93 ; 145 ; soviet
    advance through Europe, 152
Budapest, 42, 67, 134 ; soviet
    advance through Europe, 152,
    154
Buell, (Union Offensive), 15
Buffalo, R, 44
Bug, R, 67, 77, 119
Bukovina, 67
Bulair, feint attack by RN division,
    86
Bulgaria, 41-2, 54, 56-7, 64, 67,
    69, 80-2, 84, 87, 93 ; military
    casualties 1914-18, 100 ;
    civilian casualties and
    expenditure 1914-18, 101, 104,
    110, 118, 134, 141, 145 ; soviet
    advance through Europe, 152
Bulgarians of Kazan, 58
Bull Run
    First Battle of, 15, 19, 21-2
    River, 12, 20-3
    Second Battle of, 15, 20-1, 23
Buq Buq, 133
Burao, 34
Burgas, 56-7
Burgos, (Nationalist HQ) military
    revolt in 1936, 115
Burke's Station, 30
Burkesville, 16, 30
Burma, 55, 114, 137 ; Japanese
    assault on, 138 ; casualties
    during, 138 ; Road, 137-8, 149
Burnside, (Union Offensive), 16
Burza, Polish destroyer, escapes
    to Britain despite German naval

surveillance, 119
Buzau Pass, 93

Cabanatuan, 156
Cabourg, 151
Cadiz, military revolt in, 1936, 115
Caen, 150-1
Cagayan,.156
Cagliari, Axis air and naval base,
    139, 147
Cairo, (Africa), 59-60, 139
Cairo, (USA), 13, 15
Calabria, 38
Calais, 66, 72, 98, 124-5 ; German
    embarkation port, 127-8
Calais, Pas de, used as decoy for
    'D' Day allied invasion, 150
Calcutta, 59, 114
California, 10
California, USS, 136
Callao, naval bombardment, 36
Calpulalpam, Battle of, 37
Caltanisetta, 146
Cambrai, 66, 76 ; British tank-
    spearheaded offensive, 95 ; 96,
    98-9
Camden, 17
Cameroon, 35
Camerunes, Battle of, 37
Campania, 38
Campbell I, 55
Canada, 10, 31, 43, 55
Canary Is, 43, 79, 130-1
Candia, (also Heraklion), 134 ;
    Axis air base, 139
Canea, 134
Cantabrian, Mts, 2
Cantaing, 95
Canterbury, 128
Canton, 17, 59 ; island, 61 ;
    communist uprising suppressed
    by nationalists, 1927, 112 ;
    Japanese troops capture major
    sea port, 1938, 113
Cape Colony, 49
Cape Girdeau, 13
Cape Helles, 86
Cape Verde Is, 79, 130-1
Cardiff, during 'Blitz', 129
Carentan, 151
Caribbean Sea, 4-5
Carinthia, 42
Carniola, 42
Carnoy, 91
Carolinas, campaign, 19
Caroline Islands, 43, 55, 69, 137,
    148, 155
Carpathian Mts, 2
Carpentaria, Gulf of, 37
Casablanca, 'Operation Torch',
    144, 145
Caspian Sea, 2-3, 6, 41, 58-60

Cassel, 98, 107
Castel Benito Airfield, 1941,
    Rommel arrives to command
    German Africa Korps in Libya,
    132, 139
Catania, Axis air and naval base,
    139, 146
Catingas, 5
Catterick RAF station, 126
Caucasus Front, (Russo-Turkish
    war), 41
Caucasus Mts, 2
Cavite, 156
Cebu, 156
Cedar Bluff, (Union Surrender), 16
Cedar Run, Battle of, 21
Celebes, 137, 155
Celles, 152
Cemetery Hill, 28
Cemetery Ridge, 28
Central Sierras, 2
Cernavoda, 93
Cetinje, 56, 134
Ceylon, 43, 55, 114
Chad, Lake, 6
Châlons, 40, 70, 76
Chalons-sur-Marne, 98
Chambersburg, 12
Chambersburg Pike, 28
Champ, 90
Champion Hill, 26 ; Battle of, 16
Champneuville, 90
Chanak, 84, 86
Chancellor's House, 27
Chancellorsville, 12 ; Battle of, 14,
    16, 20-1, 27
Changsha, Battle of, 1930,
    Nationalists defeat communists
    who flee west, 112
Chantilly, 98
Charlemagne, French battleship
    used in Dardanelles, 84
Charleroi, 66, 70, 72, 98, 124, 152
Charleston, 13, 15-17
Charleville-Mézières, 98
Charlotte, 13
Charlottesville, 12, 21
Charney, 90
Chatalja, 56-7 ; lines, 41
Château-Thierry, 66, 71, 97-8
Chatham, Island, 43, 55
Châtillon, 40
Chattahoochee, River, 29
Chattancourt, 90
Chattanooga, 13, 15-8 ; campaign
    19, 29
Chaulnes, 72, 91, 96, 98
Chaumont, 40
Chauny, 98
Cheat, Mt, Battle of, 20
Cheat, R, 12
Chefoo, 59
Chemin des Dames, 97-8

Chemulpo, 48, 51
Cherbourg, 125 ; German
    embarkation port, 127 ; 150-1
Chesapeake Bay, 12, 18-20
Cheyennes, 31
Chickamauga, Battle of, 16
Chickasaw Bayou, Battle of, 15
Chickasaw Bluffs, 19, 26
Chickasaw Landing, 17
Chickahominy, R, 12, 21
Chile, 36, 43
Chimborazo, Mt, 5
China, 48, 51, 59-60, 69 ; 1926-
    33, period marked by rivalry
    between Communists and
    Nationalists, and Japanese
    intervention, 112 ; 1933-39, 113
    114, 137-8, 149 ; military
    casualties 1939-45, 158 ;
    civilian casualties and
    expenditure 1939-45, 159
Chindwin, R, 138
Chinese City, 50
Chinkiang, 59
Chins, (Burmese tribe), 138
Chocolate Hill, 86
Christiansand, 123
Christmas I, 55
Chungking, 113, 137
Chunuk Bair, 86
Church Fenton, RAF station, 126
Cincinnati, 15
Citronelle, (Taylor surrenders to
    Canby), 17
City Point, 12, 30
Clarksburg, 15
Clarksville, 13
Claye Souilly, (HQ, French Sixth
    Army, First Battle of Marne) 71
Clement, SS, victim of Graf
    Spee, 120-1
Clercken, 73
Clermont, 98
Clignon, R, 71
Clinton, 26
Clutha, R, 7
Clydeside, during Blitz, 129
Coblenz, 40, 99, 107
Cocos Islands, 55
Cold Harbour, 12 ; Battle of, 17
Colenso, Battle of, 49
Cologne, 70, 76, 99, 107, 154
Colombo, 59
Colorado, R, 31
Colorado, Territory, 10
Coltishall, RAF station, 126
Columbia, (S. America), 36
Columbia, (USA), 13, 17
Columbia, Bridge, 21
Columbia, R, 4, 41
Columbus, (Georgia), 13
Columbus, (Illinois), 13
Comanches, 31

Combles, 96
Comines, 94
Como, 147, 154
Compiègne, 66, 70, 72, 76, 97-8
Conde, 97
Congo, 45
Congo, Belgian, 45
Congo, French, 35, 55
Congo, R, 6
Connaught, 108
Connecticut, 10
Conrad's Stores, 21
Consenvoye, 90
Constantinople, 41, 54, 56-7, 60,
    84, 86, 105
Constanza, 93
Cook Is, 55
Cook, Mt, 7
Copenhagen, 123
Coral Sea, 7
Corfu, 57, 134
Corinth, (Greece), 134
Corinth, (USA) 13 ; Battle of, 15
Cork, (also Cobh), (British naval
    base until 1938), 108
Corleone, 146
Corregidor, 156
Corsica, 38, 132, 141, 147
Cortemarck, 73
Costa Rica, 37
Couckelaere, 73
Coulommiers, (GHQ, BEF, First
    battle of the Marne), 71 ; (HQ,
    RFC) 98
Courcelette, 91
Courselles, 151
Courtrai, 66, 98
Coventry, devastated by German
    bombers (despite British
    knowledge of impending
    attack), 129
Coxyde, 73
Cracow, 42, 67, 77, 106, 119, 152,
    154
Craiova, 93
Craonne, 72, 97
Crécy, 71
Creil, 98
Cremona, 147
Crete, 54, 132, British naval losses
    off, 133 ; airborne attack by
    Axis powers, 134, 139, 141
Crna, 87
Croatia-Slavonia, 42
Cromarty, 88
Cross Keys, Battle of, 21
Crouy, 71
Croxton's Raid, 17
Cuba, 4, 37, 43
Cubango, R, 6
Cub Run, Bridge, 22
Cub Run, R, 22
Cuinchy, 96

Culgoa, R, 7
Culpeper Court House, 12
Culps Hill, 28
Cumberland, (Virginia), 12 ; army of the, 19 ; Gap, 16 ; mountains, 13 ; river, 12, 18-9
Cumberland, HMS, role in Battle of River Plate, 120-1
Curragh Camp, (1914, British Army officers resign commissions upon orders to stand ready for possible Ulster revolt, 108
Curtis, (Union offensive), 15
Cuvilly, 97
Cyprus, 55, 141
Cyrenaica, 54
Czechoslovakia, 106, 110 ; model democracy troubled by minorities, 111 ; 118, 119, 141, 145 ; soviet advance through Europe, 152, 154
Czernowitz, 42, 67, 92

Dakar, 79, 120-1
Dakota, Territory,10
Dalmatia, 42
Dalni, 51
Dalton, 13, 17, 29
Damascus, 60
Damloup, 90
Dammartin, 71
Danube, R, 2, 41-2, 56-8, 65, 67, 87, 93, 134, 154
Danville, 13
Danville Railroad, 30
Danzig, 67, 77, 106-7 ; attacked by Germans, Sept. 1939, 118 ; claimed as part of German Reich, 119 ; 152, 154
Dardanelles, 53 ; allied fleet fails to force passage through, 83 ; fiasco in, 84 ; 85-6
Dardanos, 84
Darling, R, 7
Darmstadt, 39
Davao, 156
Davies Strait, 4
Davis, (Union Offensive), 15
Dawkin's Branch, R, 23
Deal, 125, 128
Deauville, 126
Debden RAF station, 126
Debreczen, 42
Decatur, 13
Dedeagach, 56-7
De Flores Island, 120-1
Delaware, 10, 12, 15-7
Delhi, 59, 114
De Lobos Island, 120-1
Demicourt, 95
Dendi, Mt, 6

Deniecourt, 91
Denmark, 43, 64-5, 80-2, 88-9, 118-9, 123, 141, 154
Derna, 53, 132-3 ; axis naval base, 139
Dervishes, 47
Desna, R, 67
De Totts Battery, 86
Deutsch Eylau, 74
Deutschland, false name used by *Graf Spee*, 120-1
Diamantina, R, 7
Dickebusch, 75, 94, 96
Diedenhofen, (also Thionville), 70, 98
Dieppe, 40, 66 ; German embarkation port, 127 ; 128, 151
Dieuze, 98
Digby, RAF station, 126
Dijon, 40, 70
Dinant, 70, 98, 124, 152
Dinard, 126
Dinaric Alps, 2
Dinwiddie Court House, 30
Dives, R, 151
Dixmude, 66, 72-3
Dnieper, R, 2-3, 58, 67
Dniester, R, 2-3, 58, 67, 77, 92
Dobrudja, 57, 67, 93
Dodecanese, 53-4, 56
Dodecanese Is, occupied by Italy, 1912, 109
Dogger Bank, Battle of, 83
Dompierre, 91
Don, R, 2-3, 58
Don Cossacks, 58
Donegal, 108
Dongo, 147
Dongola, 34
Doric Star, SS, victim of *Graf Spee*, 120-1
Dormans, 71, 98
Douai, 66, 76, 96, 98
Doullens, 72, 98
Dover, 125, 128 ; straits of, 150
Down, 108
Drakensberg, 6
Drama, 57
Drava, R, 42, 67
Dresden, SMS, 107, 154 ; joins *Graf Spee's* force, 78
Drillancourt, 90
Drina, R, 56-7, 87
Drocourt, 66
Dublin, (Easter 1916, rising is put down by British ; ringleaders executed), 108
Dubno, 92
Ducie Island, 55
Duckport, 26
Duero, R, 115
Düna, R, 58
Dunkirk, 66, 70, 72, 98-9, 124 ;

operations in vicinity of, 1940, 125 ; by June 1940, over 338,000 allied troops have embarked from, 125 ; German embarkation port, 127 ; 128 ; with Calais as decoy allied invasion on 'D Day', 150
Dun Laoghaire, 108
Durazzo, 56-7, 87
Düren, 99
Durham Station, 17
Düsseldorf, 76
Dutch Harbour, 137, 148, 155
Duxford, RAF station, 126
Dvina, R, 58, 67,77
Dvinsk, 67, 77
Dymchurch, 128

Early's Raid, 17
Eastbourne, 128
East China Sea, 48, 51
Easter I, 78
East Indies, Dutch, 43. 137
Ebro, R, 2, 115
Echternacht, 152
Egeiga, 47
Eger, 42
Egmont, Mt, 7
Egypt (and Sudan), 34, 43, 45, 53, 55, 59-60, 64, 132-3, 139, 142, 145
Eire, neutral during Second World War, 129 ; 141
El Agheila, 132-3
El Alamein, Battle of, 133 ; 139, 142-3 ; 'Operation Torch', 144 ; Oct 1942, battle marks commencement of allied advances and victories, 145
Elands Laagte, Battle of, 49
Elba, 147
Elbe, R, 2, 42, 89, 107, 154
Elbing, 74
El Imayid, 143
Elk Run, 21
Ellice Is, 55
Elverdinghe, 75, 94
Elys Ford, 27
Emden SMS, destroyed by HMAS *Sydney*, 78 ; detaches from main force to raid Indian Ocean, 78
England, 125
English Channel, over 100 small craft involved in evacuation of Dunkirk, (243 lost), 125
Eniwetok, 78
Enna, 146
Enos, 41, 56-7
Enterprise, USS, 148
Épernay, 66, 71, 98
Épinal, 40, 69-70, 76

Equador, (also Ecuador), 36, 43
Erfurt, 107, 154
Ergene, R, 57
Eritrea, 45, 60 ; 1890, declared an
    Italian province, 109
Erzerum, 41
Escaut, R, 72
Eshowe, 34
Eski Keni, 86
Eski-Shehr, Battle of, 105
Esnes, 90
Éstaires, 96
Esternay, 71
Estonia, 104, 106, 110, 123 ;
    occupied by USSR Sept, 1939-
    June 1941, 135 ; 141 ; soviet
    advance through Europe, 152
Estrées, 96-7
Étaples, German embarkation port,
    127-8
Etchingham, 128
Etna, Mt, 146
Etowah, R, 29
Eupen, 152
Euphrates, R, 3, 60
Europe, physical features of, 2 ;
    79, 120-1, 130-1 ; German
    occupied, 139 ; in 1945, 160
Everest, Mt, 3
Ewa, attacked concurrently with
    Pearl Harbour, 136
Exeter HMS, role in battle of
    River Plate, 120-1
Eyre, Lake, 7

Fagaras, 93
Falaise, 151
Falkland Is, 43, 55
Falling Waters, Battle of, 21
Falmouth, 16, 25
Famagusta, British naval base, 139
Fanning Island, 55
Farm Ford, 22
Farmville, 30
Farragut (Union offensive), 15, 16,
    17
Fashoda, 34, 45
Faverolles, 71
Fay, 91
Fedala, 'Operation Torch', 144
Fère Champenoise, 98
Fère-en-Tardenois, 71
Fermanagh (Boundary problem
    resolved 1925), 108
Fernandina, 15
Festubert, 76
Fetterman Massacre, 31
Feuillères, 91
Fez, 54
Fezzan, 54
Fiji Islands, 43, 55
Filton RAF Station, 126

Finke, R, 7
Finland, 58, 64, 104, 110-11,
    122-3, partially occupied by
    USSR Sept, 1939-June, 1941,
    135, 140-2, 152
Fismes, 98
Fiume, 42 ; 1919-21, occupied by
    volunteer patriots 1924,
    becomes Italian ; 109
Five Forks, 30
Flaucourt, 91
Flensburg, 154
Flers, 91
Flesquières, 95
Flinders, R, 7
Flint Island, 55
Florence, 147, 154
Florence (Alabama), 13
Florida, 10, 13, 15, 16, 17
Foggia, 139, airfield complex, 147
Fokshani, 93
Folkestone, 125, 128
Fontaine, 95
Foochow, 112
Forbidden city, 50
Forges, 90
Formidable HMS, sole British
    aircraft carrier off Greece, dive-
    bombed and put out of action,
    133
Formosa, 51, 69, 112, 137
Forrest's Raid, 17
Fort Belleville, 90
Fort Belrupt, 90
Fort Bois Bourros, 90
Fort Butte à la Rose, 16
Fort Chana, 90
Fort Chaume, 90
Fort Choisel, 90
Fort Donelson, 13, 15, (taken by
    Grant, February, 1862) 18
Fort Douaumont, 90
Fort Eben-Emael, 124
Fort Fisher, 17
Fort Henry, 15, (taken by Grant,
    February, 1862) 18
Fort Jackson and St Philip, 15
Fort Macon, 15
Fort Marre, 90
Fort Monroe, 12
Fort Pillow, 13, 17
Fort Royal, 15
Fort St Michel, 90
Fort Sartelles, 90
Fort Smith, 15
Fort Souville, 90
Fort Stedman, 30
Fort Sumter, opening shots of
    war fired here, 12 April, 1861,
    15
    bombardment of, 10
Fort Tavannes, 90
Fort Thiaumont, 90

Fort Vacherauville, 90
Fort Vaux, 90
Fort Wagner, Battle of and
    evacuation, 16
Fortescue River, 7
Foucacourt, 91
France, 39, 40, 43, 54-5, 64-5,
    68-9, 72, 80-2, 98-9, military
    casualties 1914-18, 100 ;
    civilian casualties and
    expenditure 1914-18, 101, 110 ;
    fearful of a remilitarized
    Germany, 111 ;
    non-interventionist during
    Spanish Civil War, 115, 118 ;
    Sichelschnitt, 124 ; fall of, 1940,
    125, 126, 127 ; German
    occupied, 128-9, 139, 141, 145,
    150-1, 154 ; military casualties
    1939-45, 158 ; civilian
    casualties and expenditure
    1939-45, 159 ; 1945,
    previously leading international
    power, now much reduced in
    status, 160
Frankfort, (USA) 13, 15
Frankfurt, 99, 107, 154
Franklin, 13, 21 ; Battle of, 17
Frayser's Farm, Battle of, 21
Frederick, 12
Fredericksburg, 12, 15-16, 21, 27 ;
    Battle of, 20-1, 25
Freetown, 79 ; allied base
    during second battle of
    Atlantic, 131
French Empire in North Africa, 53
Frezenberg, 75, 94
Fricourt, 91
Friedrich der Grosse, SMS
    (Scheer's flagship), plan of,
    88-9
Fromelles, 96
Front Royal, 21 ; Battle of, 21
Furnes, 73, 125

Gaines' Mill, Battle of, 21
Galatz, 93
Galicia, 42, 65
Gallipoli, 56 ; Turks resist allied
    invasion, 80 ; Peninsular, 84, 85 ;
    Fiasco, 86
Gambia, 45, 55
Gambia, R, 6
Ganges, R, 3
Garfield, (Union Offensive), 15
Gascoyne, R, 7
Gateshead, during Blitz, 129
Gaulois, French battleship, use in
    Dardanelles, 84
Gavrelle, 96
Gazala, 133
Gdynia, 199

Gela, 146
Gellivare, (Swedish iron ore zone), 123
Genoa, 38 ; 1941, bombarded by British force 'H' (from Gibraltar), 132 ; Axis naval base, 139, 147, 154 ; Gulf of, 154
Georgetown, 17 ; allied base during second battle of Atlantic, 131
Georgia, 10, 13, 15-17
Georgina, R, 7
Germana Ford, 27
Germany, (Prussia until 1870), 40, 42, 54-5, 64-9, 76, 80-1 ; short of food and goods, 82, 88-9, 98-9 ; military casualties 1914-18, 100 ; civilian casualties and expenditure 1914-18, 101, 106 ; Weimar Republic, 107, 110 ; Nazi, under Hitler, intent on securing *Lebensraum* in the East, 111, 118-121, 123-6, 135, 141, 145, 151-2 ; at bay, Jan-May 1945, 154 ; military casualties 1939-45, 158 ; civilian casualties and expenditure 1939-45, 159 ; 1945, previously leading international power, now much reduced in status, 160
Gettysburg, 12 ; Battle of, 14 ; 16, 20, 28
Gettysburg and Hanover Railway, 28
Gheluvelt, 75, 94
Ghent, 66, 72, 76, 98-9, 124, 126
Ghistelles, 73
Gibraltar, 43, 55, 79 ; allied base during second battle of Atlantic, 131 ; British air and naval base, 139 ; 'Operation Torch', 144
Gie, 99
Gilbert Is, 55, 155
Ginchy, 91
Givenchy, 66
Glasgow, during Blitz, 129
Godavari, R, 3
Gold, US ship, used as a troop carrier in 'Overlord', 150
Gold Coast, 35, 43, 45, 55
Golden Horde, 58
Goldsboro, 17
Gonnelieu, 95
Goodwin Sands, 125
Gordosville, 12, 21
Gorizia-Gradisca, 42
Gorlice, 77
Goryn, R, 92
Gostivar, 87
Gouzeaucourt, 95
Gozo, 139

Graf Spee, Admiral, German pocket battleship ; cruise of and dates, 120-1 ; total tonnage sunk by as a commerce raider, 120-1 ; victims of, 120-1 ; gun ranges, 120-1 ; enters neutral harbour to seek refuge from pursuers, (HMS *Ajax*, *Exeter* and *Achilles*) 120-1 ; changes name to confuse allies, 120-1 ; damaged, flees along Plate estuary, 120-1 ; risk of internment, 120-1
Graincourt, 95
Grand Gulf, 26
Grand Junction, 26
Grand Morin, 66, 71
Grant, (Union Offensive) 15-17
Graudenz 74, 76, 119
Gravelines, 125
Gravelotte-St Privat, Battle of, 40
Gravenstafel, 75, 94
Gravesend, 128
Graz, 42
Great Bear Lake, 4
Great Dividing Range, 7
Great Lakes, 4, 31
Great Plains, 4
Great Salt Lake, 4, 31
Great Slave Lake, 4
Great Victoria Desert, 7
Greece, 54, 56-7, 64, 69, 80-1, 87 ; military casualties 1914-18, 100 ; civilian casualties and expenditure 1914-18, 101, 110 ; British naval losses off, 133 ; surrendered to Germans, 134, 139, 141, 145
Green Hill, 86
Greenland, 4. 43, 78-9, 130, 140
Greensboro, 13
Greenville, 13
Grenada, 13
Grenoble, 125
Grevena, 56
Grierson's Raid, 16
Grodno, 67-8, 77, 106, 119 ; soviet advance through Europe, 152
Grom, Polish destroyer, escapes to Britain despite German naval surveillance, 119
Groveton, 22-3
Groveton Ridge, 23
Guadalajara, Battle of, 115
Guadalcanal, 155
Guadalquivir, R, 115
Guam, 61, 137, 148, 155
Guatemala, 37
Guernica, 1937, devastated by German aircraft, 115
Guernsey, 150
Guiana, 36 ; highlands, 5

Guiana, British, 43, 55
Guiana, French, 43, 55
Guildford, 128
Guinea, Spanish, 45
Guise, 70, 98
Gumbinnen, 74
Gury, 97
Gusayatin, (HQ Russian 7th Army) 9,2

Haarlem, 126
Hadramaut, 60
Haggerstown, 12, 20
Haggerstown Road, 28
Hague, The, 124, 151
Hagushi, 157
Hai-Cheng, Battle of, 48
Haifa, British Naval Base, 139
Hainan, 137
Halfaya Pass, 133
Halifax, (USA) 79 ; allied base during second battle of Atlantic, 131
Halleck, (Union Offensive) 15
Ham, 96, 98
Hamburg, 107, 154
Hamilton's Crossing, 25
Hampton Roads, 12
Hangchow, 112
Hancock, 12, 21
Hankow, 112-3
Hanover, (USA) 12
Hanover Junction, 12
Hanover Road, 28
Hanover, (Germany) 39, 107, 154
Harbin, Battle of, 51
Hard Times, 26
Hardee, (Confederate Retreat) 17
Harpers Ferry, 12, 17
Harrisonburg, 12, 21
Hasselt, 99
Hastings, 128
Hatcher's Run, 30
Hatteras Inlet, (Confederate surrender), 15
Haumont, 90
Havrincourt, 95
Hawaii, 61, 136
Hawaiian Is, 61, 78, 137, 155
Haynes Bluff, 26
Hazebrouck, 72, 98
Hazel Run, 25
Hejaz, 60
Helena, 17
Heligoland Bight, 89
Heligoland North, 89
Helsingfors, 58
Helsinki, 122
Henry House, 22-3
Heraklion, (*see* Candia)
Herat, 60
Herbecourt, 91

Herero, 35
Hermannstadt, 93
Hermies, 95
Herne Bay, 125
Herron, (Union Offensive) 15
Herzegovina, 41-2, 54
Hesse, 39
Hickham, attacked concurrently with Pearl Harbor, 136
Hill 10, 86
Hill 60, 75, 86
Hill Q, 86
Hilton Head Island, 17
Himalayas, 3
Hindenburg Line, 66
Hindman, (Confederate Offensive), 15
Hindu Kush, 3
Hinges, 96
Holland, 43, 65-6, 70, 76, 98-9, 124, 126
Hiroshima, Aug 1945, USA drops atomic bomb; civilian casualties over 148,000, 155
Hirson, 76, 98
Hiryu, Japanese ship, 148
Hodeida, 60
Hohenzollern, 39
Hokkaido Island, 137
Hollebeke, 75, 94
Holstein, 39
Homs, 53
Hondschoote, (King Albert's HQ) 98
Honduras, 37
Honduras, British, 43, 55
Hong Kong, 43, 55, 59
Honnecourt, 95
Honolulu, 61, 137
Honshu, 48, 137
Hood, (Confederate Offensive) 17
Hooge, 75, 94, 96
Hope Island, 140
Hornchurch, RAF station, 126
Hornet, USS, 148
Horns Reef, 89
Hottentot, 35
Houffalize, 152
Houtem, 94
Houthulst, Forest of, 73, 75, 94
Howland I, 61
Howth, 1914, Irish volunteers smuggle in arms, 108
Hudson Bay, 4
Hull, during Blitz, 129
Humaita, Battle of, 36
Humboldt, 13
Hungary, 42, 106, 110, 118-19, 134; controlled by Germany, 135; 141, 145; soviet advance through Europe, 152, 154
Hun Ho, R, 50
Huntsman, SS, victim of Graf

Spee, 120-1
Hwang Ho, R, 3, 112-13
Hythe, 128

Ibar, R, 56-7, 87
Iceland, 43, 79, 130, 140
Iheya, 157
Illinois, 10, 13, 15-16
Iloilo, 156
Imperial City, 50
Inchy, 95
Indaw, 138, 149
Indefatigable, HMS, 88
India, 43, 55, 59-60; strife in pre-1939, 114, 137-8, 149
Indian Ocean, 3, 6-7
Indiana, 10, 13, 15-16
Indigirka, R, 3
Indo-China, French, 43, 55, 137-8, 149
Indus, R, 3, 60
Inflexible, HMS, mined in Dardanelles, 84
Innsbruck, 42, 154
Inönü, Battles of, 105
Insterburg, 74
Invergordon, 88
Invincible, HMS, sunk, 88
Ionian Islands, 134
Iowa, 10
Iraq, 140
Ireland, 64; before and after Treaty of 1921, 108
Irish Free State, (becomes Eire in 1937), 108
Iron Duke, HMS, Jellicoe's flagship, plan of, 88-9
Irrawaddy, R, 3, 138, 149
Irresistible, HMS, mined in Dardanelles, 84
Irtysh, R, 3
Irwinsville, 17
Isandhlwana, Battle of, 34, 44
Isfahan, 60
Isigny, 151
Iskur, R, 56
Island No 10, (Confederate surrender) 15
Ismail, 93
Ismailia, 46
Istria, 42
Italy, 42, 53-4, 56, 64-5, 69, 80-2; military casualties 1914-18, 100; civilian casualties and expenditure 1914-18, 101, 109-10; fascist under Mussolini, bent on overseas conquest, 111, 118, 125, 132, 141-2; 'Operation Torch', 144, 145 campaign in 1943-45, 147; conquest of Sicily, 146, 154; military casualties 1939-45, 158;

civilian casualties and expenditure 1939-45, 159
Iuka, Battle of, 15
Ivangorod, 77
Iwojima, 137, 155; campaign, 157; US casualties at, 157; number of Japanese surrenders at, 157
Izena, 157
Izmid, 105

Jackson, (Mississippi), 13, 26; Battle of, 16
Jackson, (Tennessee), 17
Jackson's Valley Campaign, 15
Jacksonville, 15, 17; Confederate surrender, 13
Jade Bay, base of German fleet in Battle of Jutland, 88
Jamaica, 4, 43, 55
James, R, 18, 20-1, 30; crossing of, 12
Janina, 56-7
Jan Mayen, 140
Japan; Sea of, 48, 51, 59, 69; military casualties 1914-18, 100; civilian casualties and expenditure 1914-18, 101, 136-7, 148, 155; military casualties 1939-45, 158; civilian casualties and expenditure 1939-45, 159
Japura, R, 5
Jaroslav, 67
Jassy, Rumanian final stand, 93
Java, 155; Battle of, 137
Jebel Surgham, 47
Jefferson City, 13
Jenkin's Ferry, Battle of, 17
Jersey, 150
Jerusalem, 60
Jetersville, 30
Jiddah, 60
Johannesburg, 49
Johnston, (Union Retreat), 17
Johnston I, 61
Jonesboro, 17
Juba, R, 6
Juno, US ship, used as troop carrier in 'Overlord', 150
Jurva, R, 5
Jutland, Battle of, 83
Jutland Bank, 88-9

Kabul, 60, 114
Kachanik, 87
Kaga, Japanese ship, 148
Kalafat, 93
Kalahari Desert, 6
Kalamata, 134
Kalewa, 138, 149

Kalish, 119
Kambula, Battle of, 44
Kamenets-Podolski, HQ Russian
   9th Army, 92
Kamerun, 45, 55
Kandalaksha, 122
Kaneohe, attacked concurrently
   with Pearl Harbor, 136
Kansas, 10
Karachi, 59-60
Karakal, 93
Karakol Dagh, 86
Karlsruhe, SMS, 78
Kars, 41, 58-9, 105
Kasai, R, 6
Kashins, (Burmese tribe), 138
Kashmir, 1919-20, British
   operations against tribesmen
   and guerrillas, 114
Kassa, 42
Kassel, 39, 154
Katowice, 107
Kavak Tepe, 86
Kavalla, 57
Kazan, 58
Kelly's Ford, 27
Kemmel, 94
Kenesaw Mt, First and Second
   Battles of, 17
Kengtung, 138, 149
Kenley, RAF station, 126
Kent, 125
Kentucky, 10, 13, 15-17
Kenya, Mt, 6
Kerama, 157
Kermadec Islands, 55
Kernstown, 21 ; Battle of, 21
Kerreri, 47
Keyem, 73
Kharkov, 58, 104, 135
Khartoum, 34
Kherson, 58
Kholm, 152
Khyber Pass, 114
Kidney Ridge, 143
Kiel, 154 ; Canal, 65, 88, 154
Kiev, 58-9, 67, 104, 106, 135, 152
Kilid Bahr, 84, 86
Kilimanjaro, Mt, 6
Kimberley, 49
Kimpolung, 92
King s County, (renamed Offaly),
   108
Kingston, 29
Kingstown, (renamed Dun
   Laoghaire), 108
Kirby Smith, (Confederate
   Offensive) 15 ; (Confederate
   Retreat) 17
Kiretch Tepe Sirt, 86
Kirk Kilisse, 56-7
Kirton-in-Lindsey, RAF station,
   126

Kishinev, 67
Kiska, 137, 148, 155
Kitchener's Wood, 75
Knokke, Fort of, 73
Knoxville, 13, 15-17
Koja Chemen Tepe, 86
Kola, 58
Kolberg, 107, 154
Kolomea, 92
Kolozsvar, 42
Konia, 105
Koningsberg, 67-8, 74, 76, 152,
   154
Korea, 48, 51, 69
Korean Strait, 48
Koskiusko, Mt, 7
Kovel, 92
Kovno, 67-8, 77
Kozlov, 104
Kragujevac, Serbian military
   centre and arsenal, 87
Krasnovodsk, 58
Krilov, 92
Krim, 58
Krishna, R, 3
Krithia, 86
Krivoi Rog, 152
Kronstadt, 49, 58, 93 ; ship
   canal, 58
Kruiseecke, 75, 94
Kuban, R, 58
Kumanovo, 56
Kum Kale, 84
Kunlun, Mts, 3
Kuriles, 136-7
Kurnanovo, 87
Kursk, 135
Kustendil, 56, 87
Kutno, 119
Kuty, 92
Kuwait, 59
Kwango, R, 6
Kwangtung Peninsular, Battle of
   48, 51
Kyushu, 48, 137

La Bassée, 66, 72, 96 ; canal, 96 ;
   98
La Boiselle, 91
Laccadives, 43
Lachlan, R, 7
Ladoga, Lake, 2, 104, 122, 135
Ladysmith, 49
La Fère, 66, 70, 72, 96-7
La Ferté, 98
La Ferté Milon, 71
La Ferté-sous-Jouarre, 71
Lagny, 71, 97
La Grange, 16
Lahore, 59
Lai-Kha, 138, 149
Laing's Nek, Battle of, 34, 49

Lala Baba, 86
Landrecies, 66
Langemarck, 73, 75, 94
Langres, 70
Laon, 66, 70, 72, 76, 97-8
La Panne, 125
Larissa, 56-7, 134
Larne, April 1914, rifles smuggled
   in from Germany, 108
La Rochelle, Axis naval base, 139
Lashio, 138, 149
Lassigny, 96
Latvia, 104, 106, 110, 118-9, 123 ;
   occupied by USSR Sept, 1939-
   June 1941, 135, 141 ; soviet
   advance through Europe, 152
Lebanon, 16
Le Cateau, 66, 70, 98
Lee, (Confederate offensive)
   15-16 ;
   (Confederate retreat) 17
Leech Lake, Battle of, 31
Leeward Is, 43
Leffinghe, 73
Legaspi, 156
Leghorn, Axis air base, 139, 147
Le Havre, 40, 124, 150-1
Leinster, 108
Leipzig, 107, 154
Leipzig, SMS, joins *Graf Spee*'s
   force, 78
Leix, 108
Le Mans, Battle of, 40
Lemberg, 42, 67, 77, 104, 106,
   119
Le Mort Homme, 90
Lena, R, 3
Leningrad, 122 ; never taken by
   Germans, 135, 141-2, 152
Lens, 66, 72, 76, 96, 98
Le Sars, 91
Lesboeufs, 91
Le Shima, Japanese airfield, 157
Lessay, 151
Le Transloy, 91
Lewis Ford, 22
Lexington, 15, 21 ; (Confederate
   Offensive), 13
Leyte, 156
Liao Ho, R, 3
Liao Yang, Battle of, 51
Libau, 67, 77
Liberia, 45
Libya, 45 ; 1911-12, conquered by
   Italy, 109 ; 1912-25, ceded by
   Italy to Britain, 109, 132-3,
   139, 142
Libyan Desert, 6
Licata, 146
Liege, 66, 68, 70, 76, 98-9, 124,
   152
Lihons, 91
Lille, 40, 66, 70, 72, 76, 96 ;

canal, 96, 98-9, 125, 150
Lim, R, 56-7
Lima, Battle of, 36
Limpopo, R, 6
Lingayen, 156
Linhpa, 138
Linz, 42
Lion, HMS, Beatty's flag-ship, plan of, 88
Lippe, 39
Lisbon, 115
Lithuania, 58, 104, 106, 110, 118-19, 123 ; occupied by USSR, Sept, 1939-June, 1941, 135, 141 ; soviet advance through Europe, 152
Little Big Horn, Battle of, 31
Little Rock, 13
Liverpool, during Blitz, 129 ; allied base during second battle of Atlantic, 131
Lizy, 71
LLanos, Mts, 5
Lodz, 67, 119, 154
Lofoten Islands, 123
Loikaw, 138, 149
Loire, R, 40, 65, 151
Lombardy, 38
Lombartzyde, 73
London, 128 ; heaviest raid of Blitz, 129, 141, 151
Londonderry, 108
Longstreet, 16
Longwy, 66, 98
Loo, 73
Loos, 76, 96
Lorient, first German 'U-boat' base on Atlantic coast, 130 ; Axis naval base, 139 ; retained by Germans until 1945, 151
Lorraine, 39-40
Lotzen, 74
Louisiana, 10, 13, 15-17
Louisville, 13
Louvain, 66, 70, 98, 151
Louvemont, 90
Lowestoft, 83
Loznitsa, 87
Luayon, 156
Lubeck, 154
Lublin, 67, 119 ; soviet advance through Europe, 152
Lucca, 38
Lucknow, 59
Lule Burgas, 56
Lulea, 123
Lüneburg, 154
Luneville, 66
Luray, 21
Lusitania, SS, 79
Lutsk, 67, 92
Lutzow, SMS, escapes from Jutland, 88 ; Hipper's flagship,

plan of, 88 ; sunk, 89
Luxembourg, 39-40, 64-5, 68-70, 76, 98-9, 110, 118, 124-6, 141, 151-2, 154
Luzon, 61, 155-6
Lvov, (*see* Lemberg)
Lynchburg, 12, 17
Lyon, (Union Offensive), 15
Lyons, 125, 145
Lys, R, 66, 68, 70, 72, 94 ; German offensives, 1918, 96 ; 98

Maas, R, 124
Maastricht, 124, 151
McClellan, (Union offensive) 15
McCullogh, (Confederate offensive) 15
McDowell, 12
MacKenzie, R, 4
McKinley, Mt, 4
Macon, (Georgia), 13, 17
Macquarie I, 55
Macquarie, R, 7
Madagascar, 6, 34, 43, 45, 55
Madeira, 43, 130
Madeira, R, 5
Madras, 59, 114
Madrid, besieged at intervals 1936-39, 115 ; surrenders to Nationalists, civil war ends, 115
Mafeking, 49
Magdeburg, 154
Magenta, Battle of, 38
Magersfontein, Battle of, 49
Magwe, 138, 149
Maidos, 86
Main, R, 154
Maine, (USA) 10
Mainz, 99, 107, 154
Majuba Hill, Battle of, 34
Majunga, 34
Malabang, 156
Malaga, 115
Malancourt, 90
Malay States, 55 ; Battle of, 137
Malden I, 43, 55
Maldives, 43
Maldon, 128
Maleme, 134
Malines, 98
Malmédy, 98, 152
Malta, 43, 55 ; 1941, British submarines commence operations against axis shipping plying between Italy and Libya, 132 ; defiant, pre-1942, 139 ; awarded George Cross, 139 ; 141, 147
Malvern Hill, Battle of, 21
Manassas Gap, 12, 22
Manassas Junction, 12, 21-2
Manassas Railway, 22

Manchester, during Blitz, 129
Manchuria, 48, 137
Mandalay, 138, 149
Manila, 137, 156
Mannekensvere, 73
Mannheim, 40, 99
Marche, 152
Marchelpot, 91
Marcoing, 95
Mareuil, HQ 1st German Army at
Marne, 71
Margate, 125, 128
Mariana Islands, 43, 55, 69, 136, 148, 155
Marienburg, 74
Marietta, 13
Maritsa, R, 56-7
Marle, 98
Marmara, Sea of, 86
Marne, R, 40, 65-6, 68, 70 ; first battle of, 71 ; 97-8, 124
Maros, R. 42
Marquesas Islands, 43, 55
Marra, 6
Marre, 90
Marsala, 38, 146
Marseilles, 125
Marshall Islands, 55, 69, 136-7, 148, 155
Martinpuich, 91
Martinsburg, 12
Marye's Hill, 25
Maryland, 10, 12, 15-17 ; strategic importance of, 11 ; US battleship, 136
Masbate, 156
Masnières, 95
Mason-Dixon Line, 10
Massachusetts, 10
Massacre Canyon, 31
Massanutten, Mts, 12, 21
Massapnax, R, 25
Massawa, 34
Massuria, 67
Masurian Lakes, 74, 76
Matapan, Cape, Battle of, 1941, British sink 3 Italian cruisers and 2 destroyers ; battleship *Vittorio Veneto* escapes, 132
Mattapony, R, 12
Matz, 91
Maubeuge, 66, 68, 70, 72, 98, 124
Maucourt, 90
Maungkan, 138, 149
Maurepas, 91
Mauretania, 35
Mauritius, 43, 55
Mawlaik, 138, 149
M'Dowell, 21 ; Battle of, 21
Meade, 16
Meaux, 66, 71, 98
Mecca, 60
Mechanicsville, Battle of, 21

Mechili, 133
Mechum's River Station, 21
Mecklenburg Schwerin, 39
Mecklenburg Strelitz, 39
Medina, 60
Mediterranean Sea, 2-3, 6
Mehdia, 'Operation Torch', 144-5
Meiktila, 149
Mekong, R, 3
Melilla, 34 ; July, 1936, Franco
    arrives to command Spanish
    Nationalist forces, 115
Melun, 70
Memel, 58, 67, 77, 106-7 ;
    annexed by Germany, 1939,
    118-9 ; soviet advance through
    Europe, 152 ; 154
Memphis, 15-17, 26
Mendere, R, 86
Menin Road, 75, 94, 96
Merckem, 73
Meridian, 13, 17
Merignac, Axis air base, 139
Mersa Matruh, 133
Merv, 60
Merville, 96, 151
Meshed, 60
Messina, 146-7
Messines, 66, 72, 94, 96
Metemma, Battle of, 34
Meteren, 96
Metz, 66, 69-70, 76, 95, 98-9 ;
    Battle of, 40
Meuse, R, 66, 70 ; splits front
    into two, allowing Germans
    two consecutive opening
    attacks, 90 ; 98, 124, 152
Mexico, 10-11, 37, 43 ; city, 37 ;
    gulf of, 4, 10-11, 13, 37, 79,
    130-1
Mézières, 66, 76
Michigan, 10
Middelkerke, 73
Middleburg, 49
Middle Wallop RAF station, 126
Midia, 56-7
Midway I, 61, 148 ; Battle of, 137
Mikuna, Japanese ship, 148
Milan, 147, 154
Milazzo, Battle of, 38
Milliken's Bend, 26
Mindanao, 61, 155-6
Mindoro, 156
Mine Road, 25
Mine Run, Battle of, 16
Minnesota, 10
Minsk, 58, 67, 104, 106, 135 ;
    soviet advance through Europe,
    152
Miraumont, 91, 96
Miskolcz, 42
Mississippi, 10, 13, 15-17 ; military
    division of the, 19 ; River, 4, 11,

13, 15-19, 26, 31
Missouri, 10, 13, 15-17 ; River, 4,
    15, 31
Mitrovitsa, 87
Mo, 123
Mobile, 13, 17 ; Bay, Battle of, 17 ;
    Flats, 17
Modder, River, 49 ; Battle of, 49
Modena, 38
Moeuvres, 95
Moldavia, 67, 93
Moltke, SMS, 89
Monastir, 56, 87, 134
Mongolia, 59, 137
Monroe, 13, 26 ; fortress, 15
Mons, 66, 70, 72, 76, 98-9
Monschau, 152
Montauban, 91
Montdidier, 66, 96-8
Monte Cassino, 147
Montenegro, 41-2, 56-7, 64, 67,
    69, 80-2, 87 ; military casualties
    1914-18, 100 ; civilian
    casualties and expenditure
    1914-18, 101
Monterey, 21
Montfaucon, 90
Montgomery, (Confederate
    capital), 13
Montivideo, Graf Spee flees to,
    120-1
Montmédy, 98
Montmirail, 98
Montmort, HQ 2nd German Army,
    First Battle of the Marne, 71
Montreuil, Haig's GHQ, 98
Montrose, 16
Moorefield, 21
Morava, R, 57, 87
Moravia, 39, 42, 119
Morgan's Raid, 16
Morhange, 70
Morocco, 45, 53-4, 64, 139 ;
    'Operation Torch', 144 ;
Morocco, Spanish, 45, 115, 139 ;
    'Operation Torch', 144 ; 145
Mortigny, 97
Morval, 91
Moscow, 58-9, 67, 104 ; never
    taken by Germans, 135 ; 141-2,
    152
Moselle, R, 40, 66, 70, 98, 124
Mosjön, 123
Moulmein, 138, 149
Mount Jackson, 21
Mozambique, 43, 45
Msus, 132-3
Mughla, 105
Mülhausen, 70
Munich, 1920, Hitler forms
    Nationalist Socialist Party ;
    107 ; 1923, 'Putsch' fails, 107 ;
    1924, Hitler imprisoned and

writes Mein Kampf, 107
Munster, 108
Münster, 107
Murchison, R, 7
Murfreesboro, 13, 16
Murmansk, 104 ; never taken by
    Germans, 135 ; 140
Murray, R, 7
Muscat, 60
Myitkyina, 138

Nagasaki, Aug, 1945, US drops
    atomic bomb, 155
Nago, 157
Naha, 157
Namsos, 123
Namur, 66, 68, 70, 76, 98-9, 124,
    152
Nanchang, 1927, Communist
    uprising suppressed by
    Nationalists, 112
Nancy, 66, 70, 76, 98-9
Nanking, 112-3
Nantes, 125, 151
Nanteuil, 71
Naples, Axis naval base, 139, 145,
    147
Narbada, R, 3
Narew, R, 67, 77
Narva, 67
Narvik, 123
Nashville, 15-17 ; (Union
    offensvie) 13
Nassau, 39
Natal, 45, 49
Natchez, 13, 26
Nauplia, 134
Nebraska Territory, 10
Needle Gun, first tried out, 39
Negro, R, 5
Negros, 156
Neisse, R, 154
Nejd, 60
Nepal, 114
'Neptune', code name for naval
    moves during Operation
    'Overlord', 150
Nesle, 96, 98
Netherlands, 39-40, 64, 68, 72
    81-2, 110, 118 ; capitulates,
    124 ; 141, 151-2, 154
Neufchâteau, 98
Neuve Chapelle, 66, 76, 96
Nevada, territory, 10
Nevada, US battleship, 136
Newbern, (Confederate surrender),
    15
New Caledonia, 43, 55
New Carthage, 26
Newcastle, during Blitz, 129
Newfoundland, 79, 130
New Guinea, 55, 137, 155

New Hampshire, 10
Newhaven, 128
New Hebrides, 55
New Jersey, 12, 15
New Madrid, 13
Newmarket, (USA) 12, 21-2
New Mexico Territory, 10
New Orleans, 13, 15-16, 26 ;
    Kirby Smith surrenders to Canby,
    17
Newtin Beech, SS victim of *Graf
    Spee*, 120-1
New York, 10, 79
New Zealand, 7, 43, 55, 78
Nicaragua, 37
Nice, 38
Nicholson's Nek, Battle of, 49
Nicobar Is, 55
Nieman, R, 58, 65, 67-8, 77
Nieuport, 66, 70, 72 ; flooding of
    sluices, 73 ; 98, 125
Niger, R, 6
Nigeria, 45, 55
Nigeria, Northern, 35
Nigeria, North-western 35
Nigeria, Southern, 35
Nikolaiev, 67
Nile, R, 6, 34, 46-7, 60 ; valley, 34
Ningoo, 59
Nis, 56-7, 87
Nishi, 157
Nizhni-Novgorod, 58
Norfolk, 15 ; (Confederate
    surrender), 12
Norfolk, 43, 55
Normandy, 150
North America, physical features
    of, 4
North Carolina, 10, 13, 15-7
Northern Ireland, (the Six
    Counties), 108, 129
North Mts, 12
Northolt RAF station, 126
North Sea, 59, 65
North Weald RAF station, 126
North-West Frontier, 114
Norway, 64, 81-2, 110-11, 122-3,
    135, 140-2
Nottingham, during Blitz, 129
Novgorod, 58
Novgorod Severski, 58
Novibazar, Sanjak of, 42, 87
Novo-Georgievsk, 77
Novorossisk, Axis naval base, 139
Noyon, 66, 76, 96-8
Nuits St Georges, Battle of, 40
Nun's Copse, 75
Nuremberg, 107, 154
Nurnberg, SMS, 78
Nyasa, Lake, 6
Nyasaland, 45
Nyon, Sept, 1937, 9-power
    conference held ; anti-

submarine naval patrol zones
    established, 115

Oahu, (Pearl Harbor), 136
Ob, R, 3
Ocean, HMS, mined in
    Dardanelles, 84
Ocean Beach, 86
Oder, R, 2, 107, 154
Odessa, 58, 67 ; bombarded by
    Turko-German warships, 1915,
    83 ; 84, 93, 104 ; Axis naval
    base, 139 ; 152
Odon, R, 151
Offaly, 108
Ohio, 10, 15-17 ; River, 4, 15-19
Oise, R, 40, 66, 68, 70, 72, 97,
    124
Ojos del Salado, Mt, 5
Okhotsk, Sea of, 59
Okinawa, 155, campaign, 157
Oklahoma, USS, 136
Old Cold Harbor, 21
Oldenburg, 39
Olustee, Battle of, 17
Omaha, USS, used as troop carrier
    in 'Overlord', 150
Oman, 60
Omdurman, Battle of, 34, 47
Omsk, 59
Onega, Lake, 2, 104
Oostanaula, R, 29
Oosttaverne, 94
Oran, 142 ; Operation Torch', 144,
    145
Orange Court House, 12
Orange Free State, 45, 49
Orange, R, 6, 49
Oregon, 10
Orel, 58
Orinoco, R, 5
Orizaba, 37
Orkanie, 84
Orléans, broad front policy of
    attack by allies, 151
Ormoz, 156
Ornes, 90, 151
Orsova, 42, 87, 93
Orzel, Polish destroyer, escapes
    to Britain despite German naval
    surveillance, 119
Oslo, 123
Ostend, 66, 70, 72 ; mines laid off
    coast to protect flotilla against
    U-boats, 73 ; 98, 125 ; German
    embarkation port, 127 ; 151
Ottoman Empire, 42, 54, 56-7, 60
Ouchy, 54
Oulu, 122
Ourcq, R, 71, 97
Ourthe, R, 152
Oviedo, 1936, military revolt, 115

Oxford, (UK), 128
Oxford, (USA), 15

Pachino, 146
Paducah, 13, 17
Pagan I, 78
Paietwa, 138
Pakhoi, 59
Palau Is, 55, 69
Palawan, 156
Palermo, 146
Palestine, 139
Paletwa, 149
Palmyra I, 55, 61
Pampas Gran Chaco, 5
Pamunkey, R, 12
Panama, 36, 61, 79 ; canal zone,
    61
Panay, 156
Pantellaria, 139, 147
Panther, SMS, 54
Papal States, 38
Paraguay, 36 ; River, 5
Parana, R, 5
Parang, 156
Paris, 39-40, 65-6, 68, 70, 98-9,
    124-6, 145, 150-1
Parma, 38
Passchendaele, 73, 75 ; Battle of,
    (Third Ypres), 94
Patay, Battle of, 40
Patras, 134, 145
Paumotu Is, 43, 55
Pea Ridge, Battle of, 15
Pearl Harbor, Battle of, 136-7,
    148, 155
Pearl, R, 26
Pecs, 42
Pei Ho, R, 50
Peiping, (*see* Peking)
Peking, 48, 50, 59 ; captured by
    Nationalists, name changed to
    Peiping, 112 ; July, 1937, clash
    sparks off Japanese invasion
    of China, 113 ; plan of, 50
Pembrey RAF station, 126
Pennsylvania, 10, 12, 15-17 ;
    strategic importance of, 11
Pennsylvania, US battleship, 136
Pensacola, 13, 15
Perm, 58 ; Battle of, 104
Péronne, 66, 76, 91, 96, 98
Perryville, Battle of, 15
Persia, (Iran), 59-60, 140
Persian Gulf, 60
Perthes, 76
Peru, 36, 43
Pervyse, 73
Peshawar, 114
Pesaro, 147
Petersburg, 12, 17, 30 ; siege of,
    18, 20

Petit Morin, R, 66, 71
Petrograd, 104
Petsamo, USSR secures access to Norwegian border, 122
Philadelphia, 12
Philippine Is, 43, 61, 137, 155; reconquest of, 156
Philippopolis, 41
Phoenix I, 55
Piedmont, 38
Pietsang, 50
Pilckem, 73, 75, 94
Pilcomao, R, 5
Pilsen, 42
Pindus, Mts, 2
Pinsk, 67, 104, 119
Piraeus, 134; axis naval base, 139
Pitcairn I, 43, 55
Piteschi, 93
Plank Road, 25
Plate, River, Battle of, 120-1
Pleasant Hill, Battle of, 17
Plevna, 41
Ploesti, 93; oil region important during soviet advance through Europe, 152
Plovdiv, 56
Plum, R, 28
Plymouth, during Blitz, 129
Po, River, 38, 42, 65, 147, 154
Podgoritsa, 87
Poelcapelle, 73, 75, 94, 96
Pola, 42, 154
Poland, 39, 58, 64-5, 67, 77, 104, 106, 110, 118; invasion of by Germany and USSR, 119; controlled by Germany and USSR, 135; 141, 145; soviet advance through Europe, 152; 154; approx. 4,500,000 Poles killed during 1939-45, 159
Polygon Wood, 75
Pomerania, 39
Pommern, SMS, sunk ,89
Pongola, R, 44
Pontecorvo, 38
Pontic, Mt Range, 2
Pontoise, 98
Poperinghe, 96, 125
Popocatepetl, Mt, 4
Port Arthur, 48, 51
Port Gibson, 13, 26; Battle of, 16, 26
Port Guinea, 45
Port Hudson, 13, 16, 26
Port Pulaski, (Confederate surrender) 15
Port Republic, 21
Port Said, 46, 79; British naval base, 139
Porter, (Union offensive) 17
Portertown, 24
Porto Princessa, 156

Portsmouth, 128; during Blitz, 129; 150
Portugal, 43, 64, 80-2, 110; 1928, dictatorship established, 115, 139, 142; 'Operation Torch', 144, 145
Posen, 39, 107, 154
Potijze, 75, 94
Potomac, R, 12, 15-6, 18-19, 20-1, 24, 27
Pozières, 91
Poznan, 119
Pozsony, 42
Prague, 42, 154
Prairie Green, Battle of, 15
Prairies, 4
Prasnysz, 67
Predeal Pass, 93
Prestonburg, Battle of, 15
Pretoria, 49
Preveza, 56
Price, (Confederate offensive) 17; (Confederate retreat) 15
Pripet Marshes, 106, 119
Pripet, R, 58, 67, 77, 92
Pristina, 87
Prizren, 87
Prome, 138, 149
Provins, Pétain's GQG, 98
Prussia, East, 39, 65, 67, 77, 107, 118-19; dominated by Germany, 135, 141; soviet advance through Europe, 152, 154
Prussia, West, 39
Pruth, R, 41, 58, 67, 92-3
Przemysl, 42, 67, 77, 119
Pskov, 58, 67
Puebla, Battle of, 37
Puerto Rico, (also Porto Rico), 61
Pumpkinvine Creek, 29
Punjab, British operations against tribesmen and guerrillas, 114
Punta del Este, 120-1
Purus, R, 5
Pusan, 48
Putumayo, R, 5
Pyongyang, Battle of, 48
Pyrenees, Mts, 2

Qaret el Abd, 143
Qaret el Himeimat, 143
Qatar, 60
Qattara Depression, 133, 141
Queen Mary, SS, 88
Queen's County, (renamed Leix), 108
Quetta, 59

Rabat, 'Operation Torch', 144
Rabaul, 155
Radom, 67, 119

Ragil, 143
Ragusa, 42, 134
Rakaia, R, 7
Raleigh, 17
Ram, 87
Ramscapelle, 73
Ramsgate, 125, 128
Rancourt, 91
Rangitata, R, 7
Rangoon, 138, 149
Rapidan, R, 12, 19, 21, 27
Rappahannock, R, 12, 18-19, 21, 25, 27
Ravenna, 147
Rawalpindi, 1919, Peace Treaty between Afghans and British, 114
Raymond, Battle of, 16, 26
Red, R, (China), 3
Red, R, (USA), 4, 13, 26, 31
Red Sea, 3, 6, 34, 59-60
Remagen, 151
Resaca, 29
Rethal, 98
Rethondes, 97
Rethymno, 134
Reunion, 43, 55
Reuss, 39
Reval, 51, 106
Revel, 67
Reykjavik, allied air base during second battle of Atlantic, 131, 140
Rheims, 66, 70, 72, 76, 97-9, 124
Rhine, R, 2, 39-40, 65, 70, 76, 99, 107, 118, 124, 151-2
Rhineland, 118
Rhode Island, 10
Rhodes, 53-4; 1940, British fleet attacks targets and repels Italians, 132; 'E' boat sortie, 132, 133; Axis air base, 139
Rhodesia, 55
Rhodesia, Northern, 45
Rhodesia, Southern, 45
Rhone, R, 2, 65
Ribecourt, 95, 97
Richmond, 10, 15, 17-18, 27, 30; abandoned, 20; strategic importance of, 12; battle of, 15
Richmond, Mt, Battle of, 15
Richmond, R, 21
Riencourt, 96
Riga, 58, 67, 77; treaty drafted in favour of Poland during Russo-Polish war, 106, 135, 152
Rimini, 147
Rio de Janeiro, naval bombardment, 36
Rio de Oro, 45
Rio de la Plata, (see River Plate)
Rio Grande, 4, 31; River, 31, 37
River Clyde, HMS, at Gallipoli, 86

Roanoke Island, (Confederate surrender), 15
Robinson House, 22
Rock Creek, 28
Rockfish Gap, 12
Rocky Mts, 4
Rome, (Italy), 118, 141, 145. 147
  Battle of, 38 ; Axis air base, 139
Rome, (USA), 13, 29
Romney 21
Rorke's Drift, Battle of, 34, 44
Rosebud, Battle of, 31
Rosecrans, 15-16
Rostock, 154
Rostov, 104, 135
Rosyth, 88
Rother Thurn Pass, 93
Rotterdam, heavily bombed by Luftwaffe, 124
Rouen, 40, 66, 124, 151
Roulers, 72-3
Roumania, (also Rominia and Rumania), 42, 56-7, 64, 67, 69, 80 ;
  eliminated from war, 81 ; 82, 84, 87, 92-3 ; military casualties 1914-18, 100 ; civilian casualties and expenditure 1914-18, 101 ; 104, 106, 110-11, 118-19, 134 ; controlled by USSR and Germany, 135 ; 141, 145 ; soviet advance through Europe, 152
Rovno, 67 ; HQ Russian 8th Army, 92
Rovsheim, 122
Royan, 125
Roye, 72, 98
Ruhr, 151
Ruhr, R, 124
Rumilly, 95
Russia, 39, 41-3, 51, 54, 56-7, 60, 64-5, 67-9, 74, 77, 80-2, 84, 93 ; military casualties 1914-18, 100 ; civilian casualties and expenditure 1914-18, 101 ; civil war, 104-5 ;
  (post Revolution see USSR)
Rustchuk, 41, 93
Rustenburg, 49
Ruweisat Ridge, 143
Rye, 128
Ryuku Islands, 51, 137
Rzhev, 58

Saar, 1928, US occupation force return home, 107, 118, 151
Saarbrücken, 40, 98
Saarburg, 70
Sabine Cross-Roads, Battle of, 17
Sadowa, (Koniggratz), Battle of, 39

Sahara Desert, 6
Sahara, Northern, 35
St Augustine, (Confederate surrender), 15
St Cloud, 126
St Dizier, 98
St Eloi, 75, 94
St Eval, RAF station, 126
St Georges, 73
St Gond, Marsh of, 71
St Helena, 43, 55
St Jean, 75, 94
St John's, allied base during second battle of Atlantic, 131
St Julien, 75, 94
St Lawrence, R, 4
St Lo, 151
St Louis, 13, 15
Ste Mère Église, parachute site for 'D Day', 151
St Mihiel, 66, 70, 76, 98
St Nazaire, retained by Germans until 1945, 151
St Omer, 72, 98
St Petersburg, (Petrograd), 58-8, 67
St Pal, 72, 98
St Quentin, 66, 76, 96 ; Battle of, 40, 70
St Trend, 152
St Vith, 152
Sajama, Mt, 5
Sakhalin, 51, 137
Sakkaria, R, 105
Salem Church, 27
Salerno, 147
Salisbury, 17
Salonika, 41, 54, 56-7 ; allies land here to assist Serbians, 1915, 87 ; 134 ; Axis naval base, 139
Salvador, 37
Salween, R, 3, 138, 149
Salzburg, 42, 154
Samaket Gaballa, 143
Samar, 156
Samara, 58
Samarkand, 60
Sambre, R, 66, 70, 72, 98, 124, 152
Samoa Islands, 55, 78
San, R, 67, 77, 119
Sandomir, 119
Sandwich Group, 55
San Giovanni di Medua, 87
Sangro, R, 147
San Stephano, 41, 146
Sao Francisco, R, 5
Saone, R, 70
Sarajevo, 42, 57, 134
Saratov, 58, 104
Sardinia, 38, 109, 132, 141, 147 ; Kingdom of, 38
Sari Bair, 86

Saskatchewan, R, 4
Sava, River, 41-2, 67, 87
Savannah, 13, 17, 19
Savoy, 38
Saxony, 39 ; Duchies of, 39
Scandinavian Highlands, 2
Scapa Flow, 88
Scarpanto, 1940, British fleet attacks targets and repels Italian 'E' boat sortie, 132-3
Scarpa, River, 72, 98
Scheer, Admiral, false name used by *Graf Spee*, 120-1
Schelde, R, 66, 72, 98, 124
Scheldt, R, 70
Schleswig, 39
Schleswig, North, 107
Schofield, 17
Schoorbakke, 73
Schoore, 73
Scoglottie, 146
Scutari, 56-7, 87
Sebastopol, 58, 84, 104, 135 ; axis naval base, 139, 152
Sedan, 66, 70, 76, 124 ; Battle of, 40
Sedd el Bahr, 84
Sedgewick, Battle of, 24
Seine, R, 2, 40, 65-6, 70, 98, 124, 150-1
Selles, R, 151
Selma, 17
Selvas, 5
Seminary Ridge, 28
Senegal, 43, 45 ; R, 6
Senlis, 97-8
Senova, Battle of, 41
Seoul, 48
Serbia, 41-2, 56-6, 64-5, 67, 69, 80-2 ; attacked by Austro-German-Bulgarian forces, 87 ; military casualties 1914-18, 100 ; civilian casualties and expenditure 1914-18, 101
Sereth, R, 92-3
Serre, 91
Serres, 57
Seven Days' Battles, 15, 20-1
Seville, 1936, military revolt in, 115
Sevres, 126
Seychelles, 43, 55
Seydlitz, SMS, 89
Seymour, (Union offensive), 17
Sezanne, 71
Shabatz, 87
Shanghai, 59 ; 1932, occupied by Japanese forces, 112 ; 1937, captured by Japanese following intensive aerial bombardment, 113
Shantung, occupied by Japanese, 112

Sharpsburg, 21, 24
Shebeli (also Scebeli) West, R, 6
Sheffield during Blitz, 129
Shenandoah, River, 12, 19, 21
Sherman, (Union offensive), 15-17
Sherman and McClernand, 16
Shikoku, 137
Shiloh, Battle of, 13, 15, 18-19
Shimonoseki, Treaty of, 48
Ship Island, 15
Shipka Pass, 41
Shreveport, 17
Shrewsbury Forest, 75
Shumla, 41
Shuri, 157
Shwebo, 138, 149
Siam, 114
Sian, 1936, Nationalist troops
    mutiny at HQ, 113
Sicilies, Kingdom of the two, 38
Sicily, 38, 109, 132, 139, 141 ;
    'Operation Torch', 144 ;
    conquest of, 146 ; following
    capitulation 'Mafia' begin to
    dominate economy, 147
Sidi Abd el Rahman, 143
Sidi Barrani, 132
Sidi Rezegh, 133
Siegfried Line Forts, 111
Sierra Leone, 43, 45, 55
Sierra Morena, 2
Sierra Nevada, 2
Sigel, (Union retreat), 15
Sikiang, R, 3
Silesia, 39, 42
Silistria, 41, 93
Singapore, 43, 55, 59, 137
Sinkiang, 59
Sinope, 105
Sioux, 31
Sistova, 93
Sittang, 138, 149
Sizran, 104
Skagerrak, German name for the
    Battle of Jutland, 88
Skoplje, 56-7, 87, 134
Slim Buttes, Battle of, 31
Slovakia, 119 ; controlled by
    Germany, 135
Sluch, R, 92
Slype, 73
Smith, (Union offensive), 17
Smolensk, 58, 67, 104, 135
Smyrna, 60, 105
Smyrna-Adalia Region, 1919,
    abortive Italian attempt to
    establish control, 109
Snake, R, 4
Society Is, 43
Society of Righteous Harmonious
    Fists, (see Boxer Rebellion)
Sofia, 41, 56-7, 87, 134
Soghanli Dere, 86

Soissons, 66, 72, 76, 97-8
Sokoto, 35
Soldau, 74
Solferino, Battle of, 38
Solomon Is, 55
Somaliland, 35
Somaliland, British, 45, 55, 60 ;
    1925, ceded to Italians, 109
Somaliland, French, 45, 55, 60
Somaliland, Italian, 45, 60 ; 1889,
    becomes Italian, 109
Somme, R, 40, 66, 68, 70, 72, 91 ;
    Battle of, 91 ; German
    offensives 1918, 96 ; 98, 124
Songhwan, Battle of, 48
Sortavala, 122
Soryu, Japanese ship, 148
South America, 77, 120-1, 130-1,
    160 ; physical features of, 5
Southampton, 128 ; during 'Blitz',
    129
South Carolina, 10, 13, 15-7
South China Sea, 3
South Mts, 12
Southside Railroad, 30
Spa, 98
Spain, 43, 53-4, 64, 80-2, 110 ;
    beset by internal unrest, 111 ;
    Axis training ground, 1936-39,
    115 ; training ground for
    Luftwaffe, 118, 125, 139, 141-2 ;
    'Operation Torch', 144, 145
Spalato, 42
Spanish Morocco, 34
Speier, 99
Spezia, 147
Sphakia, 134
Spichern, Battle of, 40
Spion Kop, Battle of, 49
Spitzbergen, 140
Spottsylvania, 12
Springfield, 15
Staden, 73
Stafford Heights, 25
Stalingrad, 141-2 ; never taken
    by Germans, 135
Stanislau, 67, 92
Stanislavov, 119
Stanmore, HQ, RAF Fighter
    Command, 127
Starkville, 16
Staunton, 12, 21
Stavanger, 123
Stavelot, 152
Steele, (Union offensive), 17
Steenbeek, R, 94
Steenstraat, 73, 75, 94
Steenwerck, 96
Stettin, 154
Steveson, 13
Stewart I, 7
Stokhod, R, 92
Stone Bridge, 22-3

Stoneman's Raids, 17
Stones, River, Battle of, 15
Stormberg, Battle of, 49
Strasburg, (USA) 12, 21
Strassburg, (France) 70, 99, 124
Streight's Raid, 16
Streonshalh, SS, victim of Graf
    Spee, 120-1
Struma, R, 41
Stuttgart, 107, 154
Styr, R, 92
Styria, 42
Suakin, 34
Suchow, 112
Suda Bay, Axis naval base, 139
Sudan, Anglo-Egyptian, 45
Sudetenland, (later West
    Czechoslovakia, 1939),
    annexed by Germany, 118
Sudley Ford, 22-3
Sudley Springs Ford, 22-3
Suez, 46
Suez Canal, 6, 46 ; 1941,
    Germans drop accoustic and
    magnetic mines, closing canal
    for three weeks, 132 ; British
    air base, 139
Suffren, French battleship, used
    in Dardanelles, 84
Sullom Voe, allied air base, 140
Sumatra, 137, 155
Suribachi, Mt, 157
Surmelin, R, 71
Susquehanna, R, 12
Suvla Bay, 86
Swatow, 59
Swaziland, 45
Sweden, 64-5 81-2 104, 110-11,
    118-19, 122-3, 135, 140-2, 154
Sweetwater Canal, 46
Swift Run Gap, 12
Switzerland, 39-40, 42, 54, 64-5,
    69, 80-2, 110, 118, 125, 139,
    141-2, 145, 147, 151, 154
Sword, US ship, used as troop
    carrier in 'Overlord', 150
Sydney, HMAS, destroys SMS
    Emden, 78
Sydney, (USA), allied base
    during second battle of
    Atlantic, 131
Syracuse, 146
Syria, 139
Szeged, 42, 154
Szurduk Vulkan Pass, 93

Tacna, Battle of, 36
Tagus, R, 2, 115
Tairoa, SS, victim of Graf Spee,
    120-1
Tako, 157
Taku, 50

Talawa Hill, Battle of, 49
Tallinn, 152
Tamatave, 34
Tananarivo, 34
Taneytown Road, 28
Tanganyika, Lake, 6
Tangier, 54, 115; 'Operation Torch', 144
Tangmere RAF station, 126
Tannenberg, 67; Battle of, 68; campaign, 74
Tapajoz, R, 5
Tapqaeauku, (also Tapuaenuku), 7
Taranto, 1940, British aircraft inflict heavy damage on Italian naval units, 132; Axis air and naval base, 139, 147
Tarlac, 156
Tarnopol, 42, 67, 92, 106
Tarnow, 77
Tartar City, 50
Tartars, 58
Tashkent, 59-60
Tasman Sea, 7
Tasmania, 7, 43
Taunglau, 138, 149
Taupo, Lake, 7
Taurus Mts, 2
Taylor, 16
Tecomovaca, Battle of, 37
Tehran, 59-60, 140
Tekke Burnu, 84
Tekke Tepe, 86
Telegraph Road, 25
Tel-el-Kebir, Battle of, 34, 46
Temesvar, 42
Tennessee, 10, 13, 15-7; Army of the, 19; River, 4, 11, 15-9, 29;
Tennessee, USS, 136
Tenterden, 128
Terek, R, 58
Termini Imerese, 146
Teruel, Battle of, 115
Tervaete, 73
Teschen, 42
Texas, 10
Thailand, 137-8, 149
Thames, R, 128
Thermopylae, 134
Thielt, 98
Thiepval, 91
Thierville, 90
Thionville, (see Diedenhofen)
Thorn, 77, 119
Thourout, 73
Thrace, 105
Tibesti, 6
Tibet, 59, 137
Tientsin, 50
Tiflis, 58
Tigris, R, 3, 60
Tirana 56-7 134
Tisza, R, 67

Tobol, R, 3
Tobruk, 53, 132; 1941, March-May, besieged but not overrun, 133; 1941, Nov-Dec relieved by British, 133; Axis naval base, 139; 145
Tocantins, R, 5
Togo, 45, 55
Tokelau Is, 55
Tokyo, 137; March 1945, US bombers devastate, 155
Toledo, military revolt, 1936, 115
Tomashov, 119
Tonga, 55
Tornio, 122
Toul 40, 69-70, 76, 98
Toulon, 125, 142, 145
Toulouse, 125
Toungoo, 138, 149
Tournai, 66, 98
Tours, 40
Tralee Bay, 1916, Sir Roger Casement lands from German submarine, 108
Trans-Jordan, 139
Transvaal, 45, 49
Transylvania, 42, 67
Transylvanian Alps, 2
Trapani, Axis naval base, 139; 146
Trent, 42
Trevanion, SS, victim of Graf Spee, 120-1
Trier, 40, 70, 98
Trieste, 42, 134, 147, 154
Trinidad, 43
Tripoli, 35, 45, 53-4, 64, 132; Axis naval base, 139; 'Operation Torch', 144; 145
Tripolitania, 54
Tristan da Cunha, 43, 55
Trondheim, 123
Troyes, 40
Tsaribrod, 87
Tsaritsyn, 104
Tsinan, 112
Tsingtau, 51, 55, 69, 78
Tsugen, 157
Tsushima, Battle of, 51
Tugela Drift, 44
Tugela, R, 44
Tula, 104
Tumen, R, 48
Tungchow, 50, 59
Tunis, 45, 54; British naval base, 139; 'Operation Torch', 144, 145
Tunisia, 34, 53, 64, 132, 139, 141; 'Operation Torch', 144, 145, 147
Tunja, River, 56-7
Tupelo, 13; Battle of, 17
Turin, Axis air base, 139; 147, 154
Turkestan, 59-60
Turkey, 41, 43, 53, 64, 80-2, 84; military casualties 1914-18, 100;

civilian casualties and expenditure 1914-18, 101; 104-5, 110; anxious to remain aloof from Great Power disputes, 111; 133-4, 139, 141-2, 145
Turnhouse RAF station, 126
Turturkai, 93
Turukhansk, 59
Tuscaloosa, 13, 17
Tuscany, 38
Tutuila, 61
Tver, 58
Tyrol, 39, 42
Tyrone, 108

Ubangi, R, 6
Uckfield, 128
Ufa, 58
Uganda, 45
Ukraine, 58
Uleaborg, 58
Ulster, 1912, Carson's Ulster Volunteers drill openly in defiance of British Govt, 108
Ulundi, Battle of, 34, 44
Umfolozi, R, 44
Umgoni, R, 44
Union Church, 16
Union City, 17
Unorganized Territory, (USA 1861), 10
Ural Mts, 2-3
Ural, R, 3, 58
Uralsk, 58
Uruguay, 36, 43, 120-1; R, 5
Uruguayana, Battle of, 36
USA (United States of America), 37, 43, 78-9; military casualties 1914-18, 100; civilian casualties and expenditure 1914-18, 101, 120-1, 130-1, 137; military casualties 1939-45, 158; civilian casualties and expenditure 1939-45, 159; 1945, sole possessor of atomic bomb, thus world's leading military power; largest air force and navy in world; leading industrial and manufacturing nation; territory untouched by war, 160
U.S. Ford, 27
Ushak, 105
Ushanti, 35
USSR (Union of Soviet Socialist Republics), 4, 106, 110; Communist under Stalin; anxious to industrialize; 111; worried about German-Japanese liason; 111; 118-19, 122-3; German assault on, 135,

137, 140-2, 145 ; advance through Europe, 152 ; military casualties 1939-45, 158 ; civilian casualties and expenditure 1939-45, 159 ; 1945, largest army in world, but no atomic bomb ; virtually self-sufficient in raw materials but much of industry in ruins following German occupation, 160
Ustiug, 58
Usworth RAF station, 126
Utah, Territory, 10
Utah, USS, 136 ; used as troop carrier in 'Overlord', 150
Uxbridge, HQ No. 11 Group, 127
Uzhitse, 87

Vaal, R, 6, 49
Vadso, 123
Vailly, 72
Valencia, March 1939, surrenders to Nationalists, civil war ends, 115
Valenciennes, 66
Valjevo, 87
Valley Pike, 21
Valognes, 151
Valona, Axis air base, 139
Valparaiso, naval bombardment, 36
Van Dorn, (Confederate retreat), 15
Vardar, R, 41, 56-7, 87
Varna, 41, 93
Velés, 57, 87
Vendhuile, 95
Venetia, 38
Venezuela, 36
Venice, Axis naval base, 139 ; 147, 154
Ventnor, 127
Vera Cruz, 37
Verbrandenmolen, 75, 94
Verdun, 66, 70, 76 ; Battle of, 90 ; 98-9
Vereeniging, 49
Verkhoyansk, 59
Verlorenhoek, 75
Vermont, 10
Verona, 147
Verrines, 71
Verse, R, 97
Verviers, 152
Vervins, 98
Vesle, R, 66, 68, 72, 97
Viborg, 122
Vichy, 125, 141
Vicksburg, 13, 15-18 ; campaign, 26 ; siege of, 19
Victoria, Lake, 6
Viels Maison, (HQ French 5th

Army, first battle of the Marne), 71
Vienna, 39, 42, 154
Vierstraat, 75, 94
Viga, 156
Villa Belmonte, April 1945, Mussolini killed by partisans, 147
Villacoublay, 126
Villers Guislain, 95
Villiers Cotterets, 71, 97
Vilna, 58, 67-8 ; Russian offensive in Russo-Polish war, 106 ; territory around taken from Lithuania by Poland, 106 ; 119 ; soviet advance through Europe, 152
Vimy, 66, 72
Vinaroz, 115
Vire, R, 151
Virgin Is, 61
Virginia, 10, 12, 15-17 ; West, 15-17
Vistula, R, 2, 65, 67, 74, 76, 106, 119, 154
Vitebsk, 153
Vitry-le-François, 98
Vittorio Veneto, Italian battleship escapes from battle off Cape Matapan, 132
Vladivostok, 51, 59
Vlamertinghe, 75
Vlodava, 119
Volga, R, 2-3, 58
Volhynia, 58
Volochisk, HQ Russian 11th Army, 92
Vologda, 58
Volturno, 147 ; Battle of, 38
Voormezeele, 75
Vorarlberg, 42
Voronezh, 58
Vorskha, R, 67
Vyatka, 104

Wadai, 35
Waikato, R, 7
Waitiki, R, 7
Wake, I, 61, 136-7, 148, 155
Waldeck, 39
Walvisch Bay, 43, 55
Warneton, 94
Warrenton, 26 ; Junction, 12
Warsaw, 58-9, 67, 77 ; Battle of, 106 ; 119 ; soviet advance through Europe, 152 ; rising fails Aug-Sept 1944, 152 ; 154
Warta, R, 119
Washington DC, 10, 12, 15, 17-19 ; Strategic importance of, 11 ; territory, 10, 20-1

Washita, Battle of, 31
Waza, 138
Wei Hai Wei, 51, 55, 59 ; Battle of, 48
Weimar Republic, 1919, new constitution formed, 107
Wervicq, 94
Weser, R, 107
Westende, 73
Westhoek, 75
West Indies, 79, 130
Westphalia, 39
West Point, 12
Westroosebeke, 73, 75
West Virginia, USS, 136
Weymouth, 150
Wheeler, advance attack prior to Pearl Harbor, 136
White Bird, Battle of, 31
White House Bridge, 21
White, R, 44
Wick RAF station, 126
Wieltje, 73, 75
Wilderness ; Battle of, 17 ; campaign, 18, 20 ; tavern, 27
Wilhelmshaven, 120-1
Wilk, Polish submarine, escapes to Britain despite German naval surveillance, 119
Willow Springs, Battle of, 31
Wilmington, 12, 17
Wilson's Creek, Battle of, 15
Wilson's Raid, 17
Winchester, (USA), 12, 20-1 ; Battle of, 17, 21
Windward Is, 43
Winnipeg, Lake, 4
'Wipers', (see Ypres)
Wisconsin, 10
Wittering RAF station, 126
Worms, 99
Wörth, Battle of, 40
Worthing, 128
Woumrn, 73
Wounded Knee, 31
Wu, R, 3
Wuchang, 112
Wulverghem, 94
Wurttemburg, 39
Wytschaete, 75, 94

Yalu, R, 48 ; Battle of, 51
Yambol, 56
Yangtse, R, 3, 112-13
Yangtsun, 50 ; Battle of, 50
Yarmouth, bombarded by German warships, 83
Yasoo, R, 26
Yellow Sea, 48
Yellowstone, R, 31
Yemen, 60
Yenisei, R, 3

Yingkow, Battle of, 48
Yonne, R. 40, 70
York, (USA), 12 ; R, 12
Yorktown, 12
Yorktown, USS, 148
Young's Branch, R. 23
Ypres, 66, 70, 72-3, 76 ; salient, 75 ; 94, 96, 98
Ypres-Comines Canal, 75
Yser, R. 70, 72-3, 98 ; Battle of the, 73
Yser-Ypres Canal, 75
Ytres, 96

Yugoslavia, 110-11, 118 ;
following Coup d'Etat, Axis
forces invaded and overran
country, 145 ; 147 ;
soviet advance through Europe,
152 ; 154
Yukon, R, 4

Zagreb, 134, 154
Zajecar, 57
Zambezi, R, 6
Zamboanga, 156

Zandvoorde, 94
Zanzibar, 55
Zara, 1919-24, disputed with
Yugoslavia, 109
Zariba, 47
Zarren, 73
Zeebrugge, 66, 98, 125
Zeerust, 49
Zillebeke, 75, 94
Zonnebeke, 75, 94
Zululand, 44

Supplementary Index

Africa :
scramble for, pre-1914, 45 ;
strife in, 1860-99, 34, 1899-
1914, 35
Allies :
advances ; into Germany 1918,
99 ; into Mediterranean and
Balkans, 1942-5, 145 ; into
Pacific 1943-5, 155
convoy routes in Atlantic, 79 ;
bombardment and destruction
of fleet in Dardanelles, 84 ;
landings in Gallipoli, 1915, 86 ;
offensives, 1918, 98
shore-based aircraft, arctic
maximum range, 140
submarines in Dardanelles, 86
American Civil War :
1861-5, 10-31 ; issues behind,
10 ; opposing forces in, and
manpower of states, 11 ; war
aims, 11 ; strategy, 11 ; Eastern
theatre of war, 12 ; military
organization of combatant sides,
14
Anti-submarine net laid by Turks
in Dardanelles, 86
'Anvil' (Dragoon), operation, 145
Arcadia conference : Roosevelt and
Churchill decide that war
against Germany is first
priority, 142
Armee d'Alsace, 70
Armies :

of the world, 1906, 52
positions of in Russian Civil
war, 104
Armistice line, 11 Nov, 1918, 99
Army Groups :
Jilinsky, 74
German, at *Sichelscnitt*, 124
North, 119
South, 119
Arras Gruppe, 95
Atlantic, First battle of, 79 ;
second battle of, 130-1
Austria-Hungary, 1867-1918, 42
Austrian armies in Brusilov
offensive, 92
Avalanche, Operation, 145
Axis advance on Balkan Flank, 134

Balkan League, 54
Balkans, 1905-12, Crises in, 54
Balkan War :
First : 1912-13, 56
Second : 1913, 57
'Barbarosa', 135 ; delayed by
Balkan campaign, 135
Beseler Group, 72
Bielaya Smert, Finnish Ski patrols,
122
Black and Tans : special force of
armed police sent to Ireland by
British Govt, 108
Blitz, 129
Blücher, German offensive, 97

Boer, (or S. African) war,
1899-1902, 49
Bologna division, 143
Bolsheviks, 104
Brescia division, 143
British Empire, 1914, 55
British Expeditionary Force, 71 ;
transferred to Flanders to
shorten supply route from
England, 72
British influence in Asia, pre-1914,
59
British naval losses off Greece and
Crete, 1941, 133
Brunhild, defence line, 98
Brusilov offensive, 92
Bucharest, Treaty of, 57
Bulge, Battle of the, 152
Busigny Gruppe, 95

Caesar line, 147
Carbonit, moored mines, use in
Dardanelles, 84
Caspian route, (indirect), 140
Casualties :
at the Somme, 91, 96 ; at the
Lys, 96 ; military 1914-18, 100 ;
civilian 1914-18, 101 ; military
1939-45, 158 ; civilian 1939-45,
159
Caudry Gruppe, 95
Central America, strife in,
1861-1900, 37

Chinese Nationalist Capital, moves westward as Japanese armies advance, 113
Chlorine Gas, released during Ypres salient, 75
Commonwealth troops, contribution to war effort, 145
Communists in China defeat Japanese force, Sept. 1937, 113
Congress of Berlin, 1878, 43
Convoys, Arctic, 140
Convoy system, plan of, 79
Cossacks, in Russo-Polish war, 106

Devers, allied drive, 1944, 151
Dynamo, operation, 1940, 125

Eastern Front:
    in outline, 1914-18, 67; 1916, Russia launches major offensive, 81; Russian final offensive, 82
Enigma code, 129
Europe:
    in 1914, 64; the middle years, 1915-17, land events, 1915, 80; 1916, 81; 1917, 82; naval events 1915-17, 83; in 1925, 110; between the world wars, 111; under the Axis, 141; western liberation of, 150; pre-invasion strategy of, 150
Expenditure, 1914-18, 101; 1939-45, 159

Fall Gelb, (Plan Yellow), 1940, 124
Flandern, defence line, 98
France, (North), and Low Countries, liberation of, 151
Franco-Prussian War, 1870-1, 40
French armies, prelude to trench warfare, 72
French Empire, 1914, 55

Georgette, German offensive, 96
German advance into Russia halted by onset of winter, 80
German armies:
    gap between at first battle of the Marne, 71; gap closed by 5th Army, 72; prelude to trench warfare, 72; advance on Konnigsberg, 74
German attempt to sever allied sea link with England, (Battle of the Yser), 73
Germany's biggest gain at Ypres, 75

German commanders at battle of the Marne, 1914, 70
German Empire, 1914, 55
Germany, unification of, 39
Gneisenau, German offensive, 97
Gothic line, 145
Graeco-Turkish War, 1919-22, position of armies. (Turks, Armenians, Greeks, Nationalists, Italians), 105
Graf Spee, German pocket battleship, cruise of, Aug.-Dec 1939, 120-1
Gustav line, 145, 147

Hermann, defence line, 98
Hitler's road to war, 1936-9, territories gained, first exploratory move, 118
Hunding, defence line, 98
Husky, operation, 145; conquest of Sicily, results in Mediterranean becoming under allied control again, 146

Irish Free State, 1922-3, civil war between Govt and extremists, 108
Italian expansion, 1889-1939, 109
Italian front:
    1915, offensives on, 80; 1916, main actions, 81-2
Italian troops; over 1,000,000 fighting for Germans outside Italy, 1943, 147
Italo-Turkish war, 1911-12, 53
Italy, campaign in, 147
Italy, unification of, 38

Japanese conquests, 1941-2, 137
Jews, killed 1939-45, 159
Jutland Bank, (known as Skagerrak to Germans) confrontation of British and German battle fleets, 88; approach of rival fleets, 88; plan of Beatty versus Hipper, 88; plan of Jellicoe versus Scheer, 88; second clash of fleets, 89; details of casualties etc, 89

Kamikaze pilots, 157
Kriemhild, 98

Lebensraum, 111
Linsingen army group, 92
Little Entente, between Rumania, Czechoslavia and Yugoslavia,

111
London Peace Conference, 1912, 57
Long March, 1934-5, Chinese communists march 6,000 miles to establish new base for future operations in North China, 113
Luftwaffe; training ground in Spain, 118; during Battle of Britain, 126; losses during Battle of Britain, 127; during Blitz, 129

Maginot line, 124-5
Mannerheim line, 122
Mareth line, 145
Marine fusiliers, 72
Mediterranean, 1940-1, 132
Messines, Battle of, 94
Michael, German offensive, 96
Middle-East, pre-1914, 60
Mines and Minesweepers, use of in Dardanelles, 85; laying of mines, 85
Mobile eastern front, 1915, 77
Mustard gas, used for first time by Germans, 94

Navies of the world, 1906, 52; Japanese at Pearl Harbor, 136
Nieuport sluices, flooding of to stem German advance to Channel ports, 73
Normandy, allied assault on, 151; losses, 151
North, the, (Federal States), 11; war aims, 11; available manpower of, 11; strategy of, 11; general factors, 11; union naval blockade, 15-16
North Africa, 1905-12, crises in, 54; 1940-1, 132
North Sea, strategic position unchanged after Battle of Jutland, 89

Oceanic, warfare, world scene 1914, 78
Occupation of German colonies by Australian forces, 78
Outbreak of American civil war at Fort Sumter, 15
'Overlord', Operation, 150; allied dispositions and movements, 150; chain of command, 150

RAF Fighter Command during Battle of Britain, 126; losses during Battle of Britain, 127
Railway, importance of during

American civil war, 11
Ramcke division, 143
Richmond-Petersburg-Appomattox retreat, 30
Rumanian campaign, 1916, 93 ; Rumania weak in aircraft, artillery, ammunition, trench guns and poison gas, 93
Russian army :
  in Tannenberg campaign, 74 ; gap between in Tannenberg campaign, 74 ; in Brusilov offensive, 92
Russian civil war, 1917-22, 104
Russian influence in Asia, pre-1914, 58
Russo-Japanese war, 1904-5, 51
Russo-Polish war, 1920, 106
Russo-Turkish war, 1877-8, 41

Schlieffen plan, 1914, 124
'Sealion', code name for German plan to invade Britain, 128
Serbia, overwhelmed by Austro-German-Bulgarian invasion, 80, 87
Serbian refugees withdraw through Albania and are evacuated to Corfu, 87
'Shingle', operation, 145
Sichelschnitt, (Cut of the Sickle), 124 ; role of German paratroops, 124
Siegfried, defence line, 98
Sinn Fein, (Ourselves alone), 108
Sino-Japanese war, 48
Skagerrak, German name for Battle of Jutland, 88
Slavery, issue in American civil war, 10
Smoke, used to obscure sight in battle, 88 ; used as cover under

which to fire torpedoes, 89
South, the, (Confederate States), 11 ; available manpower of, 11 ; general factors, 11 ; risks taken by, 11 ; strategy of, 11 ; war aims, 11
South Africa, (or Boer) War, 1899-1902, 49
South America, strife in, 1864-95, 36
Soviet anti-German buffer zone, creation of, 135
Soviet-Finnish war, 122
Soviet tidal wave advance, 1944, 153 ; soviet armies organized into 'Fronts' ; no retreat by Germans on personal instructions from Hitler, 153
Spanish civil war, 115
State's rights in American civil war, 10
Static Western Front, 1915, rail network under German control, 76
Strategy, 1942 ; American, British, Soviet and German viewpoints, 142
Submarines attack British, French, Soviet and Spanish shipping, 1937, 115
Superpowers of the World, 1945, 160

Taxis, used to carry troops to first battle of the Marne, 71
Third Reich, 118
Third Ypres, (see Passchendaele)
Timok army, 87
'Torch', operation, Nov 1942, 144
Trawlers used by allies as minesweepers, 85
Trench warfare :

prelude to, 72
sets in, 80
Trento division, 143
Turkish shore gunners in Dardanelles, 85

U-boat routes, 1915-17, 83
USA, possessions of, pre-1914, 61
USSR, allied aid to 140

Verdun, Battle of, 90

War plans and concentrations, 1914, 65
Weimar Republic, 'Germany following Treaty of Versailles', 107
Weserubung Nord und Sud, German invasion of Norway and Denmark, 123
Western Front :
  in outline, 1914-18, 66 ; 1915, main actions of, 80 ; 1916, main actions of, 81 ; 1917, main actions of, 82
White man versus Red man, 31
Wotan, defence line, 98

Young Turkey Party, 54
Ypres, Cathedral and Cloth Hall, 75
Ypres salient, 75 ; rapid rifle fire used to convince Germans of existence of machine guns, 75

Zones, in allied advance into Germany, 1918, 99
Zulu battle formation, 44
Zulu war, 1879, 44

Index of People

Abdullah, Mohammed ben, 35
Alexander, Sir Harold, (later Field-Marshal), 146
Arabi Pasha, 46

Ataturk, Mustafa Kemal, 105

Banks, N. P, 26

Beatty, Earl, 88
Beauregard, P. G. T. de, 22
Bismarck, Otto von, 39
Blaskowitz, General Johannes

von, 154
Bock, Field-Marshal Fedor von, 119, 135
Böhm-Ermolli, Baron Edward von, 92
Bothmer, Count Felix von, 92
Bradley, Omar, General, 150, 154
Brusilov, General Alexsei, 92
Bülow, General von, 70-1
Burnside, General Ambrose E, 25
Burrough, Admiral HM, 144
Byng, Viscount, 95

Cetawayo, 44
Chernyakhovsky, General Ivan, 154
Churchill, Winston, 142
Clark, Mark, General, 144, 154
Conneau, General, 72
Crerar, General H.D.C, 150
Cunningham, Admiral, 144, 146

Davis, Jefferson, 10
d'Esperey, Franchet, 71
Dempsey, General Miles, 150
De Mitry, General, 72-3
Denikin, General Anton, 104
Devers, General Jacob, 151, 154
Diaz, Porfirio, 37
Doolittle, General James H, 144
Doubleday, Abner, 25
Dowding, Lord, 126
Dutov, A, 104

Early, Jubal A, 25, 27
Eisenhower, General Dwight, 144, 146, 150
Evan-Thomas, Rear-Admiral Hugh, 88
Evert, General, 92
Ewell, Richard S, 28

Falkenhayn, General Erich von, 93
Franklin, William B, 25
Franz-Joseph, Emperor, 93
Fredendall, General Lloyd R, 144
French, Sir John, 71

Gallwitz, General, 87
Gandhi, Mahatma, 114
Garibaldi, Giuseppe, 38
Geiger, General Roy S, 157
Goering, Hermann, 126
Graham, Sir Gerald, 46
Grant, Ulysses, S, 26
Grierson, General Benjamin H, 26

Hamley, Lieut-General Sir

Edward, 46
Hausen, General Max von, 70
Hausser, General Paul, 154
Heeringen, General Josias von, 70
Herron, General Francis Jay, 26
Heth, General Henry, 28
Hewitt, Admiral Henry K, 144
Hill, General Ambrose, 25
Hill, General Daniel H, 25
Himmler, Heinrich, 154
Hipper, Admiral Franz von, 88
Hitler, Adolf, 111, 118, 135, 142
Hodge, General John R, 157
Hood, General John Bell, 25
Hood, Rear-Admiral Horace, 88
Hooker, General Joseph, 25, 27
Howard, General Oliver Otis, 27

Jackson, Thomas J, 'Stonewall', 21, 25, 27
Jellicoe, Earl, 88
Jerram, Vice-Admiral Sir Martyn, 88
Jeshonnek, General Hans, 126
Jilinsky, General Yakov, 74
Joffre, Field-Marshal Joseph, 76
Johnston, General Albert S, 22, 26

Kaledin, General, 92
Kesselring, Field-Marshal Albert, 154
Kluck, General Alexander von, 70-1
Koltchak, Admiral Alexander, 104
Koniev, Marshal Ivan, 154
Kövess, General Hermann, 87
Krasnov, General Peter, 104

Lane, James H, 25
Langsdorff, Captain, 120-1
Lechitsky, General Platon, 92
Lee, General Robert E, 20, 25, 27
Leeb, Field-Marshal Wilhelm, von, 135
Lenin, 82
Lesh, General, 92
Lincoln, Abraham, 10, 14
Longstreet, General James, 25, 27
Lowe, Drury, 46

MacArthur, General Douglas, 155
McClernand, General John, 26
McDowell, General Irvin, 22
Mackensen, Field-Marshal August von, 93
McLaws, General Lafayette, 25
McPherson, General James Birdseye, 26, 46
Malinovsky, Marshal Rodion Y,

154
Marwitz, General Georg von der, 95
Maunoury, General Michel Joseph, 71
Maximilian, President of Mexico, 37
Meade, General George Gordon, 25, 27
Model, General Walther, 154
Moltke, Count Helmuth von, 70, 124
Montgomery, Field-Marshal, 146, 150, 154
Mussolini, Benito, 111, 118, 147

Nimitz, Admiral Chester W, 155

Patton, General George S, 144, 146, 150
Pemberton, General John Clifford, 26
Petrov, General Ivan, 154
Pflanzer-Baltin, General Karl von, 92
Porter, Admiral David, 26
Pulhallo von Brlog, General, 92

Rennenkampf, General Pavel, 74
Reynolds, General John Fulton, 25, 27
Rokossovsky, Marshal Konstantin, 154
Rommel, Field-Marshal Erwin, 133
Roosevelt, Theodore, 142
Rundstedt, Field-Marshal Karl von, 119, 135
Rupprecht of Bavaria, Crown Prince, 70
Ryder, General Charles, 144

Sakharov, General, 92
Samsonov, General Alexander, 74
Scheer, Vice-Admiral Reinhard, 88-9
Schmidt, General Harry, 157
Schörner, General Ferdinand, 154
Sedgwick, General John, 27
Shcherbachev, General, 92
Sherman William, T, 19, 26
Sickles, General Daniel Edgar, 27
Sitting Bull, 31
Slocum, General Henry, 27
Smith, William Farrar, 25
Spee, Admiral Graf von, 78
Stalin, Joseph, 111, 135
Stoneman, General George, 27
Stuart, General Jeb, 25, 27
Sumner, General Edwin Vose, 25

Sultan of Turkey, 54

Tedder, Marshal of the RAF Lord, 146
Tolbukhin, General F. I, 154

Troutbridge, Commodore Thomas H, 144

Weichs, General Maximilian von, 154

Wilhelm II, Kaiser, 54
Wilhelm, Crown Prince of Germany, 70
Wrangel, Baron Petr, 104
Wurttemberg, Grand Duke of, 70, 73